THOUGH YOU MAY NOT KNOW IT, BOOKS THAT YOU MAY NEVER HAVE READ ARE PROFOUNDLY AFFECTING YOUR LIFE AND LIFE AROUND YOU IN AMERICA TO-DAY.

The call for revolutionary action by Thomas Paine . . . the argument for civil disobedience by Thoreau . . . the dissection of governmental corruption by Lincoln Steffens . . . the analysis of American racism by Gunnar Myrdal . . . the chilling warning against ecological disaster by Rachel Carson . . . these are but a few of the books that have left a lasting impression upon America. From the moment of their publication, their influence began to be felt—an influence that has never ceased to operate in American society.

Taking a brilliant cross-section of works in virtually every area of thought—political, economic, scientific, judicial, sociological, and literary—Dr. Robert B. Downs, former President of the American Library Association and head of the University of Illinois Library, gives a superb explication of each of these fascinating works and charts their effects upon the complex fabric of our emerging and evolving nation.

ROBERT B. DOWNS is the author of *Books That Changed the World,* a distinguished guide to world literature that has sold nearly half a million copies in its Mentor edition.

MENTOR and SIGNET CLASSIC Titles
of Related Interest

BOOKS
That Changed
America

by Robert B. Downs

A MENTOR BOOK from
NEW AMERICAN LIBRARY
TIMES MIRROR
New York and Scarborough, Ontario

Library of Congress Catalog Card Number: 71-84430

This is an authorized reprint of a hardcover edition published
by The Macmillan Company.

 MENTOR TRADEMARK REG. U.S. PAT. OFF. AND FOREIGN COUNTRIES
REGISTERED TRADEMARK—MARCA REGISTRADA
HECHO EN CHICAGO, U.S.A.

SIGNET, SIGNET CLASSICS, SIGNETTE, MENTOR, AND PLUME BOOKS
are published *in the United States* by
The New American Library, Inc.,
1301 Avenue of the Americas, New York, New York 10019,
in Canada by The New American Library of Canada Limited,
81 Mack Avenue, Scarborough, 704, Ontario

FIRST PRINTING, SEPTEMBER, 1971

PRINTED IN THE UNITED STATES OF AMERICA

Contents

INTRODUCTION IX

1 CLARION CALL FOR REVOLUTION 17
   Thomas Paine's *Common Sense*

2 THE WAY WEST 30
   Meriwether Lewis and William Clark's
   History of the Expedition

3 LATTER-DAY SAINT 42
   Joseph Smith's *The Book of Mormon*

4 CASE OF THE WOUNDED STOMACH 52
   William Beaumont's *Experiments and Observations
   on the Gastric Juice and the Physiology of Digestion*

5 WAVE OF THE FUTURE 63
   Alexis de Tocqueville's *Democracy in America*

6 EVANGELIST FOR PUBLIC SCHOOLS 74
   Horace Mann's *Annual Reports*

7 PROFESSIONAL HOMICIDE 86
   Oliver Wendell Holmes' *The Contagiousness of
   Puerperal Fever*

8 STATE VERSUS INDIVIDUAL 96
   Henry David Thoreau's *Resistance to Civil
   Government*

9 BLACK MAN'S ILIAD 108
   Harriet Beecher Stowe's *Uncle Tom's Cabin*

10 AMERICAN UTOPIA 119
      Edward Bellamy's *Looking Backward, 2000–1887*

11 RULING THE WAVES 130
      Alfred T. Mahan's *The Influence of Sea Power upon History, 1660–1783*

12 THE RECEDING FRONTIER 142
      Frederick Jackson Turner's *The Significance of the Frontier in American History*

13 MUNICIPAL MUCKRAKER 152
      Lincoln Steffens' *The Shame of the Cities*

14 HORRORS OF THE STOCKYARDS 164
      Upton Sinclair's *The Jungle*

15 REVOLUTION IN MEDICAL SCHOOLS 172
      Abraham Flexner's *Medical Education in the United States and Canada*

16 AMERICA'S MOST USEFUL CITIZEN 185
      Jane Addams' *Twenty Years at Hull-House*

17 SCIENCE OF EFFICIENCY 196
      Frederick Winslow Taylor's *The Principles of Scientific Management*

18 ECONOMIC DETERMINISM IN PHILADELPHIA 207
      Charles A. Beard's *An Economic Interpretation of the Constitution of the United States*

19 THE GREAT DEBUNKER 219
      Henry Louis Mencken's *Prejudices*

20 LEGAL MIND AT WORK 229
      Benjamin N. Cardozo's *The Nature of the Judicial Process*

21 VENTURE IN CONTEMPORARY ANTHROPOLOGY 238
      Robert S. and Helen Merrell Lynd's *Middletown*

22 NATION WITHIN A NATION 252
      W. J. Cash's *The Mind of the South*

23   DEED VERSUS CREED   262
        Gunnar Myrdal's *An American Dilemma*

24   PRIVATE OPULENCE AND PUBLIC POVERTY   274
        John Kenneth Galbraith's *The Affluent Society*

25   UPSETTING THE BALANCE OF NATURE   283
        Rachel Carson's *Silent Spring*

     BIBLIOGRAPHICAL NOTES   292

     INDEX   295

Introduction

THE PROPOSITION advanced in the present work, with supporting evidence, is that a nation's economic and social thought, political actions, scientific progress, and religious beliefs—in short, its culture and civilization—may be profoundly affected by the written word, or, more specifically, that certain seminal books have played key roles in shaping the American world of today.

The aim here is not to produce a list of "best" books, "great" books, or literary gems, a favorite pastime of literary critics, but instead to identify those writings which have exerted the greatest impact on our national history, direct or indirect.

Previous attempts to name the books of greatest influence have been made, two by the present author in his *Books That Changed the World* and *Molders of the Modern Mind.* In an article for *Publishers' Weekly* in 1935, Edward Weeks, John Dewey, and Charles A. Beard each selected the twenty-five most influential books since 1885—a fifty-year period. The sole title of American origin on which all three agreed was Edward Bellamy's *Looking Backward.* Two of the trio named James' *The Principles of Psychology*, Mahan's *The Influence of Sea Power upon History,* Veblen's *The Theory of the Leisure Class,* Adams' *The Education of Henry Adams*, and Lewis' *Main Street* and *Babbitt.*

A similar approach was followed by Malcolm Cowley and Bernard Smith a few years later, 1939, in their *Books That Changed Our Minds.* On the basis of a poll of educators, historians, critics, lecturers, and publicists, a dozen titles came to the top as having had most weight, in the judgment of the panelists, in shaping the American mind, though a total of 134 different books were mentioned by the individuals polled. Seven native Americans emerged in the select group: Adams' *The Education of Henry Adams,* Turner's *The Frontier in American His-*

tory, Sumner's *Folkways,* Veblen's *Business Enterprise,* Dewey's *Studies in Logical Theory,* Beard's *Economic Interpretation of the Constitution,* and Parrington's *Main Currents in American Thought.*

A more recent venture, by Rochelle Girson in the *Saturday Review,* 1964, followed the same technique: Twenty-seven historians, economists, political analysts, educators, social scientists, and philosophers were asked what books published during the past four decades had, in their view, most significantly altered the direction of our society. Among the experts in the symposium were Sir Denis Brogan, Stuart Chase, William O. Douglas, Sidney Hook, Walter Lippmann, and Allan Nevins. Titles receiving four or more votes each included Myrdal's *An American Dilemma,* Wiener's *Cybernetics,* Riesman's *The Lonely Crowd,* Kinsey's *Sexual Behavior* (male and female), Steinbeck's *The Grapes of Wrath,* Spock's *The Common Sense Book of Baby and Child Care,* Galbraith's *The Affluent Society,* Berle and Means' *The Modern Corporation and Private Property,* Niebuhr's *The Nature and Destiny of Man,* and Carson's *Silent Spring.* The remainder of a long list trailed off to votes of three, two, or one.

A famous list of older titles is the Grolier Club's *One Hundred Influential American Books Printed Before 1900,* which were exhibited at the Grolier Club in New York in 1947. The record begins with *The Bay Psalm Book,* printed at Cambridge, Massachusetts, in 1640, and concludes with Thorstein Veblen's *The Theory of the Leisure Class,* in 1897. A project sponsored by the Carnegie Corporation, and edited by Eric Larrabee, was published under the title *American Panorama* in 1957. Therein fifteen critics reviewed a total of 350 books designed to present "a picture of present-day American civilization and its origins." Sets of the books selected were distributed to the British Commonwealth countries where the corporation is active. Similar in nature and purpose is a recent publication, *USA in Books, an Introductory Collection: a Bibliography,* 1968, an annotated list of 250 titles; sets of the works recommended have been distributed by the United States Information Agency to all U.S. Information libraries abroad. The announced aim is "to show the spirit and reality of the American people—their social and political institutions, their scientific and technological development, their artistic expression, hopes and dreams."

It is readily apparent from an examination of the foregoing efforts to single out those books of most marked influence that a unanimous verdict is exceedingly difficult to achieve on any given work. Inevitably, selection is highly personal and subjective. Nevertheless, there is sufficient consensus on the twenty-five titles selected for discussion in the present volume to believe that all would rank high in a vote by any knowledgeable and impartial jury.

Is there any reasonable doubt that books do, in fact, change history? Overwhelming support exists for the thesis that under certain conditions or circumstances given books have been dynamic and vital, and were capable of changing the whole direction of events, sometimes for good, sometimes for evil. From a worldwide vantage point, skeptics might consider the impact of Karl Marx's *Das Kapital* on the socialist movement, Hitler's *Mein Kampf* on fascism, or, closer home, Tom Paine's *Common Sense* on the American Revolution, Harriet Beecher Stowe's *Uncle Tom's Cabin* on the American Civil War, and Thoreau's *Civil Disobedience* on the independence movement in backward countries and as a technique for social protest.

The testimony of dictators is also convincing. Witness the Nazis' book-burning orgies at Nuremberg in the nineteen thirties and the frequent destruction by Communist mobs abroad of American information libraries. In his book *Variety of Men*, C. P. Snow offers observations on Joseph Stalin's well-documented respect for writers and writing:

> Stalin . . . was deeply read in Russian literature and in Russian literary history. . . . He knew, more completely than any westerner, the role of the nineteenth century writers as an unofficial opposition. I suspect he felt, in a way no westerner could, the magical efficacy of literature. In his struggle for power, he had other forces to look after. But once he had gained power, then this was one among many forces to be looked after: it was not going to endanger either himself or his state.

Denigrators of books, such as Marshall McLuhan, would have us believe that books are obsolescent, being rapidly superseded by the newer media. Thus they would hold that books have had their day—possibly significant and influential in earlier eras, but now on the way to becoming museum pieces. The spuriousness of the argument can be easily demonstrated by citing three books published in the nineteen sixties, all of which have had a direct impact on current events: Rachel Carson's *Silent Spring*, which called dramatic attention to the perils of indiscriminate use of chemical preparations in agriculture and elsewhere; Ralph Nader's *Unsafe at Any Speed*, which forced the automobile industry to produce safer cars; and Jessica Mitford's *The American Way of Death*, which had a marked effect on the funeral business.

The measurement of influence is a perplexing question. A book which sells in the millions of copies may make little or no impact on popular thought or behavior, while another work, of limited circulation, may shake the world. Einstein's *Relativity* is a classical example. A plausible theory of communications has been advanced by Elmo Roper, who holds that most ideas are formulated by a few great thinkers and are then communicated to ever increasing numbers of people by various disseminators until the masses are aware of them. Roper assumes that the entire populace can be divided into six concentric groups. The smallest, innermost group, called "the great thinkers," consists of a handful of highly intellectual individuals. At this level, the great ideas and philosophies which eventually gain wide acceptance are born. Surrounding the elite group are "the great disciples"—individuals who do not orginate the great ideas, but who are in accord with them and become effective protagonists for them. A third and still larger group, "the great disseminators," is composed of individuals who have access to national or in some instances international forums to expound the ideas received from the brain trust above. From here on the task of spreading new thought is passed on successively to "lesser disseminators," the "politically active" (in a broad sense), and the "politically inert."

Of the authors included in *Books That Changed America,* perhaps a majority belong in the category of "great disseminators." When Tom Paine was writing *Common Sense,* the American Revolution was already primed for explosion, and civil war was in the air when Harriet Beecher Stowe's *Uncle Tom's Cabin* appeared. Civil disobedience was at least as ancient as biblical times when Thoreau gave new dimensions to the concept. Joseph Smith was deeply under the influence of the Bible and biblical commentators when he dictated *The Book of Mormon;* Edward Bellamy's utopia followed a tradition going back to Plato's *Republic;* and Turner's theory of the frontier had been expounded by a number of farsighted American leaders before his day.

Thus, here is a temptation to revert to the old saw that there is nothing new under the sun. On the other hand, probably without exception, the twenty-five authors (or twenty-seven, including joint authors) dealt with in the present work brought new interpretations to ideas they found floating in the air, dramatized situations, and caught the public imagination with their manner of expression. And in certain instances, in William Beaumont's experiments in human digestion, for example, new and revolutionary ideas were produced.

The emphasis in the selection of titles for *Books That Changed America* is on the social sciences, rather than science or the humanities. The three works of fiction included—Bellamy's *Looking Backward,* Sinclair's *The Jungle,* and Stowe's *Uncle Tom's Cabin*—are essentially sociological treatises in fictional guise. Three works pertain to the field of medicine—Beaumont's *Experiments,* Holmes' *Contagiousness of Puerperal Fever,* and Flexner's *Medical Education*—but only the first can be classified as a scientific medical work; the others have vital social messages to impart. The reason for the stress on the social sciences, and to a more limited extent on science, is easily explainable. It is simply the fact that the influence of books in these areas is, as a rule, more direct and more easily measurable than that of the important books in such fields as literature and philosophy.

A total of more than eighty titles were seriously considered for selection in the present work, and the task of reducing the list to twenty-five was by no means easy. Among the strong runners-up, finally eliminated for space or other reasons, were Horatio Alger, whose *Ragged Dick* and its successors inspired several generations of upcoming young businessmen; Bryce's *American Commonwealth,* a classic of American government; Dana's *Two Years Before the Mast,* an epic that did much to improve conditions at sea for American sailors; Benjamin Franklin's memoirs, the most widely read of all American autobiographies; Henry George's *Progress and Poverty,* one of the most influential of American works on economics; the Kinsey reports, which brought a sane approach to the most important aspect of human relations; Dr. Spock's *Common Sense Book of Baby and Child Care*, with its "tranquilizing effect on parental anxieties" and its permissive philosophy; Herman Melville's *Moby Dick*, "The Great American Novel"; Mark Twain's *Huckleberry Finn*, the nearest thing that we have to a national epic; and John Steinbeck's *The Grapes of Wrath*, which aroused the nation to major problems of social injustices and helped to focus attention on the war against poverty. These are a few of the considerable number of books whose impact on American history during the past two centuries can be convincingly documented.

It will be noted that two non-Americans appear among the selected authors: Alexis de Tocqueville, a Frenchman, and Gunnar Myrdal, a Swede. The acuteness of observation, the objectivity, and the depth of penetration of these two writers in dealing with problems of American democracy have scarely ever been equaled. America has, in fact, gained (and occasionally suffered) much from foreign critics, e.g., Mrs. Trollope's *Domestic Manners of the Americans*, Charles Dickens' *American Notes*, Lord Bryce's *American Commonwealth*, Frederick Marryat's *A Diary in America*, Rudyard Kipling's *American Notes*, and many more. The range is from the querulous and superficial to the profound; the nineteenth-century Tocqueville and the twentieth-century Myrdal clearly belong in the latter category.

Somewhat irrelevant, but of human interest, are the sex and age of the authors included. Among the twenty-seven are four women—Jane Addams, Rachel Carson, Helen Lynd, and Harriet Beecher Stowe. At the time their books were published, not one of the total group was beyond the mid-fifties in age. Two were in their twenties, Upton Sinclair and Joseph Smith; thirteen in their thirties: Beard, Bellamy, Cash, William Clark, Holmes, Meriwether Lewis, Helen and Robert Lynd, Paine, Lincoln Steffens, Thoreau, Tocqueville, and Turner; seven in the forties: Beaumont, Flexner, Mann, Mencken, Myrdal, Stowe, and Taylor; Admiral Mahan, Galbraith, and Jane Addams were barely fifty, Cardozo was fifty-one and Rachel Carson fifty-five. If any conclusions can be drawn from these limited data, they are that sex is not a significant factor in the writing of books of great influence, but the most productive period for authors is the thirty to fifty age bracket. Only four of the twenty-seven were under thirty or over fifty.

A few of the select group are known principally for a single book: Joseph Smith, Lewis and Clark, Beaumont, Tocqueville, Turner, and W. J. Cash are examples. Others were prolific, notably Charles Beard, H. L. Mencken, Harriet Beecher Stowe, Oliver Wendell Holmes, Upton Sinclair, and J. K. Galbraith. The remainder fall between the two extremes. Further, the titles by which several of the writers are represented in the present work do not exhaust, by any means, the books for which they are famous. Illustrations are Paine's *Age of Reason* and *Rights of Man*, Thoreau's *Walden*, Mencken's *American Language*, Beard's *Rise of American Civilization*, Steffens' *Autobiography*, and Rachel Carson's *The Sea Around Us*.

As one reviews these twenty-five power-laden books a query frequently comes to mind: Did the times make the book, or vice versa, i.e., was a particular work influential chiefly because the time was ripe for it? Would the book have been equally significant in another era, or could it even have been written at any other date? The conclusion is inescapable that the times produced the book in nearly every instance. In some other period, the work would not have been produced at all, or if it had appeared, would have attracted little attention.

The secret of success of the chosen books is that the world was ready to receive them and in toto they carried messages appealing to millions of people. Sometimes the influence was beneficent, sometimes harmful. Disregarding moral values, the twenty-five books demonstrate conclusively that books are dynamic and powerful instruments, tools, or weapons.

R. B. D.

1–CLARION CALL FOR REVOLUTION

THOMAS PAINE'S *CommonSense*

FEW FIGURES in American history are as controversial as Thomas Paine and few made contributions as notable as his toward the beginning of the United States as a nation. To dismiss Paine, as did Theodore Roosevelt, as "a filthy little atheist" (he was none of the three) is totally unfair to a man who played a major role in inspiring the American Revolution, who had a direct hand in drafting the Declaration of Independence, and who was instrumental in maintaining the morale of George Washington's troops at their lowest ebb.

The first thirty-seven years of Tom Paine's career were marked by a series of failures, giving virtually no evidence of future greatness. He came into the world in 1737 in the village of Thetford, England, the son of Quaker parents. At the age of thirteen, he left the local grammar school to serve an apprenticeship in his father's trade of corset making. Soon tiring of the dullness and drudgery of the work, Tom staged his first rebellion, running away to join the crew of a privateer. His father overtook him on board and brought him back to stay-making. Again the boy ran away and this time saw enough service at sea to cure any romantic illusions. In the years that followed, matters went from bad to worse: two unfortunate marriages, one ending in the wife's early death and the other in separation; two periods of employment in the excise service, the last leading to discharge for serving as spokesman for the grossly underpaid customs officers; earning a pittance as a schoolmaster; operating an unsuccessful tobacco shop; and ending up in London in hiding to avoid imprisonment for debt.

While in London, Paine had the good fortune to meet

Benjamin Franklin, stationed there as political agent for the American colonies. Franklin was attracted by Paine's character and abilities and urged him to migrate to America and make a new start. Paine's interest in science, electrical experiments, and practical inventions had drawn the two men together. Paine proceeded to accept Franklin's advice and arrived in Philadelphia in late 1774, armed with a letter of introduction to Franklin's son-in-law, Richard Bache.

The New World produced a transformation in Paine. Prior to coming to America, he had written only one piece of propaganda, *The Case of the Officers of Excise*, in which he had argued for better pay for the excisemen. His varied experience in England, as shopworker, sailor, tradesman, revenue officer, and teacher, however, had fitted him well for the part of master propagandist which he would play in future. He had witnessed at first hand the misery, poverty, and insecurity of the lower classes in England, in contrast to the conspicuous wealth of the royalty and nobility. During his term of government duty, Paine had also become acquainted with widespread public corruption. He sailed for America disillusioned with the European scene, but filled with dreams of liberty, ready to fight for democratic principles.

Within a short time after Paine's arrival in Philadelphia, a printer and bookseller named Robert Aitken began publication of the *Pennsylvania Magazine*. Paine wrote extensively for the first issue of the new periodical, following which he was appointed its editor. During the ensuing eighteen months, he wrote on a variety of radical causes, denouncing Negro slavery, the custom of dueling, cruelty to animals, and hereditary titles, and advocating women's rights, old-age pensions, rational divorce laws, national and international copyright, international federation, and republican equality. One of Paine's first articles condemned Negro slavery as a monstrous evil, in these words:

> Certainly one may, with as much reason and decency, plead for murder, robbery, lewdness, and barbarity, as for this practice. They are not more contrary to the natural dictates of conscience and feelings of humanity; nay, they are all comprehended in it.

Paine was one of the first, and perhaps the first, to

advocate complete freedom for the United States. Nine months before the Declaration of Independence he wrote: "I hesitate not for a moment to believe that the Almighty will finally separate America from Britain. Call it Independency or what you will, if it is the cause of God and humanity it will go on."

Events in the American colonies had been building up toward an explosion. A year before Paine landed in Philadelphia, Sam Adams and his Boston patriots threw the British tea into the ocean, as punishment for which the Boston port was ordered closed until the East India Company was compensated for the lost tea. The economic hardship caused in Boston by this move led to the meeting of the First Continental Congress, in September 1774. The Congress declared grievances, stated principles, and criticized British policies, but disclaimed any idea of independence. George III was determined, in any case, to suppress ruthlessly any disloyal actions or sentiments. Whatever the consequences, the king said, the colonists must be compelled to absolute obedience. On orders from Downing Street, Admiral Graves' fleet made a bonfire of Portland, Maine, in 1775; ten weeks later the town of Norfolk, Virginia, was burned to the ground by the royal governor, Lord Dunmore, who also issued an order freeing all slaves who would take up arms against their masters.

Then came the battles of Concord and Lexington, in April 1775, when British redcoats fought colonial minutemen, clashes which began the war for independence. In May, the Second Continental Congress convened, to create the Continental Army, to appoint George Washington commander in chief, and in general to serve as a center for consultation and protest for the thirteen colonies. Even so, as Charles A. and Mary R. Beard have observed, "months after the first blood was shed, strong men continued to express their affection for England and to hope for a peaceful way out of the prolonged deadlock." Men of such diverse tempers as Washington, Jefferson, and John Adams clung to the hope of a reconciliation with England.

In this confused state of affairs, one man saw clearly the direction in which events were trending and came through with a bold, uncompromising stand—separation from England and establishment of an independent republican government. This was the essence of Tom Paine's celebrated pamphlet *Common Sense*. Deeply stirred by the prevailing controversies, and especially the beginning of hostilities at Concord and Lexington, Paine had begun putting his convictions on paper in the autumn of 1775. A publisher was found for him by Dr. Benjamin Rush, and a Philadelphia newspaper of January 10, 1776, carried the following advertisement:

> This day was published and is now selling by Robert Bell in Third Street, price two shillings, Common Sense, addressed to the inhabitants of North America.

The anonymous eighty-page pamphlet was identified merely as "Written by an Englishman," and attributed at first to Franklin, John Adams, or Samuel Adams.

In his introduction, Paine holds that "The cause of America is in a great measure the cause of all mankind," for the principles involved were universal. Moreover, "the laying of a country desolate with fire and sword, declaring war against the natural rights of all mankind, and extirpating the defenders thereof from the face of the earth is the concern of every man to whom nature has given the power of feeling."

The first part of *Common Sense* treats of the nature of society and of government, making a clear distinction between the two. "Society is produced by our wants," it is remarked, "and government by our wickedness. . . . Society in every state is a blessing, but government even in its best state is but a necessary evil, in its worst state an intolerable one. . . . Government, like dress, is the badge of lost innocence; the palaces of kings are built on the ruins of the bowers of paradise." Nevertheless, the simplest society finds it necessary eventually to establish "some form of government to supply the defect of moral virtue." As population increases, government becomes more complex, but the end always, insists Paine, should be "freedom and security."

Paine next examines "the so much boasted constitution of England," from the point of view of these objectives, and concludes, "that it was noble for the dark and slavish times in which it was erected is granted. When the world was overrun with tyranny, the least remove therefrom was a glorious rescue. But that it is imperfect, subject to convulsions, and incapable of producing what it seems to promise is easily demonstrated . . . the constitution of England is so exceedingly complex that the nation may suffer for years together without being able to discover in which part the fault lies."

The concept of monarchy and hereditary succession is bitterly attacked by Paine. He is contemptuous of a social system which sets up a king to rule over human beings. "Male and female are the distinctions of nature," he points out, "good and bad the distinctions of heaven, but how a race of men came into the world so exalted above the rest, and distinguished like some new species, is worth inquiring into, and whether they are the means of happiness or of misery to mankind." The institution of monarchy is condemned on two grounds—natural rights and scriptural authority:

Government by kings was first introduced into the world by the heathens, from whom the children of Israel copied the custom. It was the most prosperous invention the devil ever set on foot for the promotion of idolatry. The heathens paid divine honors to their deceased kings, and the Christian world has improved on the plan by doing the same to their living ones. . . . To the evils of monarchy we have added that of hereditary succession; and as the first is a degradation and lessening of ourselves, so the second, claimed as a matter of right, is an insult and imposition on posterity. . . . One of the strongest natural proofs of the folly of hereditary rights in kings is that nature disproves it, otherwise she would not so frequently turn it into ridicule by giving mankind an *ass* for a *lion*.

George III, in particular, is denounced by Paine as the "Royal Brute of Great Britain," and the "greatest enemy this continent hath, or can have." In fact, "England since the conquest has known some few good monarchs, but groaned beneath a much larger number of bad ones; yet no man in his senses can say that their claim under William the Conqueror is a very honorable one. A French bastard landing with an armed banditti and establishing himself king of England against the consent of the natives is in plain terms a very paltry, rascally original. It certainly has no divinity in it." After the battle of Lexington, Paine declared, "I rejected the hardened, sullen-tempered Pharaoh of England forever and disdain the wretch that, with the pretended title of father of his people, can unfeelingly hear of their slaughter and composedly sleep with their blood upon his soul."

As seen by Paine, the king performs no constructive or useful function: "In England a king hath little more to do than to make war and give away places; which, in plain terms, is to impoverish the nation and set it together by the ears. A pretty business, indeed, for a man to be allowed eight hundred thousand sterling a year for, and worshipped into the bargain! Of more worth is one honest man to society, and in the sight of God, than all the crowned ruffians that ever lived."

If the monarchy ensured a race of good and wise men, it would not be objectionable, but as a matter of fact, asserted Paine, "it opens a door to the *foolish,* the *wicked,* and the *improper,*" for "Men who look upon themselves born to reign, and others to obey, soon grow insolent; selected from the rest of mankind their minds are early poisoned by importance . . . when they succeed to the government are often the most ignorant and unfit of any throughout the dominions." Permitting underage and overage kings to sit on the throne also has numerous disadvantages. In the first instance, the actual administration of the country is carried on by a regent, and in the other it is subject to the whims of a senile, worn-out monarch.

Having effectively disposed of monarchical government, Paine proceeded to "Some thoughts on the present state of the American affairs." Economic arguments for separation from Britain were stressed. To the Tories' contention that the American colonies had flourished because of their connection with England, Paine rejoined:

America would have flourished as much, and probably much more, had no European power had anything to do with her. The commerce by which she has enriched herself are the necessaries of life and will always have a market while eating is the custom in Europe. . . . I challenge the warmest advocate for reconciliation to show a single advantage that this continent can reap by being connected with Great Britain. . . . Our corn will fetch its price in any market in Europe, and our imported goods must be paid for, buy them where we will.

The claim that Britain had protected the colonies against the Spanish, French, and Indians, Paine dismissed with the comment: "She would have defended Turkey from the same motives, viz., for the sake of trade and dominion," and, in any case, the defense was "at our expense as well as her own."

One of the strongest ties holding the colonies against separation, Paine recognized, was a sentimental conception of Britain as the mother country. If this were true, "Then the more shame upon her conduct. Even brutes do not devour their young nor savages make war upon their families . . . the phrase 'parent' or 'mother country' has been jesuitically adopted by the king and his parasites with a low papistical design of gaining an unfair bias on the credulous weakness of our minds. Europe, and not England, is the parent country of America." The New World, Paine pointed out, "has been the asylum for the persecuted lovers of civil and religious liberty from *every part* of Europe . . . and it is so far true of England that the same tyranny which drove the first emigrants from home pursues their descendants still."

Foreshadowing George Washington's Farewell Address twenty years later, warning the American people "to steer clear of permanent alliances with any portion of the foreign world," and Thomas Jefferson's policy of "Peace, commerce, and honest friendship with all nations— entangling alliances with none," Paine held that there would be numerous drawbacks to continued British rule:

> . . . because any submission to or dependence on Great Britain tends directly to involve this continent in European wars and quarrels and sets us at variance with nations which would otherwise seek our friendship and against whom we have neither anger nor complaint. As Europe is our market for trade, we ought to form no partial connection with any part of it. It is the true interest of America to steer clear of European contentions, which she can never do while, by her dependence on Britain, she is made the makeweight in the scale of British politics. Europe is too thickly planted with kingdoms to be long at peace; and whenever a war breaks out between England and any foreign power, the trade of America goes to ruin *because of her connection with Britain.*

The manifold inconveniences of British government were reviewed by Paine and the conclusion reached that:

... it is not in the power of Britain to do this continent justice. The business of it will soon be too
weighty and intricate to be managed with any toler-
able degree of convenience by a power so distant
from us and so very ignorant of us; for if they cannot
conquer us, they cannot govern us. To be always
running three or four thousand miles with a tale or a
petition, waiting four or five months for an answer,
which, when obtained, requires five or six more to
explain it in, will in a few years be looked upon as
folly and childishness. . . . There is something very
absurd in supposing a continent to be perpetually
governed by an island. In no instance has nature
made the satellite larger than its primary planet.

To the skeptics and fainthearted who still held out for
restoring harmony and bringing about reconciliation,
Paine made an impassioned plea:

Can ye restore to us the time that is past? Can ye
give to prostitution its former innocence? Neither can
ye reconcile Britain and America. The last cord now
is broken, the people of England are presenting addresses against us. There are injuries which nature
cannot forgive; she would cease to be nature if she
did. As well can the lover forgive the ravisher of his
mistress as the continent forgive the murders of Britain.

While the rest of the world was burdened with oppression, America should open her doors wide to freedom, and
prepare an asylum for persecuted mankind. "The sun
never shined on a cause of greater worth," wrote Paine.
" 'Tis not the affair of a city, a county, a province, or a
kingdom, but of a continent—of at least one-eighth part
of the habitable globe. 'Tis not the concern of a day, a
year, or an age; posterity are virtually involved in the
contest, and will be more or less even to the end of time
by the proceedings now. Now is the seedtime of continental union, faith, and honor."

His final chapter was devoted by Paine to some practical considerations on "the present ability of America,"
designed to convince the colonists that they had the manpower, manufacturing experience, and natural resources to
wage a successful war. There was already in existence a

large body of armed and disciplined men. A navy as powerful as Britain's could be constructed in a brief time; tar, timber, iron, and cordage were available in quantity, and "Ship building is America's greatest pride, and in which she will, in time, excel the whole world." A fleet was needed in any case, for the colonies' defense and protection, in view of the fact that the English navy "three or four thousand miles off can be of little use, and on sudden emergencies, none at all."

In the light of the religious controversies in which he subsequently became involved, it is of interest to note Paine's religious views at this stage in his career:

> As to religion, I hold it to be the indispensable duty of all government to protect all conscientious professors thereof, and I know of no other business which government has to do therewith. . . . For myself, I fully and conscientiously believe that it is the will of the Almighty that there should be diversity of religious opinions among us. It affords a larger field for our Christian kindness. Were we all of one way of thinking, our religious dispositions would want matter for probation; and on this liberal principle I look on the various denominations among us to be like children of the same family, differing only in what is called their Christian names.

Summing up his case like an expert attorney-at-law, Paine enumerated the factors which had convinced him that "nothing can settle our affairs so expeditiously as an open and determined declaration for independence." These were: (1) As long as America was regarded as a subject of Britain, no other nation would attempt to mediate the differences between them; (2) no aid could be expected from France or Spain in repairing the breach and strengthening the connection between Britain and America, because such a step would be to their disadvantage; (3) while the Americans acknowledged themselves to be the subjects of Britain, they would, in the eyes of foreign nations, be considered rebels, and therefore would win little sympathy; (4) if the Americans would prepare a manifesto setting forth their grievances against Britain, and their intention of breaking off all connections with her, sending copies of the declaration to other countries, expressing their peaceable disposition toward them and their desire to establish trade relations, the results would be highy favorable.

Paine closed his argument by asserting that:

> . . . until an independence is declared, the continent will feel itself like a man who continues putting off some unpleasant duty from day to day, yet knows it must be done, hates to set about it, wishes it were over, and is continually haunted with the thoughts of its necessity.
>
> Wherefore, instead of gazing at each other with suspicious or doubtful curiosity, let each of us hold out to his neighbor the hearty hand of friendship and unite in drawing a line which, like an act of oblivion, shall bury in forgetfulness every former dissention. Let the name of Whig and Tory be extinct, and let none other be heard among us than those of *a good citizen, an open and resolute friend, and a virtuous supporter of the rights of mankind and of the free and independent states of America.*

This was Tom Paine's revolutionary message communicated to the American people by *Common Sense*—a mixture of reasonable, realistic, and practical contentions and of demagogic, emotional, and violently partisan appeals.

The response was immediate and phenomenal. Within three months, 120,000 copies of *Common Sense* had been sold, and the total sales may have reached a half-million copies—the American best seller of all time in relation to population, then about two and a half million.

George Washington wrote to Joseph Reed: "A few more such flaming arguments as were exhibited at Falmouth and Norfolk [burned by the British], added to the sound doctrine and unanswerable reasoning contained in the pamphlet *Common Sense*, will not leave numbers at a loss to decide on the propriety of a separation." Two months later, in another letter to Reed, Washington commented: "By private letters which I have lately received from Virginia, I find *Common Sense* is working a wonderful change in the minds of men."

Soon after *Common Sense* was issued, Major General Lee wrote to Washington: "Have you seen the pamphlet, *Common Sense*? I never saw such a masterly, irresistible performance. It will, if I mistake not, in concurrence with the transcendent folly and wickedness of the ministry, give the *coup-de-grace* to Great Britain. In short, I own myself convinced by its arguments of the necessity of separation."

In his *History of the American Revolution,* Sir George Trevelyan states: "It would be difficult to name any human composition which has had an effect at once so instant, so extended and so lasting. . . . It was pirated, parodied and imitated, and translated into the language of every country where the new republic had well-wishers . . . according to contemporary newspapers *Common Sense* turned thousands to independence who before could not endure the thought. It worked nothing short of miracles and turned Tories into Whigs."

Benjamin Franklin noted of *Common Sense,* "I own it has convinced me," and William Henry Drayton reported that "this declaration came like an explosion of thunder upon the members of the Continental Congress."

Within a few months after the appearance of *Common Sense,* most of the states had instructed their delegates to vote for independence, only Maryland hesitating and New York opposing. On July 4, 1776, less than six months from the date when Paine's famous pamphlet came off the press, the Continental Congress, meeting in the State House at Philadelphia, proclaimed the independence of the United States of America. Though Paine did not write the Declaration, he was closely associated with Thomas Jefferson while it was being composed, and except for the omission of an antislavery clause which Paine advocated, the principles for which he stood were incorporated in the celebrated manifesto.

Soon after the Declaration of Independence, Paine enlisted in the Revolutionary Army, but Washington, realizing his superb talents for propaganda, assigned him to the writing of a series of papers entitled *The American Crisis,* designed to inspire the troops and to hearten any discouraged patriots. The opening paragraph of the first *Crisis* is characteristic:

These are the times that try men's souls. The summer soldier and the sunshine patriot will, in this crisis, shrink from the service of their country; but he that stands it *now* deserves the love and thanks of man and woman. Tyranny, like hell, is not easily conquered; yet we have this consolation with us, that the harder the conflict, the more glorious the triumph.

The *Crisis* papers were read by practically everyone, in and out of the Army. They aided immensely in keeping the struggle for independence alive when it seemed headed for disaster because of apathy, Loyalist opposition, lack of recruits, shortage of supplies, and inefficient organization.

Paine's biographer, Alfred Owen Aldridge, found that the influence of *Common Sense* extended far beyond the continental borders of America. In the same year that it was published in Philadelphia, a French translation appeared and was widely popular. During the Revolution of 1789 it was issued in Spanish to vindicate the new French republic. Later it was retranslated and circulated in Latin America, where it became highly influential in the independence movements of Venezuela, Mexico, and Ecuador.

The Revolution over, in 1783, Paine turned to mechanical inventions, designing the first iron suspension bridge, and experimenting with steam power. The decision was made to consult engineers in France and England on some of the technical problems, and in 1787 Paine went to Europe, where he remained for fifteen years.

Soon after his arrival abroad, the French Revolution erupted, an event which Paine hailed with enthusiasm as further justification of his democratic ideas. In defense of the Revolution, replying to Edmund Burke's attacks, he produced his classic *The Rights of Man*. Forced hurriedly to leave England to avoid arrest for treason, because of the doctrines expressed therein, Paine fled to France, where he had been elected to the Convention as a member representing Calais. In an attempt to save Louis XVI from execution, Paine broke with such extremists as Robespierre and Marat. When these elements took over the government, Paine was arrested, deprived of his honorary citizenship, imprisoned for ten months, and narrowly escaped the guillotine. Released from prison through the intercession of the American ambassador, James Monroe, he was nursed back to health in Monroe's home.

The great work of this period was *The Age of Reason*, sometimes described as "the atheist's bible." Actually, Paine was a pious deist, believing in one God and a hereafter, and *The Age of Reason,* though highly critical of the Old Testament, had been written to check the strong tide of atheism sweeping France in the Revolutionary era. Nevertheless, theologians and orthodox religious groups roundly condemned Paine as a dangerous radical and unbeliever.

When Paine returned to America in 1802, he found himself received not as a Revolutionary hero, but virtually ostracized by political leaders and churchgoers, due to his authorship of *The Age of Reason* and his radical political theories. In New Rochelle, New York, where he settled, he was denied the right to vote on the ground that he was not an American citizen. An attempt was even made to murder him. After seven incredible years of abuse, hatred, neglect, poverty, and ill health, he died in 1809, at the age of seventy-two. He was denied burial in a Quaker cemetery.

This was the man who perhaps more than any other deserves the title, "Founder of American Independence," who first used the phrase "The United States of America," who foresaw that "The United States of America will sound as pompously in history as the Kingdom of Great Britain," and who proclaimed, "The cause of America is, in a great measure, the cause of all mankind." No better index to Paine's character can be found than in his reply to Franklin's remark, "Where liberty is, there is my country." "Where liberty is not," said Paine, "there is mine."

Even in his own time, the hymn of hate and misrepresentation was not universal. Andrew Jackson dared to say, "Thomas Paine needs no monument made by hands; he has erected a monument in the hearts of all lovers of liberty."

2—THE WAY WEST

MERIWETHER LEWIS AND WILLIAM CLARK'S
History of the Expedition Under the Command of Captains Lewis and Clark

FOR AT LEAST twenty years before he became President of the United States, Thomas Jefferson had thought and dreamed of an overland expedition to the Pacific. In Great Britain's formal recognition of the United States in 1784, the new nation's western boundary was specified as the Mississippi. Three nations—France, Britain, and Spain—were in deadly rivalry for the immense unsettled territory beyond the great river. Jefferson foresaw that any valid American claim to the vast area must be supported by discovery and exploration. Proposals from Jefferson to John Ledyard, André Michaux, and George Rogers Clark to carry the American flag across the continent came to nothing, for a variety of reasons.

The great opportunity came at the dawn of the nineteenth century. Spain had ceded all the region vaguely known as Louisiana back to France. Napoleon Bonaparte was, as usual, engaged in war and preparation for war, and badly needed money. Prolonged negotiations between Talleyrand and American agents, sent to Paris by Jefferson, eventually led to a French agreement to sell the Louisiana Territory to the United States for $15,000,000. Jefferson's enemies in Congress bitterly opposed the transaction, condemning the expenditure of such a sum to acquire what they called the "Great American Desert." Nevertheless, the Senate promptly ratified the treaty, on October 19, 1803.

Under the terms of the Louisiana Purchase, the United States was to obtain the entire area drained by the Mississippi and its tributaries, or as Jefferson phrased it, *"the boundaries of interior Louisiana are the high lands enclos-*

ing all the waters which run into the Mississippi or Missouri directly or indirectly." No one, not even Jefferson, realized the enormous size of the newly acquired territory. Actually, all or most of thirteen states were being added to the Union: Louisiana, Arkansas, Oklahoma, Missouri, Kansas, Colorado, Wyoming, Montana, the Dakotas, Nebraska, Iowa, and Minnesota. No white man had ever set foot on a large portion.

Even before the United States could claim legal title to the western region, Jefferson had initiated plans for exploring country that was still almost a blank on the maps. An appropriation of $2500 was asked for and approved by Congress to finance an expedition to the West Coast. British traders were penetrating south from Canada and Spanish raiders were moving north from Mexico. It was rumored that the British were planning to hoist the Union Jack at the mouth of the Columbia River. Jefferson recognized the need for speedy action if America was to retain the new territory.

Jefferson's message to Congress outlined his purpose:

The River Missouri and the Indians inhabiting it are not as well known as is rendered desirable by their connection with the Mississippi and, consequently, with us. It is, however, understood that the country on that river is inhabited by numerous tribes, who furnish great supplies of furs and pelfry to the trade of another nation carried on in a high latitude, through an infinite number of portages and lakes shut up by ice through a long season. The commerce on that line could bear no competition with that of the Missouri, traversing a moderate climate, offering, according to the best accounts, a continued navigation from its source and, possibly, with a single portage from the Western Ocean. . . . An intelligent officer with ten or twelve chosen men, fit for the enterprise and willing to undertake it, taken from our posts where they may be spared without inconvenience, might explore the whole line, even to the Western Ocean, have conferences with the natives on the subject of commercial intercourse, get admission among them for our traders as others are admitted, agree on convenient deposits for an interchange of articles, and return with the information acquired in the course of two summers.

To head the expedition, Jefferson selected his private secretary, a fellow Virginian, Meriwether Lewis, who at age twenty-nine was an experienced soldier and diplomat and brought to his new assignment an impressive knowledge of the frontier and of Indians, a lively mind, great physical stamina, and natural qualities of leadership. In preparation for his formidable adventure, Lewis spent several months in Philadelphia and Lancaster, buying scientific instruments and learning how to take latitude and longitude, to use astronomical instruments, and to make maps; obtaining medicine from the famous Dr. Benjamin Rush of Philadelphia; and rounding up equipment from the quartermaster depot.

Jefferson suggested that Lewis select an alternate commander, as a precaution, and Lewis nominated his best friend, William Clark, a thirty-four-year-old artillery lieutenant. The choice was ideal. Clark was an experienced mapmaker, trained as an army intelligence officer, and skillful with pen and pencil in making sketches of birds, animals, and plants. Furthermore, the personalities of the two men were perfect complements—Lewis a taciturn introvert, and Clark a redhaired, convivial, friendly extrovert. It is significant that the two leaders remained warm friends throughout the expedition.

Jefferson's written directions handed to Lewis prior to his departure were most specific and placed heavy responsibilities on the captains and their men. "The object of your mission," stated Jefferson, "is to explore the Missouri river, and such principal streams of it, as, by its course and communication with the waters of the Pacific ocean, whether the Columbia, Oregon, Colorado, or any other river, may offer the most direct and practicable water-communication across the continent, for the purposes of commerce."

The President continued with orders to take observations of latitudes and longitudes, beginning at the mouth of the Missouri, at all "remarkable" points, such as the mouths of tributaries, rapids, and islands. The explorers were to become acquainted with the Indian nations, including their names and numbers and the extent of their possessions; their relations with other tribes or nations; their languages, traditions, and occupations; their food, clothing, and living arrangements; their diseases and remedies; their laws, customs, and dispositions; and the articles of commerce they possessed or desired. In all relations with the natives, they were to be treated in a "friendly and conciliatory manner."

As if this were not enough, Jefferson asked his agents to observe "the soil and face of the country, its growth and vegetable productions, especially those not of the United States; the animals of the country generally, and especially those not known in the United States; . . . the mineral productions of every kind . . . volcanic appearances; climate, as characterized by the thermometer, by the proportion of rainy, cloudy, and clear days; by lightning, hail, snow, ice; by the access and recess of frost; by the winds prevailing at different seasons; the dates at which particular plants put forth, or lose their flower or leaf; times of appearance of particular birds, reptiles, or insects."

Twenty-eight months later, Lewis and Clark had substantially accomplished the seemingly impossible mission for which Jefferson had appointed them.

The Lewis-Clark expedition mustered in Illinois, not far from the mouth of the Missouri. While Lewis was busy in St. Louis collecting every scrap of information available on the Missouri and the Indian nations inhabiting its borders, Clark spent the winter of 1803–4 enlisting and drilling men for the westward trek. The men picked were enrolled in the Army at $10 a month for privates, $15 for three sergeants, and $80 each for Lewis and Clark. Twenty-nine men were trained in the rudiments of woodcraft, nine of them recruits from Kentucky; also in the party were hunters from Virginia, farmers from Vermont, and carpenters from Pennsylvania. America had already become a melting pot, for there were Irishmen, Scots, Dutchmen, and Frenchmen, and Clark's Negro servant, York. To guard against the dangerous Indians of the plains, the captains decided to take an extra corporal and six soldiers, all to be sent back from the Mandan Indian villages. Nine rivermen were added to help row the heavy boats upstream, constituting a total company of forty-five men.

In equipment for the expedition, Lewis and Clark had apparently thought of everything. Loaded on a keelboat and two pirogues—standard river transportation—when the party left its river camp on May 14, 1804, to enter the mainstream of the Missouri, were boxes of ammunition for hunting and defense, casks of whiskey to cheer the men and the Indians they would meet en route; sacks of grain; spools of rope; a large American flag; clothing;

and even a little mill for grinding corn. There was also
a great quantity of "trade goods" for the Indians; laced
coats, ruffled calico skirts, striped silk ribbons, scarlet
cloth, gaudy handkerchiefs, medals and beads, small bells,
mirrors, knives, tomahawks, rings, brooches, brass kettles,
fishhooks, steel traps, and theatrical paint. The iron-framed
keelboat, the largest craft that had ever attempted to navi-
gate the Missouri, was fifty-five feet long and equipped
with both sails and oars.

Almost immediately, the expedition discovered how
treacherous and dangerous the Missouri, or "Big Muddy,"
could be. The second day out, it was reported, "We found
that our boat was too heavily laden in the stern, in
consequence of which she ran on logs three times to-day.
It became necessary to throw the greatest weight on the
bow of the boat, a precaution very necessary in ascending
both the Missouri and Mississippi rivers, in the beds of
which there lie great quantities of concealed timber."
Against the main current of the Missouri, oars and poles
were useless and yet the cave-ins along the banks made it
highly dangerous to approach too near the shore. The
swift current frequently turned the boat around, broke the
towline, and drove it on sandbars.

Nevertheless, in other respects, the journey for the first
several months was idyllic. There were comfortable camps
at night and the party was traversing beautiful country.
The two leaders spent the evenings working by firelight on
their journals, recording in meticulous detail the events
and observations of each day. In one entry, Lewis noted:
"In addition to the common deer, which were in great
abundance, we saw goats, elk, buffalo, antelope, the black-
tailed deer and the large wolves." Fifty-two herds of bison
were counted in a single day.

No expedition in history was ever more carefully
documented than Lewis and Clark's. Of the incidents of
each day, a conscientious journal was kept by Captain
Lewis or Captain Clark, and sometimes by both. The notes
were afterward revised and enlarged during periods of
leisure along the route. Jefferson had ordered the journals
to be kept "with great pains and accuracy and to be
entered distinctly and intelligibly." Other men in the company were also encouraged to record events, observations,
and impressions, and seven did so, four of whose accounts
have survived. None was comparable in literary quality,
however, to those of Lewis and Clark. Even the leaders'

diaries have a certain misleading quality. As Jeannette Mirsky pointed out in her *The Westward Crossings*, "They drone on and on, occupied with each pinprick of time in the making; there is a repetitious, almost tedious quality to the entries; there is a matter-of-factness, a preoccupation with soil and game, with humdrum minutiae, that obscures the continuity and the heroic mission." Yet, the cumulative effect on the reader is of firsthand participation in a great journey filled with infinite variety.

Throughout the first phase of their travels—the long haul from May 14 to October 24, 1804—the explorers were passing through the almost limitless prairies. Farther up the Missouri, few trees except willow and dwarf cottonwood were found. Ash trees disappeared beyond the Platte River, a misfortune for the boatmen, who needed new poles, oars, masts, or ax helves. For hundreds of miles the Missouri flowed between high bluffs, constantly undermining them, especially in flood periods, causing huge trees and tracts of land to collapse into the river and to be carried downstream. Gradually the prairies gave way to the great plains. Three months after leaving St. Louis, the voyagers had covered 850 miles and were in the vicinity of what is now Sioux City in Iowa. From here on the going became harder. Sandbars caught the pirogues, one man collapsed from sunstroke, Sergeant Charles Floyd died of colic, and insects almost drove the men insane. Mosquitoes bit them until they were "covered with blood and swellings," and horseflies, known as "greenheads," tormented both men and horses.

Beyond the Platte, which the party reached on July 21, was Indian country. Most of the Indian tribes they encountered were friendly, pleased with the trinkets and drinks of whiskey dealt out to them. One of the first powwows was held with a group of Oto and Missouri Indians on August 3 at a site which Clark named Council Bluffs, now a thriving Iowa city. Greater apprehensions were felt about the Sioux, farther up the Missouri, the most warlike of the tribes, who claimed a monopoly of the river trade. Placated by presents and doubtless intimidated by the well-armed explorers, the Sioux let them pass, though not without threatening attacks on several occasions. The Arikara Indians, on the other hand, were too friendly. Their squaws were "handsomer than the Sioux" and "disposed to be amorous." They were so "fond of caressing our men" that they invaded the camp to "persist in their civilities." The big black man York particularly attracted them.

By October signs of winter were coming fast in the high plains country. The Mandan villages, terminus of the boat trade from St. Louis, were reached on October 26 in cold and snow. The men set to work at once to construct winter quarters, building a log cabin about sixty feet square and naming it Fort Mandan, near the present site of Bismarck, North Dakota. In the five and a half months since leaving St. Louis, the party had traveled sixteen hundred miles up the Missouri. The next six months were spent waiting for the ice on the river to break up. The men were kept busy finding enough food and providing shelter warm enough to keep out the frigid winds (Clark recorded the temperature at forty degees below zero on January 10). Game was scarce, but hunting parties brought in sufficient meat to keep the fort well supplied. The carefully fortified camp was guarded night and day, so that, despite threats from the Sioux, there was never an attack on the company.

The boredom of the long winter for Lewis and Clark's men was relieved by the easy virtue of the Mandan women—as a consequence of which a number of the party had to be treated for veneral diseases. Throughout the course of the expedition, in fact, there were health problems, including snakebite, sunstroke, frostbite, appendicitis, dysentery, constipation, skin infections—boils, tumors, and abscesses—and gunshot wounds. For treatment, Lewis, who served as doctor, prescribed pills, poultices, bloodletting, and other remedies which he had learned from Dr. Rush, and drew upon a wide knowledge of herbs acquired from his mother, a well-known Virginia herb doctor. Mercury ointment was considered a specific for venereal disease, though it could hardly have done more than to clear up the symptoms. In any event, the men generally recovered from their various ailments despite the treatments. Sergeant Floyd was the one man lost during the entire expedition.

A fortunate occurrence for the expedition while it was encamped at Fort Mandan was the appearance of Sacajawea, wife of Toussaint Charbonneau, one of the half-breed French interpreters, whom the captains "hope may be useful as an interpreter among the Snake Indians." Sacajawea, the Bird-woman, a member of the Snake or Shoshone tribe, had been captured in her childhood from her people in the mountains by the Minnetarees, and sold as a slave to Charbonneau. Now nineteen years of age, slender, with long braids and dark hair, Sacajawea was carrying a young papoose on her back as the expedition resumed its travels. Her presence proved to be the difference between disaster and success for Lewis and Clark.

In early April 1805, Lewis wrote: "The ice in the Missouri has now nearly disappeared. I shall set out on my voyage in the course of a few days. I can see no material obstruction to our progress and feel the most perfect confidence that we shall reach the Pacific ocean this summer. For myself, individually, I enjoy better health than I have since I commenced my voyage. The party are now in fine health and excellent spirits, are attached to the enterprise and anxious to proceed. Not a whisper of discontent or murmur is to be heard among them. With such men I feel every confidence necessary to insure success." Captain Lewis was perhaps overly optimistic, for tremendous hardships faced the party before its goal was to be attained.

On April 7, when the expeditionary force embarked from Fort Mandan it numbered thirty-one men, plus Sacajawea and her infant son. The heavy longboat was left behind, and the party with all its baggage was towed in six small canoes and two large pirogues. "At the same time that we took our departure," wrote Lewis, "our barge, manned with seven soldiers, two Frenchmen, and Mr. Gravelines as pilot, sailed for the United States loaded with our presents and dispatches." From here on Lewis and Clark were plunging into unknown territory, "a country on which the foot of civilized men had never yet trodden." In the beginning snow was in the air and the skies were overcast and cold. The voyagers passed the Little Missouri, the Yellowstone, and Musselshell Rivers. Animal life was abundant—bear, buffalo, wolves, deer, elk, antelope, beaver, and prairie hens.

The explorers were now getting into the country of the grizzly bears, *Ursus horribilis,* about whose ferocity the Indians had been telling them hair-raising tales, but no white man then knew much about these creatures and Lewis and Clark were skeptical. Several actual encounters with the huge brutes, from which the explorers barely escaped with their lives, soon persuaded them of the truth of the folklore. The bears were almost unkillable with the muzzle-loading rifles of the early nineteenth century, and one was capable of running a quarter of a mile with a bullet in its heart.

Not until May 26 did Lewis record that he saw the Rocky Mountains for the first time. The party was nearing the head of "the heretofore conceived boundless Missouri." In mid-June the Great Falls of the Missouri were reached, revealing scenery so inspiring that Lewis "wished for the pencil of Salvator Rosa or the pen of Thompson, that I might be enabled to give the enlightened world some just idea of this truly magnificent and sublimely grand object, which has from the commencement of time been concealed from the view of civilized man."

Harsh realities accompanied the magnificent panorama. Ticks, mosquitoes, and rattlesnakes made life miserable. River banks caving in suddenly nearly swamped the boats. Heavy head winds made navigation dangerous. A violent hailstorm bombarded the men, and it required three weeks to portage the boats and equipment around the Falls. On July 4, the supply of whiskey ran out.

Finally, on August 12, the Missouri came to an end in a stream so narrow that it could be straddled by one of the men. The explorers' feeling of triumph was subdued, however, by, as Lewis put it, "the immense ranges of high mountains still to the West of us with their tops partially covered with snow," yet to be crossed.

Strangely, in spite of the immense amount of game surrounding them, the men saw no Indians. In five months of travel from Bismarck, North Dakota, to the foothills of the Rockies, the expedition did not meet a single human being, though there were occasional Indian signs. At the western edge of Montana, great smokes on the prairie began to be sighted, signals of a Shoshone band, but the Indians remained elusive. These were Sacajawea's people, who evidently feared the invaders and remained out of sight.

Lewis and Clark knew that they must have guides to find a way across the mountains. At last, Lewis and several picked men proceeded ahead of the main party and several days later managed to make contact with the wary Indians. After much persuasion, the Shoshones were induced to return with Lewis to rejoin the rest of his company. There, by an amazing coincidence, it was discovered that one of the Shoshones was Sacajawea's brother. Lewis bartered armaments, coats, blankets, and knives for thirty-eight horses.

After the departure of the fickle Shoshones, who shortly deserted them, the explorers wandered on through the Bitter Root Range. Snow began to block the passes, provisions ran low, and wild game vanished. Some of the horses had to be killed for meat. Finally open country was reached and the party emerged into the beautiful Clearwater Valley in Idaho. There the Nez Percés Indians befriended them, fed and nursed the exhausted men, and guided them to the Clearwater River to begin the last stage of their journey to the Pacific. Six crude canoes were constructed for the wild passage down the turbulent streams ahead. Entering the Clearwater, they paddled down to the Snake, and about the middle of October reached the mighty Columbia, which surged out of the north and turned westward. At the Short Narrows on the Columbia, the tremendous stream was compressed between rock precipices only forty-five yards apart, but the expedition shot the narrows with their canoes, to the astonishment of watching Indians, "notwithstanding the horrid appearance of this agitated gut swelling, boiling and whorling in every direction."

The great day came on November 7, 1805, when the explorers caught their first glimpse of the Pacific Ocean. With another winter at hand, Fort Clatsop was built on the south bank of the Columbia, near present-day Astoria.

After a relatively uneventful stay, through a dreary fogbound winter in Oregon, the expedition began the long trek homeward in late March of 1806. The repassage of the mountains was dangerous enough, but the return trip required only one third as long as was consumed in traveling west. They now had landmarks to guide them, and Sacajawea to serve as guide. Near where Missoula, Montana, now stands, the captains separated, Lewis leading a party to explore the north across the mountains to the Marias River and Clark riding south with another group to the headwaters of the Yellowstone. Lewis experienced the only serious mishaps. He and one of his men had to kill two Blackfeet Indians to prevent them stealing their horses and rifles—and then had to ride for their lives to escape the vengeful redskins. Two weeks later, Lewis was shot in the hip by a nearsighted member of his party who mistook him for an elk; for three weeks thereafter, the captain was unable to walk. The last entry in Lewis' journal is August 12, when he was reunited with Clark.

Swiftly the party moved downstream and on September 23, 1806, Lewis and Clark were back in St. Louis.

The nation had long since given the explorers up for dead. They had been gone two years and four months and the last communication received from them was a letter forwarded from Fort Mandan. Thomas Jefferson wrote his congratulations and cheering crowds greeted them in St. Louis. Their travels through the wilderness had covered eight thousand miles. The New York *Gazette* gazed into a clouded crystal ball and predicted that the region would never be traveled again, but the more farsighted Jefferson envisioned "a great, free and independent empire on the Columbia River."

The Lewis and Clark expedition stands as a major event in American history, solidly establishing our title to the vast Louisiana Territory and later to the Oregon country. The explorations revealed a strange and unknown world, full of exciting wonders, and pointed the way to its possibilities for future development. Lewis was an eloquent writer and Clark's maps and drawings of wildlife are invaluable. Many of the birds and animals that they discovered were new to science, among them the Rocky Mountain rat, the mountain goat, the American antelope, two new kinds of grouse, the Lewis woodpecker, and the Clark nutcracker. Theirs were the first adequate descriptions, too, of the prairie dog, the coyote, and the grizzly bear. Specimens of plants were preserved and the vocabularies of some of the Indians were recorded. The success of the expedition was due in large part to the perfect accord between the two leaders and to their combined abilities. Each had qualities complementing the other's.

Immediately following their return, Lewis and Clark began to plan for a published account of their adventures, but the publication of what has rightly been termed "this most important of all overland narratives" was attended by a series of misfortunes, climaxed by the mysterious and violent death of Lewis in a wayside inn near Nashville, Tennessee, in 1809. Difficulties in finding a printer caused further delay. Finally, a two-volume work, entitled *History of the Expedition Under the Command of Captains Lewis and Clark, to the Sources of the Missouri, Thence Across the Rocky Mountains and Down the River Columbia to the Pacific Ocean, Performed During the Years 1804-5-6, By Order of the Government of the United States,* was issued in Philadelphia in 1814, with an introduction by Thomas Jefferson. The book was edited by Nicholas Biddle of Philadelphia, assisted by Paul Allen, assistant editor of the *Port Folio* magazine. The edition has been criticized on various counts, in particular the deliberate omission of natural history descriptions, that is, the accounts of the animals, birds, fish, and reptiles encountered by the explorers; the cutting of the original manuscript from 900,000 to 370,000 words; the substitution of Biddle's elegant vocabulary and phrases for Lewis' more colorful and natural style; and a general over-refinement. On the other hand, the authoritative *Literary History of the United States,* after characterizing the book as "one of the great travel narratives of the world," defended Biddle in these words: "The editor had the good sense to let the hard, compact prose of the journals stand with a minimum of tidying up." In one respect, at least, Biddle improved on the original. Both Lewis and Clark were atrocious spellers. Americans of their day, as one commentator stated, "not only had freedom of speech but freedom of spelling." Many words in the Lewis-Clark journals, spelled phonetically, were practically unrecognizable, and urgently demanded the attention of a good editor.

Almost exactly a century after Lewis and Clark's historical mission, their journals were edited by Reuben G. Thwaites and published under the title *Original Journals of the Lewis and Clark Expedition, 1804–1806* (New York: Dodd, Mead 1904–5, eight volumes). Another primary source of great value is Donald Jackson's collection of *Letters of the Lewis and Clark Expedition, With Related Documents, 1783–1854* (Urbana: University of Illinois Press, 1962). The Biddle edition has been reprinted many times, at home and abroad, the most useful one annotated by Elliott Coues and issued in 1893.

3-LATTER-DAY SAINT

JOSEPH SMITH'S *The Book of Mormon*

PARALLELS between the origins of the early Christian church and Mormonism are numerous. The revelations to Moses on Mount Sinai are strikingly similar to Joseph Smith's visions on the Hill Cumorah. In each religion there is the chronicle of a martyred prophet; both begin with wanderings through a wilderness and arrive, after numerous trials and tribulations, in a promised land; they start with a handful of disciples, who proliferate into a multitude.

From Moses to Joseph Smith, the phenomenon of divine revelation has played a major role in the transmission of sacred literature. The two tables of stone, containing the Ten Commandments, received by Moses from Jehovah, are comparable to the golden plates, containing *The Book of Mormon,* revealed to Joseph Smith by the angel Moroni. In like miraculous fashion, the scriptures of Islam, the Koran, were communicated to Mohammed by the angel Gabriel, through a tablet of vast size, called the "preserved table."

In the third and fourth decades of the nineteenth century, nonconformist and utopian movements were springing up throughout frontier America. Religious festivals and bizarre faiths swept entire communities. It was the heyday of the wandering evangelist, who held great campfire meetings to preach of hell and damnation. Among the eccentric manifestations of the new spirit in the land were the Shakers, the Millerites, the Campbellites, the Labadists, the Ephratists, the Rappites—in most instances, like the Mormons, communitarian, biblical cults. Each sect was convinced that it alone had had divine truth revealed to it and possessed the only authentic gospel for salvation.

In this highly charged atmosphere, so preoccupied with the supernatural and theological controversy, a new faith was born, the Church of Jesus Christ of Latter-day Saints, or Mormonism, destined for a permanence, vitality, and wide acceptance denied other sects of the era.

The miraculous origins of the Mormons are thoroughly established in American lore and tradition. The Church's roots go back to a small town in upstate New York, Palmyra, in the eighteen twenties, and to a young man, Joseph Smith, who envisaged himself as a modern-day prophet, a direct descendant of the tribes of Israel, a lineal successor to Isaiah, Hosea, and Moses.

Joseph Smith's background was humble. His father, a well-digger by trade, moved his family from place to place, no less than nineteen times in ten years. The future prophet was born in 1805 in Sharon, Vermont. In one respect—a factor which may likely have shaped Joseph's career—the parents were different. Both claimed to possess clairvoyant power, and frequently experienced supernatural visions. The mother was a fortune-teller and a believer in demonology.

The son's formal education ended with the elementary grades. At an early age, Joseph became fascinated with the study of the Bible, religions, and ethics. He became a member of a local debating society, arguing moral and ethical issues at length, and demonstrating ability as a debater and public speaker.

Palmyra was swept in 1820 by a great religious revival, with competing Methodist, Baptist, and Presbyterian evangelists stirring the people into a high state of excitement. Young Joseph Smith, then fifteen years old, was confused and disturbed by the conflicting claims and bitter controversy which marred these events. In that state of mind, he had the first of a series of visions. According to Joseph's written account, he had gone to a retired spot to pray for divine guidance. There he had been "seized upon by some power which entirely overcame me . . . so that I could not speak." A pillar of light, sweeping across the treetops, came to rest before the praying boy. The brilliant light revealed to the terror-stricken youth two glorious beings, the Savior and God the Father. Resign from the congregation, Joseph was commanded, belong to no church, but wait until the proper time, when he would found a church of his own.

More than three years passed before Joseph Smith experienced his second vision or manifestation. Actually, on this occasion there were four visions within the space of twelve hours. As he lay in his bed praying, during the night of September 21, 1823, his prayer was answered by the appearance of "a personage . . . glorious beyond description and his countenance truly like lightning." Joseph's account continues:

> He called me by name and said unto me that he was a messenger sent from the presence of God to me, and that his name was Moroni. That God had a work for me to do and that my name should be had for good and evil among all nations, kindreds, and tongues.

The angel Moroni went on to inform Joseph Smith that there was a book deposited, written upon gold plates, "giving an account of the former inhabitants of this continent, and the source from which they sprang." The vision revealed the place, near the top of Cumorah Hill, close to Palmyra, where the plates were hidden under the ground. Furthermore, deposited with the plates were "two stones in silver bows"—magic spectacles called the Urim and Thummim—fastened to a breastplate, through whose magic power Joseph would be enabled to translate the book.

Proceeding as directed by the angel, Joseph Smith climbed Cumorah and reported his remarkable discovery:

> On the west side of this hill, not far from the top, under a stone of considerable size, lay the plates, deposited in a stone box. . . . Having removed the earth and obtained a lever which I got fixed under the edge of the stone, and with a little exertion raised it up. I looked in, and indeed did I behold the plates, the Urim and Thummin, and the breastplate as stated by the messenger.

Joseph was not permitted, however, to remove the plates on his first visit. It was four years later, in fact, that the angel Moroni delivered the plates to him for translation, accompanied by the stern warning that on pain of death the plates were not to be shown to another human being until the task of translation was completed.

The skeptical and the unbelievers have from the beginning branded as incredible the events narrated by Joseph Smith, but, as V. F. Calverton remarks, "The origins of all religions are extremely dubious. . . . To expose the contradictions, fallacies, and absurdities of any religion is an easy task. The difficult task is to explain how religion, in the face of such contradictions, fallacies, and absurdities has managed to survive, and retain through the ages the support of countless millions."

The point of view of the Church of Jesus Christ of Latter-day Saints is well expressed by the Mormon historian John Henry Evans: "Mormonism has its basis on the miraculous element in religion, or it has no foundation at all on which to stand. They are fooling themselves, whether within or without the Mormon church, who think that they can accept the faith of Joseph Smith and at the same time reject the visions of Joseph Smith. No such choice is permissible. One must believe these super-normal experiences and Mormonism, or one must reject Mormonism with its visions."

In support of the genuineness and authenticity of the golden plates upon which *The Book of Mormon* is based, every edition of the work carries the signed testimonials of eyewitnesses. First, there were the Three Witnesses, as the Mormon Church has always designated them—Oliver Cowdery, David Whitmer, and Martin Harris—who were taken into the woods and who, after some hours of prayer and exhortation, signed a statement to the effect that they had seen the plates. Cynics, on the other hand, suggest that the setting and circumstances were ideal for hallucinations and hypnosis.

A second statement carries the signatures of Eight Witnesses who solemnly testified that Joseph Smith showed them the plates "which have the appearance of gold; and as many of the leaves as the said Smith has translated we did handle with our hands; and we also saw the engravings thereon, all of which has the appearance of ancient work and of curious workmanship." The precious plates were never again exposed to curious outside eyes. The moment the translation was finished, an angel appeared and carried away the plates and the magic aids used in their translation.

The plates reputedly came into Joseph's hands in September 1827, but it was not until the end of July 1829 that the manuscript of the translation was ready for the printer. The actual work of translation was largely completed during the last three months of the twenty-two-month period. According to Smith's account, he was joined in April 1829 by a former Palmyra schoolteacher, Oliver Cowdery, who agreed to serve as his amanuensis. The original text was described as written in "Reformed Egyptian Hieroglyphics." Day after day, Smith sat behind a dark screen or curtain dictating the translation to his disciple until the work was finished. The scribe did not see the plates during translation. Some concept of the magnitude of the task may be gained from the fact that the printed text ran to 590 pages containing more than a quarter of a million words—all produced by a farm laborer with only an elementary education.

Publication posed further problems. Thurlow Weed of the Rochester *Anti-Masonic Inquirer* declined the job, pronouncing it "a jumble of unintelligent absurdities," after reading a portion of the manuscript. Shortly thereafter, Egbert B. Grandin, printer of the local newspaper, the *Wayne Sentinel,* undertook to produce five thousand copies of the book on being guaranteed $3000 by Martin Harris, one of Joseph's secretaries. The printer refused to deliver the volumes until he was paid, whereupon Joseph had a revelation for Harris, "Pay the printer's debt! Release thyself from bondage!" Martin Harris sold his farm, and Grandin, paid in full, finished the printing, probably in March 1830. Joseph's father and brothers went out that spring to sell the book from farm to farm in New York State and upper Pennsylvania. In April, a month after publication of *The Book of Mormon,* Joseph Smith and his close followers organized the Church of Jesus Christ of Latter-day Saints.

Only in the first edition of *The Book of Mormon* does Joseph Smith appear as "The Author." In later editions, the title page records him as "The Translator," omitting any claims to earthly authorship.

The Book of Mormon continues the story of salvation began in the Old and New Testaments. The scene has shifted, however, from the Old to the New World, to the Americas. Joseph Smith's theory of the origin and nature of the American people is set forth in the following statement:

The history of America is unfolded from its first settlement by a colony that came from the Tower of Babel at the confusion of languages, to the beginning of the 5th Century of the Christian era. We are informed by these records that America in ancient times has been inhabited by two distinct races of people. The first were called Jaredites, and came directly from the city of Jerusalem about 600 years before Christ. They were principally Israelites of the descendants of Joseph. The Jaredites were destroyed about the time that the Israelites came from Jerusalem, who succeeded them in the inhabitance of the country. The principal nation of the second race fell in battle toward the close of the fourth century. The remnant are the Indians that now inhabit this country.

The Book of Mormon is roughly similar in structure to the Bible and emulates the language of the King James Version. It is made up of fourteen books. The first two books, Nephi I and II, cover a period from 600 to 545 B.C. and tell the central story of Lehi, a descendant of Joseph, son of Jacob, who migrated, together with his wife Sariah, his four sons (Laman, Lemuel, Sam, and Nephi), and their families and followers. Following the Lord's command, Lehi had built a ship, and embarked from Jerusalem shortly before the Babylonian captivity. Sailing eastward, with divine guidance, they landed in due course on the west coast of South America.

Chronologically, another great migration preceded that of the Lehites, though an account of it appears only near the end of *The Book of Mormon,* in the Book of Ether. This was the nation of the Jaredites, who left the Chaldean region after the destruction of the Tower of Babel. Sailing in eight barges, also with divine aid, the Jaredites crossed the Atlantic and settled in South America. For a thousand years, the Jaredites flourished, increased in numbers to some two millions, and achieved a high state of civilization in Central America and Mexico. These primeval people engaged in suicidal wars and but two survivors remained to greet the Lehites. One of the survivors was the prophet Ether, who recorded the history of his people on twenty-four plates.

Four short books—Jacob, Enos, Jarom, and Omni— carrying the record up to 130 B.C., are followed by "The

Words of Mormon." Mormon, who lived in the fourth century A.D., chronicled the history of his people, the Nephites, on golden plates, those received eventually by Joseph Smith. In the beginning, the history was recorded by Nephi, the son of Lehi, and continued by later Nephite historians. The narration fills the three main books of *The Book of Mormon*—Mosiah, Alma, and Helaman—and two shorter books—Nephi III and IV—completing the narration up to A.D. 321.

The descendants of Lehi flourished for a thousand years. Soon after Lehi's death, however, his followers split into two bitterly opposed groups, a division caused by jealousy between the two brothers Nephi and Laman. The righteous people followed Nephi, a great spiritual leader, and gradually migrated to Central and North America. The Nephites took with them the Brass Plates, similar to the Hebrew Scriptures, providing them with a religion and a written literature. A great civilization was founded by the Nephites and large cities were built by them.

The Lamanites, adherents of Laman, on the other hand, degenerated morally, intellectually, and spiritually. Laman was continually in rebellion against the Lord and broke his commandments. Because of their wickedness, the Lamanites were cursed by the Lord, who inflicted "a skin of blackness" upon them. According to Mormon doctrine, the American Indians are not Mongolian in origin, as anthropologists have concluded, but dark-skinned Israelites of the tribe of Manasseh.

In A.D. 34, fulfilling a prophecy made by Nephi, the Lord Jesus Christ Himself came down from heaven, after the resurrection. Jesus taught the people the doctrines of the Sermon on the Mount, uttered other wise teachings, and formally organized the Church. All the inhabitants were converted and for two hundred years peace prevailed between the Nephites and Lamanites. Afterward hostilities resumed and there was constant warfare between the two groups. Unfortunately for the Nephites, they too were guilty of sin and apostasy, and in punishment for their wickedness were completely wiped out by the Lamanites in a final struggle between them, at the close of the fourth century A.D. Thus their darkskinned enemies were left to inhabit the two continents until the coming of Columbus.

The Book of Moroni, the final chapter in *The Book of Mormon,* is attributed to Moroni, the son of Mormon, who completed the writing left by his father, and fourteen hundred years later transmitted the record to a Latter-day Saint, Joseph Smith, who disinterred it from the Hill Cumorah. Mormon was a militant prophet, as well as a prolific writer. The chronicle which he wrote was an abridgment, based on then existing records, of the entire history of his people from the beginning.

In a detailed analysis of the basic themes of *The Book of Mormon*, Thomas F. O'Dea comments, "It is obviously an American work growing in the soil of American concerns in terms of its basic plot and its enshrining of America as the promised land, as well as in the unconcealed secular patriotism with which it refers to the United States." There is praise for democracy, republicanism, and equality, for religious liberty and the separation of church and state. Like the Bible, *The Book of Mormon* is concerned fundamentally, however, with the problem of good and evil, telling a story of sinful people and saints, of moral lapses, repentance, and failure to keep the faith. A verse from the Book of Alma epitomizes a common thread running through *The Book of Mormon*: "Thus we see how quick the children of men do forget the Lord their God, yea, how quick to do iniquity, and to be led away by the evil one."

The Book of Mormon draws freely upon the Bible, even incorporating complete chapters from Isaiah, Malachi, and St. Matthew, and elsewhere includes quotations and paraphrases of the Scriptures. Members of the Church of Jesus Christ of Latter-day Saints take care to emphasize that *The Book of Mormon* does not replace the Old and New Testaments, but is an addition to them, giving a later sacred record of God's dealings with men.

Two other sacred books, peculiar to their faith, are recognized by Mormons, in addition to *The Book of Mormon*. These contain doctrines of present-day Mormonism. The first is *The Doctrine and Covenants*, originally published in its current form in 1876. This work consists of 136 chapters, divided into verses, containing revelations received by Joseph Smith, except for the final chapter, which is a revelation given through Brigham Young. The revelations relate to the nature of God, the church, the priesthood, the millennium, the resurrection, the state of man after death, the various grades of salvation, and other doctrines. A famous chapter, number 132, provides the authority for plural marriages, subsequently repealed by an official manifesto prohibiting polygamy, issued by the Church in 1890.

The second of the supplementary sacred books is the *Pearl of Great Price,* a small volume in five parts: The Book of Moses, The Book of Abraham, an extract from Joseph Smith's translation of the Bible (St. Matthew, Chapter 24), extracts from Joseph Smith's own story, and an official statement of belief called the "Articles of Faith."

The years following the official establishment of the Church of Jesus Christ of Latter-day Saints by Joseph Smith and his disciples, in 1830, were filled with strife and turmoil for the Mormons. They called themselves "a peculiar people" and tended to form their own communal societies separate from the "Gentiles," that is, the non-Mormons. Almost continuous persecution drove them westward to Kirtland, Ohio, where the first Mormon temple was constructed. Again, events forced them to move, this time to Independence, Missouri, and then to Nauvoo, Illinois.

Nauvoo, on the east bank of the Mississippi River, soon became a Mormon showplace—not only the largest city in the state, but also one of the most beautiful. A temple costing $600,000 was built in the center of the city, and a university was established. The population grew to twenty-five thousand. Ill-fortune, however, continued to dog the Mormons' footsteps. Intermittent guerrilla warfare blazed up between them and their hostile neighbors. Joseph Smith and his brother Hyrum were arrested and jailed in June 1844 in the nearby town of Carthage. During the night, a mob stormed the jail and shot to death both Joseph and his brother. The prophet was martyred at the age of thirty-nine.

After considerable rivalry with other claimants, Brigham Young, as the senior member of the Twelve Apostles, succeeded to the leadership. The continued bitter hostility of their neighbors convinced Young and his followers that they would have to migrate once again to virgin territory far from the Gentile world. In May 1846, Brigham Young led sixteen thousand of Nauvoo's inhabitants across the Mississippi on a long trek which ended more than a year later at the Great Salt Lake in Utah. "This is the place," Brigham Young is quoted as saying. In their ultimate refuge of Utah, the Mormons began to carve a new civilization from the frontier soil of mountain and desert—the real Promised Land.

Over the past one hundred years and more, the Church of Jesus Christ of Latter-day Saints has grown and prospered mightily. Its present membership numbers more than two million. Some five thousand proselytes and teachers are assigned to missions for two-year periods in North and South America, Europe, the Far East, and the islands of the Pacific Ocean. The Church has produced leaders of national stature and its influence is increasingly felt at home and abroad.

Throughout the history of Mormonism, the Church's most powerful and effective weapon has been *The Book of Mormon*. Other religious movements in America have come and gone and today are largely forgotten—mere footnotes in social history. The possession of their own scriptures, the reading of which has persuaded many prospective converts, has proved to be the Mormons' greatest missionary tract, giving permanence and stability to their religion, and providing them with a faith by which to live.

4–CASE OF THE WOUNDED STOMACH

WILLIAM BEAUMONT'S
*Experiments and Observations on
the Gastric Juice and the
Physiology of Digestion*

AN UNFATHOMED MYSTERY of medical science at the beginning of the nineteenth century was the physiology of digestion. The knowledge gap was not from lack of curiosity or of widespread experimentation. There were theories by the hundreds, but rarely were they based on facts. The existing understanding of the subject was summed up by William Hunter, a leading anatomist of the time, in these words: "Some physiologists will have it that the stomach is a mill, others, that it is a fermenting vat, others, again, that it is a stew pan; but in my view of the matter, it is neither a mill, a fermenting vat, nor a stew pan, but a stomach, gentlemen, a stomach."

Erroneous theories of digestion are traceable to such ancients as Hippocrates and Galen. Not until the eighteenth century were there significant advances in the knowledge of digestive physiology. The names of several pioneer experimenters of that era stand out. Réaumur, French scientist and inventor, performed the first systematic experiments on digestion in birds and mammals; for example, he persuaded a pet buzzard to swallow small perforated tubes containing fragments of sponge, to obtain samples of gastric juice. A contemporary, Lazzaro Spallanzani, Italian biologist, carried out numerous experiments on fish, frogs, snakes, cattle, horses, cats, dogs, and other animals, as well as on himself, finally proving that digestion is a chemical process, though he erroneously questioned the acid nature of the gastric juice. A third notable name is that of William Prout (1785–1850), the first English physiological chemist, who demonstrated that the

52

gastric juice contained hydrochloric acid—a major discovery.

It remained, however, for an American, "a backwoods physiologist," William Beaumont, to learn what actually happens in the stomach during the digestion of food and to present a detailed and comprehensive picture of the whole cycle of gastric digestion, in a book which Harvey Cushing, a century later, called "the most notable and original classic of American medicine."

Beaumont's opportunity to achieve medical immortality came about by a freak accident. Beaumont, a native of Lebanon, Connecticut, born in 1785, was not a medical school graduate—few doctors of the period were—but had served an apprenticeship with a practicing physician in St. Albans, Vermont. After two years of study he enlisted in the Army as an assistant surgeon. Following the War of 1812, he was stationed at Fort Mackinac, where Lake Michigan and Lake Erie join.

Mackinac, a primitive frontier community in the Michigan territory, had become a center for John Jacob Astor's American Fur Company. Early each summer, there was an influx of Indians, half-breeds, trappers, and Canadian voyageurs, bringing in their winter's collection of pelts to sell or barter at the company's retail trading post. It was in this crowded store, on the morning of June 6, 1822, that a gun went off accidentally and a young French Canadian, Alexis St. Martin, fell with a huge wound in his side. His shirt caught fire and burned until it was quenched by the flow of blood. Dr. Beaumont was sent for and arrived within a few minutes.

As described by Beaumont, the charge, consisting of powder and buck shot, was received in the left side of the nineteen-year-old youth, who had been standing not more than a yard from the muzzle of the gun. A portion of the lungs as large as a turkey's egg protruded through the external wound, lacerated and burned; below this was another protrusion resembling a portion of the stomach, "which at first sight I could not believe possible to be that organ in that situation with the subject surviving," wrote Beaumont, "but on closer examination I found it to be actually the stomach with a puncture in the protruding portion large enough to receive my forefinger." The frightful wound had torn open the chest wall, leaving a hole as large as the palm of a hand, and ribs were fractured. A mixture of food, blood, and splinters of bone escaped from the wounded stomach. Further, "The whole mass of materials forced from the musket, together with fragments of clothing and pieces of fractured ribs, were driven into the muscles and cavity of the chest."

Beaumont proceeded to render first aid, cleansing the wound and applying a superficial dressing, though he was convinced that it was impossible for the patient to survive twenty minutes. The surgeon underestimated the tenacity and toughness of the dark, wiry little half-breed. About an hour later, the wound was dressed more thoroughly— Beaumont still "not supposing it possible or probable for him to survive the operation of extracting the fractured fragments of bones and other extraneous substances, but to the utter amazement of everyone he bore it without a struggle or without sinking." Before the protruding lung could be returned into the cavity of the thorax, Beaumont was forced to cut off with a penknife the point of a fractured rib on which it was caught, and thereafter the lung had to be held in place by pressure to avoid its being forced out by coughing.

The patient was removed to the primitive base hospital, and there under Beaumont's expert care he rallied slowly, though his body was still full of shot, wadding, and splintered bone. After four months, St. Martin's miraculous tissues began to expel all foreign matter. For the better part of a year, day after day, and month after month, Beaumont continued to treat the youth, dressing the terrible wound at frequent intervals, opening successive abscesses, removing fragments of indriven cartilage or bone, as the damaged region began gradually to form healthy scar tissue.

A new kind of crisis developed some ten months following the accident. The town officials refused further assistance to the destitute patient, now a pauper without funds, relatives, or friends. Beaumont was confronted with a dilemma: He had the alternative of packing the youth off in an open bateau to his native place fifteen hundred miles away—a voyage which he could scarcely have survived—or of taking him into his own home. Impelled by motives of charity and kindness, Beaumont chose the latter course—a decision he could ill afford, since he was supporting a family on an Army surgeon's salary of forty dollars per month. Nonetheless, Beaumont moved the patient into his household, where he nursed, fed, clothed, and lodged him, while continuing with the daily dressing of the slowly healing wound. By the end of another year, Alexis had recovered his health and strength sufficiently to do household chores for the Beaumonts, but was still incapable of earning his own living. Thus began a long relationship between the military surgeon and the young French Canadian who was destined to go through life with a hole in his stomach.

After the first year, the skin tissue around the opening had healed. St. Martin, however, stubbornly refused to submit to an operation to suture the lips together. A most fortunate circumstance was that, instead of dropping back into the abdominal cavity, the rim of the stomach puncture adhered to the rim of the external wound. As a result of the union of the lacerated edges of the stomach and the intercostal muscles, a phenomenon known to medical men as gastric fistula developed. Eventually an inner coat of St. Martin's stomach folded across the opening, forming a leakproof valve. A round hole, large enough to admit the doctor's forefinger directly into the stomach, remained permanently. The valve held the food in "but was easily depressed with the finger," Beaumont reported.

Quite early in his treatment of young Alexis, Beaumont came to realize that he was being presented with a unique opportunity to explore the great mystery of human digestion. In May 1825, about three years after the gunshot episode, Beaumont began his first series of gastric experiments on the patient, who by now was fully recovered. In the daily routine of dressing the wound, Beaumont made a momentous discovery. When Alexis lay on his right side, causing the stomach to fall away from its attachment to the margins of the healing wound, "I can look directly into the cavity of the stomach," Beaumont wrote, "observe its motion, and almost see the process of digestion. I can pour in water with a funnel and put in food with a spoon, and draw them out again with a siphon. . . . The case affords an excellent opportunity for experiment upon the gastric juices and the process of digestion. It would give no pain or cause the least uneasiness to extract a gill of fluid every two or three days, for it frequently flows out spontaneously in considerable quantities; and I might introduce various digestible substances into the stomach and easily examine them during the whole process of digestion."

The walls of the fistula could be pushed apart with a thermometer, giving Beaumont a chance to peer five or six inches into the interior of the cavity. He found that the stomach walls were pale pink in color, soft and velvety-looking, and lined with a mucous coat. When a few bread crumbs were inserted, the stomach brightened in color, hundreds of tiny droplets began to rise through the mucous film and trickle down the walls—the "gastric juice," as Spallanzani had called it, tasting of hydrochloric acid. Here was the first step in the digestive process.

There followed over a period of years a variety of experiments, using all the foods found in a frontier community. The surgeon passed into the stomach through the fistula pieces of raw beef, cooked beef, fat pork, stale bread, raw sliced cabbage, and other vegetables. In all, hundreds of foodstuffs were tested with regard to the length of time required for their digestion in the stomach. The items were tied to a long piece of silk string at spaced intervals and pushed individually through the opening, which was about two and one half inches in circumference. An hour later, Beaumont withdrew the food particles and found the cabbage and bread about half-digested. At the end of a second hour, they had vanished completely along with the pork and boiled beef. Hourly examinations throughout the day showed the other foods being digested at a slower rate. The raw meat turned out to be almost wholly indigestible.

Another ingenious experiment was concerned with artificial digestion. Through a tube, as Beaumont describes the operation, he "drew off one ounce of pure gastric liquor, unmixed with any other matter, except a small proportion of mucus, into a three ounce vial. I then took a solid piece of *boiled, recently salted beef,* weighing three drachms, and put it into the liquor in the vial; corked the vial tight, and placed it in a saucepan, filled with water, raised to the temperature of 100° [found by Beaumont to be the stomach's normal temperature] and kept at that point, on a nicely regulated sand bath. In *forty minutes* digestion had distinctly commenced over the surface of the meat. In *fifty minutes* the fluid had become quite opaque and cloudy; the external texture began to seperate and become loose. In *sixty minutes* chyme began to form." Not until ten hours after the test began, however, was the meat completely digested. A similar piece of meat suspended in the stomach was fully digested in two hours.

Beaumont was the first person in history to isolate pure human gastric juice, but lacking chemical training, he was unable to analyze it. He observed, however, that the liquid is "a clear, transparent fluid; inodorous, a little saltish; and very perceptibly acid." It was concluded, too, that the gastric juice is "powerfully antiseptic," and is "the most general solvent in nature, of alimentary matter—even the hardest bone cannot withstand its action." From its behavior, Beaumont had no doubt that the fluid was a chemical agent. The gastric juice, he found, does not accumulate in the stomach during a period of fasting—thus a starving person would produce no gastric fluid—but only appears in response to the partaking of food or artificial stimulus. Beaumont suggested the possible presence of another agent in digestion, though he could not identify it. Researches by Theodor Schwann, German botanist and physiologist, a few years later isolated the substance; he gave it the name of pepsin.

In an effort to learn more about the nature of gastric juice, Beaumont sent samples for analysis to two of the leading chemists in America, Robley Dunglison of the University of Virginia and Benjamin Silliman of Yale University. The former reported that the major active ingredient was hydrochloric acid; Silliman also found hydrochloric acid present, but was otherwise vague, evading the issue with the statement that "the laws of the Creator were often incomprehensible equally in His nature and His works." A specimen sent to the famous Swedish chemist Berzelius elicited a reply too late and too indecisive to be of value.

Beaumont's investigations did not proceed smoothly and without incident in other respects. Feeling the need for a laboratory and medical library, he asked for a transfer eastward, and received an assignment to Niagara Falls, taking his patient with him. Two such different personalities, however, were incompatible, and there was constant friction between them. Alexis St. Martin resented being treated as a human guinea pig and hated the discomfort of having interminable tubes, strings, and bags moving in and out of his stomach, and being required to go on diets and fasts. His meals were frequently eaten lying down, while Beaumont watched the food pass through the gullet; he was ordered to carry small bottles under his armpits— Beaumont's method of demonstrating that animal heat is not different from ordinary heat; and many of the experiments made him ill. He was illiterate, addicted to drunken

binges, homesick for his old life in the forest, and longed
for the girl he had left behind him in Canada.

It is scarcely surprising, therefore, that in the new post,
so temptingly near his native land, St. Martin tied his
belongings in a bundle one night and vanished. Beaumont
was deeply distressed to have his promising experiments
interrupted so suddenly and apparently permanently.
While he searched without avail for his missing patient,
Alexis had gone off to marry Marie Jolly, father two
children, and to resume his career as a voyageur, in the
Indian country, for the Hudson Bay Company. Four years
passed before the truant was found, living in a village near
Montreal. Reluctantly he agreed to return, and to submit
to a new series of experiments, but only on condition that
his family accompany him and he be generously compensated. To ensure Alexis' loyalty, a detailed legal contract
was drawn up, to which the young Canadian affixed his
mark. The financial burden on Beaumont was removed by
enrolling St. Martin in the Army and assigning him to the
medical service.

The surgeon was happy to find that, despite the four-
year break, the patient's "stomach and side were in a
similar condition as when he left me in 1825. The aper-
ture was open, and his health good." As reported by
Beaumont:

> I commenced another series of experiments on the
> stomach and gastric fluids and continued them unin-
> terruptedly until March 1831. During this time, in
> the intervals of experimenting, he performed all the
> duties of a common servant, chopping wood, carrying
> burdens, etc., with little or no suffering or inconven-
> ience from the wound. He labored constantly, became
> the father of more children, and enjoyed as good
> health and as much vigor as men in general. He sub-
> sisted on crude food in abundant quantities, except
> when on a prescribed diet for particular experimental
> purposes and under special observation.

With the resumption of his experiments, Beaumont kept
a meticulous record of his observations—to appear later
in printed form—noting the movements of the stomach
during digestion, studying the effects of temperature,
sleep, and anger on the flow of gastric juice, describing the

results of starvation and of overeating. His charts represented the fluctuations of gastric secretion under a variety of conditions, and he timed the exact hours and minutes required for the digestion of numerous foods from both the animal and vegetable kingdoms. After Alexis' frequent alcoholic sprees, his stomach's condition was checked by Beaumont. Fundamental facts on human diet, nutrition, and digestion emerged from the long-drawn-out experiments.

A preliminary report on his findings was published by Beaumont in 1825 in the *Medical Recorder* under the title "A Case of Wounded Stomach." At the conclusion of his 238 experiments, there was printed in 1833, at Plattsburgh, New York, Beaumont's definitive work, *Experiments and Observations on the Gastric Juice and the Physiology of Digestion,* an octave volume of 280 pages in an edition of one thousand copies. The book was cheaply printed at the author's expense and sold by subscription for two dollars per copy. The current value on the rare book market ranges between five hundred and a thousand dollars.

Beaumont writes in an unpretentious, direct style. His "Preliminary Observations," discussing the physiology of digestion in general, fill approximately one hundred pages, divided into seven sections: Of Aliment, Of Hunger and Thirst, Of Satisfaction and Satiety, Of Mastication, Insalivation, and Deglutition, Of Digestion by the Gastric Juice, Of the Appearance of the Villous Coat and of the Motions of the Stomach, and Of Chylification and Uses of the Bile and Pancreatic Juice. The second major division of the book is a detailed description in chronological order of the experiments, followed by a brief summary of fifty-one "inferences" or conclusions.

Many of Beaumont's diverse findings have entered into general knowledge. Concerning the matter of overloading the stomach, for example, he points out, "There is always disturbance of the stomach when more food has been received than there is gastric juice to act upon it." Overeating is an all too common human failing, in the view of the author, who asserts that "the quantity of food generally taken is more than the wants of the system require; and such excess, if persevered in, generally produces not only functional aberration, but disease of the coats of the stomach." It is recognized that individual needs vary; for example, "Persons who do not exercise much, require less nutritious diet than those who are in the habit of constant labor. . . . Young people who are growing, require more nutriment in proportion to their size than those who have arrived at adult age."

Beaumont's researches support the objections of religious and temperance groups to use of alcohol and stimulating beverages. "The whole class of alcoholic liquors, whether simply fermented or distilled," he states, "may be considered as *narcotics . . .* and the use of *ardent spirits* always produces disease of the stomach, if persevered in." Water is the only fluid called for by the human system; "Even coffee and tea, the common beverages of all classes of people, have a tendency to debilitate the digestive organs."

Also having religious sanction, ancient in this instance, is the statement, "The digestibility of most meats is improved by incipient putrefaction, sufficient to render the muscular fibre slightly tender."

Among numerous other conclusions reached by Beaumont were these: Meats and "farinaceous substances" are easier to digest than vegetables; oily substances are digested with great difficulty; fish (not including shellfish) are easily digestible; condiments are non-nutritious and, except for salt and vinegar, should be avoided. Actually, in Beaumont's opinion, "the stomach is a creature of habit. It can become accustomed to any kind of diet; and sudden changes are likely to derange its healthy actions. To those accustomed to what is called high living, such as strong meats, strong drinks, and high seasoned food, of all kinds, the transition to a meat diet, which contains a considerably lowered stimulation, would probably be an imprudent change."

Moderate exercise, Beaumont found, contributes to healthy and rapid digestion. "Severe and fatiguing exercise, on the contrary, retards digestion." There is a close relation, too, between emotional states and the digestive process. Fear and anger check the flow of the gastric juices and "the latter causes an influx of bile into the stomach, which impairs its solvent properties." Bile is not present in a healthy stomach if the subject is in "an equable frame of mind."

Beaumont attempted to verify the results of his experiments during a six-month stay in Washington, D.C., where he had access to most of the available medical literature on digestion. Some authorities supported his conclusions;

others, lacking Beaumont's unique opportunities for firsthand observation, were full of beautiful but erroneous theories, mainly based on observations of animals. Beaumont pays his respects to the latter group of writers in these words:

> It is unfortunate for the interests of physiological science, that it generally falls to the lot of men of vivid imaginations, and great powers of mind, to become restive under the restraints of a tedious and *routine* mode of thinking, and to strike out into bold and original hypotheses to elucidate the operations of nature, or to account for the phenomena that are constantly submitted to their attention. The process of developing truth, by patient and persevering investigation, experiment and research, is incompatible with their notions of unrestrained genius. The drudgery of science, they leave to humbler, and more unpretending contributors. The flight of genius is, however, frequently erratic.

The reception of Beaumont's book at home and abroad was gratifying. As George Rosen brings out in detail in his *The Reception of William Beaumont's Discovery in Europe*, the Beaumont revelations were even more fully appreciated abroad during the early years after publication than they were in his native country—partially, no doubt, because of the European physicians' greater sophistication and familiarity with scientific method. German, French, and Scottish editions soon appeared, and both the medical and lay press carried numerous articles describing and evaluating the findings. Because of Beaumont's precise observations and careful recording of the experiments, there was little inclination anywhere to question his conclusions. In John F. Fulton's judgment, "William Beaumont may be ranked with Benjamin Franklin and Weir Mitchell as one of three Americans whose writings exerted a profound influence upon medical thought of Europe prior to 1900." In America, reprint editions and a second, revised edition were issued within a few years.

Perhaps the most important of Beaumont's contributions were his investigations on the influence of the psyche on gastric secretion, leading a half century later to Pavlov's famous experiments on dogs; his research on the problem of nervous dyspepsia and gastritis; and studies on the effects of intemperance and unwholesome diet on digestion. The subsequent development of studies in gastric physiology, pathology, and therapy owe a great debt to Beaumont's pioneer discoveries. A foremost historian of medicine, Sir William Osler, felt justified in calling Beaumont "the first great American physiologist."

In 1834, presumably for a visit, Alexis St. Martin was given leave to return to Canada. At approximately the same time, Beaumont was transferred by the military authorities to St. Louis, where he resided for the remainder of his career. Efforts over a period of twenty years to persuade St. Martin to return, for a continuation of the experiments, were fruitless. Thus ended the strange alliance so inadvertently begun. Alexis St. Martin outlived his partner in medical research by twenty-seven years and sired seventeen children in all; at the time of his death in 1880, he was chopping cordword for a living, having lived for fifty-eight years with a hole in his vitals. After his death, his family adamantly refused to permit an autopsy, and to ensure that he would not be dug up, buried him secretly in an unmarked grave eight feet deep.

5–WAVE OF THE FUTURE

ALEXIS DE TOCQUEVILLE'S
Democracy in America

ALEXIS DE TOCQUEVILLE's *Democracy in America* has rightly been described as the greatest work ever written on one country by the citizen of another. Tocqueville's primary concern, however, was democracy, not America. The United States was chosen by him for study because it was the first major democracy in the modern world and offered an ideal laboratory for a close examination of this "irresistible" new form of society and government.

Tocqueville was no liberal or democrat by disposition. His family belonged to the oldest Norman nobility, and had suffered the worst terrors of the French Revolution. A number of his ancestors had been sent to the guillotine. Tocqueville's own sympathies were strongly oriented toward aristocracy, but he had come to the conclusion that democracy was the inevitable political development of the nineteenth century. He determined, therefore, to find out for himself what a democratic regime had to contribute to the cause of liberty and to a solution of the problems confronting his beloved France, then still in a state of turmoil from the Revolution and from the aftermath of the Napoleonic Wars.

Tocqueville's opportunity came in 1831, at the age of twenty-six, when he and his young friend Gustave de Beaumont were commissioned by the Minister of the Interior to study the penitentiary system of the United States for any developments that might be applicable to French prisons. The official mission was conscientiously completed, though it was incidental to Tocqueville's first concern. Over a period of nine months, he and Beaumont traveled widely through New England, Canada, New

York, Philadelphia, Baltimore, Cincinnati, Tennessee, New Orleans, and Washington. Tocqueville was fascinated by the America that he found. "I confess," he wrote, "that in America I saw more than America; I sought the image of democracy itself, with its inclinations, its character, its prejudices, and its passions, in order to learn what we have to fear or to hope from its progress." It is astonishing that Tocqueville was able to grasp so thoroughly the essentials of American civilization and to write with so much depth and penetration after a visit of only nine months. The first part of his *Democracy in America* appeared in 1835, when Tocqueville was thirty, and the second half five years later.

Tocqueville was both attracted and repelled by what he saw in America. Democracy as practiced here, he concluded, was full of contradictions; liberty threatened by the tyranny of the majority; widespread educational opportunities, but too much standardization of opinion; respect for authority and personal rights, offset by a spirit of irresponsibility. Nevertheless, two beliefs were discovered to be deeply ingrained in the American people—a sense of equality and the right of the majority to rule.

Tocqueville opens his introduction to *Democracy in America* with a basic theme: "Among the novel objects that attracted my attention during my stay in the United States, nothing struck me more forcibly than the general equality of conditions." Tocqueville saw equality as the "fundamental fact" of American life and further that it reached "far beyond the political character and the laws of the country, and that it has no less empire over civil society than over the government; it creates opinions, engenders sentiments, suggests the ordinary practices of life, and modifies whatever it does not produce." Thus what most intrigued Tocqueville's interest in the study of America was not the problem of democracy in general but of a new society founded upon equality among its members. "An incredible equality reigns in America on the outside," he wrote. "All classes meet continually and no haughtiness at all results from the differences in social position. Everyone shakes hands."

The custom and practice of equality, Tocqueville decided, originated naturally in the fact that the people had come from approximately the same social level, they had no feelings of class distinctions, and the conditions of life in the New World discouraged class feelings. Democracy in America also had an economic basis, though Tocqueville visualized the rise of certain forces that would eventually undermine the principle of economic equality. Meanwhile, to an aristocrat like Tocqueville, all America seemed leveled down into one ruling middle class. To be born into an old family meant little; it conferred "neither right nor incapacity, no obligations toward the world or toward oneself."

Equalitarianism has its perils as well as its advantages, in Tocqueville's view:

> There is, in fact, a manly and lawful passion for equality, which excites men to wish all to be powerful and honored. This passion tends to elevate the humble to the rank of the great; but there exists also in the human heart a depraved taste for equality, which impels the weak to attempt to lower the powerful to their own level, and reduced men to prefer equality in slavery to inequality with freedom.

The "sovereignty of the people" brings with it another possible hazard, the tyranny of the majority. Tocqueville is much obsessed with what he regards as the despotism of the greater number. He was doubtful of the judgment of a majority of people. Popular moods could be skillfully manipulated by demagogues to gain possession of political power. Firmly established principles of good government and justice are needed to guard against the temporary aberrations of the majority. Accordingly, Tocqueville urges that "our judgement of the laws of a people, then, must not be founded exclusively upon its inclinations, since those inclinations change from age to age, but upon more elevated principles and a more general experience." Regardless of whether it is held by a monarch, an aristocracy, or a people, "unlimited power is in itself a bad and dangerous thing," and, continues Tocqueville, "I can never willingly invest any number of my fellow-creatures with that unlimited authority which I should refuse to any one of them."

Not recognized by Tocqueville, though equally perilous to democracy, is the possible tyranny of a minority. History has shown that democratic processes may be twisted, through wealth, industrial control, and political machines, to defeat the will of the majority. As George Wilson Pierson, Tocqueville's biographer, asked, "Was not the innocence and carelessness of the masses even more to be feared in a democracy than their malevolence or positive tyranny?"

The greatest threat in a popular democracy, Tocqueville holds, is to the freedom of the individual. Equality, paradoxically, may lead to servitude, because the individual counts for little in an equalitarian society. In a population which numbers millions, the individual is virtually helpless in asserting himself against any aspect of a society of which he may disapprove. Though each person is the equal of any other citizen, he may be overwhelmed by the sense of his own insignificance when he sees himself as a microscopic unit in the total body politic:

> The public has therefore among a democratic people a singular power, of which aristocratic nations could never so much as conceive an idea; for it does not persuade them to certain opinions, but enforces them, and infuses into them the faculties by a sort of enormous pressure of the minds of all upon the reason of each.

Tocqueville's most profound concern was for liberty and personal freedom, and to him the dignity and value of the individual were too important to be jeopardized. The levelers in a democratic society, he feared, were too inclined to destroy individual freedom and personal initiative by refusing to recognize that one man may be worth more than another. This was the road to a regimented society and perhaps in time to another form of tyranny.

The force of public opinion on the individual in a democracy is sometimes sinister, says Tocqueville, as it acts to suppress unpopular views. The person who holds unorthodox sentiments may ruin his political career, be ostracized and shunned by his friends, and scorned by his fellow citizens. The power of public opinion represents the rule of the commonplace, exercising a "quiet and gentle" kind of terror and intimidation, "till each nation is reduced to be nothing better than a flock of timid and industrious animals, of which the government is the shepherd." The exceptional man in a democratic society is rarely understood and seldom appreciated or welcomed. The mediocre state of literature in the United States was attributed by Tocqueville, at least in part, to this factor:

In America the majority raises formidable barriers around the liberty of opinion; within these barriers an author may write what he pleases, but woe to him if he goes beyond them. . . . He yields at length, overcome by the daily effort which he has to make, and subsides into silence, as if he felt remorse for having spoken the truth.

Three major bulwarks against democratic despotism exist, notes Tocqueville—the press, law, and religion. Concerning the first, he comments:

I think that men living in aristocracies may, strictly speaking, do without the liberty of the press; but such is not the case with those who live in democratic countries. To protect their personal independence I trust not to great political assemblies, to parliamentary privileges, or to assertion of popular sovereignty. All these things may, to a certain extent, be reconciled with personal servitude—but that servitude cannot be complete if the press is free: the press is the chiefest democratic instrument of freedom.

Other powerful deterrents to democratic corruption and excesses which particularly attracted Tocqueville, because of his own legal training, were the profession of law and the administration of justice. He recognized that the establishment of the Supreme Court, with its authority to interpret the law and the Constitution, was of basic significance in the American governmental structure. Tocqueville was amazed to discover a democracy which was willing to subordinate its authority to the supremacy of law. The judiciary had powers over legislation undreamed of in France and Britain. As seen by Tocqueville:

When the American people is intoxicated by passion, or carried away by the impetuosity of its ideas, it is checked and stopped by the almost invisible influence of its legal counsellors, who secretly oppose their aristocratic propensities to their democratic instincts, their superstitious attachment to what is antique to its love of novelty, their narrow views to its immense designs, and their habitual procrastination to its ardent impatience.

Tocqueville paid tribute also to the American jury system, which he felt exercised a powerful influence upon the national character, serving "to communicate the spirit of the judges to the minds of all the citizens" and imbuing "all classes with a respect for the thing judged, and with the notion of right."

Though he commended the role of the courts in countermanding improper actions, Tocqueville conceded that judicial procedures might be subject to abuse. The principles of democracy could be periled if in time the judiciary arrogated to itself the right of judgment over all legislative and executive acts.

Along with freedom of the press and a strong judiciary, Tocqueville named religion as a force against the possible evils of democracy. Unlike his native France, religion in America was not associated with political and social conflict. The reason, Tocqueville concluded, was the separation of church and state in America. The American clergy stood aside from political activity, thereby avoiding a corrupting influence. In the midst of the general mediocrity which accompanied "the tyranny of the majority," Tocqueville saw religion as enlightening the soul and aiding the maintenance of traditional principles.

The relationships among the federal, state, and local governments were of keen interest to Tocqueville. The peculiar conditions prevailing at the time of his visit to the United States led him into certain erroneous judgments, e.g., that the larger states were practically independent, at least in domestic affairs; the federal tie was frail and if any states wished to secede, the central power would be unable to resist effectively (disproved in the Civil War of 1861–65). Tocqueville found particularly admirable the system of decentralized administration which had developed in the United States, resting upon local bodies, town governments, and state assemblies—a striking contrast to the highly centralized government of France. The New England town meeting represented the epitome of democracy to Tocqueville. Direct participation in government at the grass roots level gave citizens "an understanding of public affairs, a knowledge of laws and precedents, a feeling for the best interests of the nation." Tocqueville approved of centralized government in matters of national interest and in the conduct of foreign relations; matters of local concern, however, should be managed locally, for local freedom brings men together and accustoms them to help one another:

> It is difficult to draw a man out of his own circle to interest him in the destiny of the state, because he does not clearly understand what influence the destiny of the state can have upon his own lot. But if it be proposed to make a road cross the end of his estate, he will see at a glance that there is a connection between this small public affair and his greatest private affairs; and he will discover, without its being shown to him, the close tie which unites private to general interest.

Decentralization of government was considered by Tocqueville as one of the most important lessons he learned for France from the study of democracy in America. The dual arrangement, combining the American federal system with local self-rule, was characterized as "one of the greatest inventions known to political science"; under this scheme, the American people had the best of two worlds: "the happiness and freedom of small nations," and at the same time wielding "the power of great nations."

A matter of special concern to Tocqueville was the difficulty in recruiting men of high caliber to run for public office under a democratic system of government. He refers to the problem in various connections:

> It is a constant fact that, at the present day, the ablest men . . . are rarely placed at the head of affairs. . . . The people not only lack that soundness of judgement which is necessary to select men really deserving of their confidence, but often have not the desire or the inclination to find them out. . . . An instinct not less strong induces able men to retire from the political arena, in which it is so difficult to retain their independence, or to advance without becoming servile. . . . Those who engage in the perplexities of political life are persons of very moderate pretensions. The pursuit of wealth generally diverts men of great talents and strong passions from the pursuit of power; and it frequently happens that a man does not undertake to direct the fortunes of the state until he has shown himself incompetent to conduct his own.

As viewed by Tocqueville, the popular dictatorship over the mind discourages great and unusual men from entering public life in democracies. The temptation to play to the galleries, to bow to the prejudices and passions of the majority, is stronger than under other forms of government. Thus, men of intelligence, integrity, and frankness avoid contests for political office rather than to sacrifice their manly qualities and their independence. The lack of an established civil service, with its security of office, also resulted, in Tocqueville's opinion, in poor selection of talent and instability in administration.

Recent commentators on political science, while acknowledging a certain validity in Tocqueville's scathing comments, tend to discount as too harsh his judgment on American officialdom.

The place of parties in the American political system was underestimated by Tocqueville—to some extent perhaps because the parties had not yet achieved in the eighteen thirties the status which they were to acquire later. In any event, there was a failure to note the growth of a two-party system, based upon patronage and spoils. Tocqueville saw parties as a necessary evil, as instruments of "agitation," and he deplored frequent elections, with their unsettling effect on governmental activities and policies.

Remarkable perception was displayed by Tocqueville in predicting the future of American industry and business and their impact on democracy. Even in the eighteen thirties, industrial changes were beginning to transform American life from an agrarian to a manufacturing society, accompanied by cheap mass production. Tocqueville prophesied the rise of an aristocracy of manufacturers. Democracy is favorable to the growth of industry for two reasons, he noted: first, because there is emphasis on material comfort and welfare for everyone, and, second, the ablest individuals are attracted to commerce because it enables them to acquire wealth without restrictions as to birth, class, and caste.

The expansion of business and industry, however, leads inevitably to the creation of a working class, and a corresponding sharp division between employers and paid laborers. The worker's tasks become highly specialized and he learns to concentrate his energy and intelligence toward the perfection of a single detail. "In proportion as the workman improves," remarks Tocqueville, "the man is degraded." The employer becomes the administrator of a vast empire and there is "no real partnership" between him and the worker. The chief object of the employers, according to Tocqueville,

> is not to govern the population, but to use it . . . the manufacturing aristocracy of our age first impoverishes and debases the men who serve it and then abandons them to be supported by the charity of the public . . . the manufacturing aristocracy which is growing up under our eyes is one of the harshest that ever existed in the world . . . the friends of democracy should keep their eyes anxiously fixed in this direction; for if ever a permanent inequality of conditions and aristocracy again penetrates into the world, it may be predicted that this is the gate which they will enter.

How to reconcile political equality and economic inequality was perceived by Tocqueville as posing a major dilemma for a democratic society. On the one hand, democracy favors the growth of an industrial economy with improved living standards for the people, but the inequalities resulting from industrialization threaten the very foundation of democracy. Tocqueville did not believe that such inequalities would be indefinitely tolerated by a democratic people, though he doubted that the "institution of property would be abolished, since it is the foundation of our social order."

A social problem of a different character was recognized by Tocqueville in the institution of slavery. The future of the United States was gravely threatened, he thought, by the existence of the black race amid the white population of America. Tocqueville confidently predicted the end of the slave system, but he did not realize the strength of the abolitionist movement and the intensity of sectional feeling which would purchase freedom for the Negroes at the price of a devastating civil war. Emancipation of the slaves would not end race prejudices or social troubles, in Tocqueville's farsighted view. "The prejudice of race appears to be stronger," he observed, "in the states which have abolished slavery than in those where it still exists; and nowhere is it so intolerant as in those states where servitude has never been known."

In no area did Tocqueville show greater discernment

than in his comments on the future history of Russia and of the United States. When he was writing, the United States was a crude upstart of a nation on the western fringes of the world, while Russia was a half-Oriental, half-feudal state which was not much more than a vast expanse of frozen steppes. Tocqueville's remarkable gift of prophecy is demonstrated in the following passage, concluding the first part of *Democracy in America*:

> There are, at the present time, two great nations in the world which seem to tend towards the same end, although they started from different points: I allude to the Russians and the Americans. . . . All other nations seem to have nearly reached their natural limits, and only to be charged with the maintenance of their power; but these are still in the act of growth. . . . The American struggles against the natural obstacles which oppose him; the adversaries of the Russians are men. . . . The Anglo-American relies upon personal interest to accomplish his ends, and gives free scope to the unguided exertions and common sense of the citizens; the Russian centers all the authority of society in a single arm: the principal instrument of the former is freedom; of the latter servitude. Their starting point is different, and their courses are not the same; yet each of them seems to be marked out by the will of Heaven to sway the destinies of half the globe.

In a letter to a friend, Tocqueville defined the "political aim" of his work: "To those for whom the word 'democracy' is synonymous with disturbance, anarchy, spoliation, and murder, I have attempted to show that the government of democracy may be reconciled with respect for property, with deference for rights, with safety to freedom, with reverence for religion; that if democratic government is less favorable than another to some of the finer parts of human nature, it has also great and noble elements."

Democracy in America was one of the most influential books of the nineteenth century. It provided strong reinforcement for liberal convictions that political equality and democratic self-government were inevitable. Much of what Tocqueville wrote about American political institutions has become outdated, but his work is a monument in the intellectual history of the West, helping to shape the thought and actions of succeeding generations of political scientists and leaders. The closing lines of *Democracy in America* are a striking reaffirmation of Tocqueville's faith in mankind.

It is true that around every man a fatal circle is traced, beyond which he cannot pass; but within the wide verge of that circle he is powerful and free; as it is with man, so with communities. The nations of our time cannot prevent the conditions of men from becoming equal, but it depends upon themselves whether the principle of equality is to lead them to servitude or freedom, to knowledge or barbarism, to prosperity or wretchedness.

6–EVANGELIST FOR PUBLIC SCHOOLS

HORACE MANN'S *Annual Reports*

ONE OF THE great ideals of the founders of the American republic was their belief in a system of universal free public education—a concept most fervently voiced by Thomas Jefferson and his followers. Jefferson was firmly convinced that no people could be free and ignorant at the same time; hence, the school is the indispensable servant of democracy.

The vision of a plan of education reaching all the people remained a dream rather than a reality for the nation as a whole until more than a century after the American Revolution. The Herculean labors of one man, Horace Mann of Massachusetts, contributed vastly to the realization of the ideal by initiating a movement whose repercussions continue to be felt at home and abroad.

When Horace Mann was made secretary to the newly established Massachusetts State Board of Education in 1837, most American states had constitutional or statutory provisions for the public support of education. Frequently, however, the laws were permissive rather than mandatory. Furthermore, if tax money was available, it was sometimes allocated to private sectarian institutions. The situation in Massachusetts, which was undoubtedly one of the most enlightened and progressive of the states, was graphically described by Mann:

Facts incontrovertibly show, that, for a series of years previous to 1837, the school system of Massachusetts had been running down. Schoolhouses had been growing old, while new ones were rarely erected. School districts were divided, so that each part was obliged to support its schools on a moiety of a fund, the whole of which was a scanty allowance. . . . The multiplicity of different books in the same school embarrassed all kinds of instruction. The business of school-keeping fell more and more into the hands of youth and inexperience; so that, in rare instances only, did the maturity of years preside over the indiscretions of the young. Not only so, but the average time during which teachers continued in the business of school-keeping was shortened; so that the children suffered under the perpetual renewals and unskillfulness of first experiments. . . . To crown the whole, and to aggravate the deterioration which it proved to exist, the private school system was rapidly absorbing the funds, patronizing the talent, and withdrawing the sympathy, which belonged to the Public Schools.

Mann was not a professional educator. He was the son of fifth-generation Massachusetts farmers, born in 1796, and grew up in extreme poverty and hardship. His teachers, he reported, "were very good people; but they were very poor teachers." Until the age of fifteen, Mann had never been to school more than eight or ten weeks in a year. Fortunately for him and for future generations, a small bequest enabled him to enroll at Brown University, where he made a brilliant record as a student. Subsequently, Mann studied law, became a highly successful attorney, and entered politics. His political career was equally distinguished, beginning with a term in the Massachusetts House of Representatives and followed by election to the State Senate; he became President of the Senate in 1836. Among other progressive legislation, Mann was sponsor of a law establishing the first state hospital for the insane.

The most important event in Mann's life was passage by the state legislature in 1837 of a bill creating a State Board of Education and Mann's appointment as its first secretary. The salary of $1500 was about one half of his income from the practice of law, but the new secretary's attitude was expressed in the statement, "The interests of a client are small compared to the interests of the next generation. Let the next generation be my client." Henceforth the advancement of public schools became his all-absorbing mission. Mann's success may be judged by the fact that he is universally referred to as "the father of the common schools," not only of Massachusetts but of the nation.

For the next twelve years after his acceptance of the secretary's position, Horace Mann's aims and accomplishments were fully summed up in a series of annual reports, documents of major educational significance, totaling about one thousand printed pages.

Each of Mann's reports develops at length one or more specific aspects of the schools' problems. In brief, their content from the first to the twelfth, 1837–48, may be summarized as follows: The first deals with the construction and hygiene of school buildings, the duties of school committees, and the need for better teachers; the second is devoted largely to the course of study and to a discussion of the methods of teaching reading, spelling, and composition; the third discusses the responsibility of the people for the improvement of common schools, child labor, the development of libraries, and the effect of reading on the formation of character; the fourth urges the establishment of union schools to take the place of the district system and emphasizes the importance of regularity and punctuality in attendance; the fifth is famous for its presentation of the advantages of education, its effect upon men, the production of property, and the increases in all the elements of human well-being; the sixth considers the enrichment of the course of study and contains one of the earliest American discussions of the educational value of a study of physiology and hygiene; the seventh records Mann's observations in European schools and contrasts American schools with them; the eighth considers the value of local and county educational institutes, the importance of music in the schools, the use of the Bible, and employment of women teachers; the ninth urges the employment of women teachers, considers the value of teachers' institutes, and discusses the motives to which the teacher should appeal; the tenth gives the history of the common school system in Massachusetts and shows the relationship which education holds to the future progress of the state; the eleventh stresses the power of the common schools to redeem the state from social evils and crimes; and the twelfth and last reviews the changes in education in Massachusetts during the twelve years of Mann's service and ends with an eloquent plea for education.

As Horace Mann pointed out so emphatically in his first

report, the common schools of Massachusetts in 1837 were in an exceedingly sad condition. State supervision was lacking. Each district controlled its own educational enterprises and a social caste or class spirit had developed. The wealthier citizens sent their children to private schools, leaving the public schools as makeshifts for the poorer classes. The teachers were so deficient in preparation that often they were unable to do simple sums in multiplication and division. Discipline was a major problem; in 1837 some three hundred teachers were driven out of their schools by unruly and disorderly pupils, whom they were unable to control, even with the use of the omnipresent whip. The schoolhouses were neglected and shabby, and the schools were operated only a few months each year. It is scarcely an exaggeration to state that the general attitude of Massachusetts citizens toward their schools, at the time Horace Mann became Secretary of the Board of Education, was one of indifference, if not outright hostility.

The patrons of private schools argued for the maintenance of these separate institutions on the ground that, as reported by Mann, "some of the children in the public school are so addicted to profanity or obscenity, so prone to trickishness or to vulgar and mischievous habits, as to render a removal of their own children from such contaminating influences an obligatory precaution," a situation which Mann felt could be remedied if the educated, intelligent members of the community would take a direct interest in public school reform.

Even the poor were indifferent or antagonistic, failing to recognize the opportunities that might be open to their children with improved education. The illiterate, poverty-stricken masses saw education not as a means to better their lot, but as a diabolical scheme to deprive them of their children's labor. "It was found," wrote Mann, "that children could be profitably employed in many kinds of labor,—in factories, in the shoemaking business, and in other mechanical employments; and this swelled the already enormous amount of non-attendance and irregularity."

Mann met the defeatist attitudes of the citizens, rich and poor, head on and with irrefutable logic. "You are all eager to learn how to rear cattle," he declared bitterly in one of his speeches, "but not children. You spend money to keep a Congress debating on tariffs or roads, but withhold it from education, on which tariffs and roads depend. If you want a wagon built you do not dream of hiring a gardener for the job. But to build the most delicate of mechanisms, a child's mind, you hire anybody or nobody. Look at your schoolhouse with its leaking roof, its cold which freezes the ink. Have you not the vision to see a bright cheerful room where eager scholars are busy at microscopes, globes, maps, books, and directed by an expert teacher who knows how to spare the rod? Can you not imagine a school as spacious as a temple, training the children of the rich and poor side by side into noble citizens?"

Mann's social and educational ideas and ideals are stated again and again in his twelve annual reports as Secretary of the Board of Education and in the ten volumes of the semimonthly *Common School Journal,* which he founded, edited, and distributed broadcast to the people of Massachusetts. Basically, Mann was a propagandist for education, with absolute faith in his cause. His writings show little concern with theory, abstract philosophy, or scientific pedagogy. Instead, he was devoted to the practical and useful.

In his fifth report particularly, Mann presented abundant statistics to prove that educated labor is far more productive and profitable than illiterate labor. His object, he wrote, was to demonstrate that "education has a market value; that it is so far an article of merchandise, that it may be turned to a pecuniary account: it may be minted, and will yield a larger amount of statutable coin than common bullion." The famous fifth report, published in 1842, goes on with a forceful and persuasive appeal to industrialists to support public education. Four principal areas were selected by Mann in marshaling his arguments on the money value and other practical advantages of education: "The worldly fortunes, the health and length of life, the manners and tastes, and the intellectual and moral character."

Years later, a leading educational authority, John D. Philbrick, observed that Mann's fifth report had "probably done more than all other publications written within the past twenty-five years to convince capitalists of the value of elementary instruction as a means of increasing the value of labor." Mann's supreme faith in popular education is epitomized in this statement: "On schools and teachers I rely more than on any other earthly instrumentality, for the prosperity and honor of the state, and for the reformation and advancement of the race. All other reforms seek to abolish specific ills; education is preventive."

Other essential features of Mann's credo may be summarized briefly. First and foremost was his conviction that education should be universal and free. "I believe," he wrote, "in the existence of a great immortal, immutable principle of natural law, a principle of divine origin . . . the absolute right to an education of every human being that comes into the world." Girls should be trained as well as boys, and the poor should have the same opportunities as the rich. The quality of education should not differ in the public schools, designed to serve all the people, and the private schools supported by the wealthy.

Mann also held firm views on the teaching and learning processes; for example, "Though much may be done by others to aid, yet the effective labor must be performed by the learner himself. Knowledge cannot be poured into a child's mind, like fluid from one vessel into another. The pupil may do something by intuition, but generally there must be a conscious effort on his part. He is not a passive recipient, but an active, voluntary agent."

Mann was fully aware that any significant improvement in the public school system depended first of all on obtaining better teachers. Before he became secretary, little attention was paid to the preparation of teachers. The obvious remedy, Mann felt, was to establish special schools for the training of teachers: "Common schools cannot prosper without normal schools. As well might we expect to have coats without a tailor and houses without a carpenter or mason, as to have an adequate supply of teachers without normal schools."

Two years after Mann became secretary, a close friend, Edmund Dwight, member of the Board of Education, offered to donate $10,000 to found a normal school, if the state would appropriate a like amount. The legislature accepted the proposal and voted to establish three schools in different parts of Massachusetts. In 1839, Lexington opened the first public training school for teachers in America. Mann sold his law library to help equip a residence hall for the future teachers. By 1842, two more schools were in regular operation. The curriculum and methods of these institutions emulated the Prussian "seminaries" for teachers. There were reviews of common school subjects from the teaching point of view, some attention to educational theory, and experience in a practice school under supervision. Despite the hostility of conservatives, incompetent teachers, and sectarian groups, the schools immediately demonstrated their usefulness and soon won general acceptance.

Another device instituted by Mann to improve teaching was to arrange for teachers' institutes to be held throughout the state. Another generous gift from his friend Edmund Dwight enabled Mann to defray the expenses of teachers attending the institutes, during an experimental period. The institutes varied in length from one week to six weeks. Typically, the members formed into classes for recitations and drill, the "most neglected portions of the common school studies" were reviewed, and the best methods of teaching each branch were demonstrated. The institutes were held during the vacation period between summer and winter schools. Horace Mann attended all of them in person and spent as much time at each as the overlapping schedules permitted. Between four and five hundred teachers attended the 1847 institutes, according to Mann's report for that year, and generally "the members appeared deeply interested in their work."

Somewhat exhausted physically and mentally by his strenuous labors on behalf of public school reform, Mann asked and received permission from the Board of Education in 1843 to visit "every one of the countries" of Europe and to study their educational systems. His aim, he stated, was to find "beacons to terrify as well as lights to guide" the American people in their efforts to solve their own educational problems. Mann's seventh report is mainly a full review of his observations and judgments on the schools which he saw in operation in England, Ireland, Scotland, Germany, Holland, and France during a five-month tour. His chief interest was to examine "schools, schoolhouses, school systems, apparatus and modes of teaching." Elementary schools, public and private, were included in his itinerary, together with normal schools, schools for teaching the blind, deaf, and dumb, schools for the reformation of juvenile offenders, charity foundations for educating the children of the poor and of criminals, and orphan establishments.

In the course of his travels, Mann found "many things abroad which we, at home, should do well to imitate." He was impressed particularly by the organization and pedagogy of the Prussian schools, their lack of corporal punishment, the scholarly competence of the schoolmasters, the use of the word method in teaching reading, and the principle of using pleasure, not pain, to motivate learning. On the whole, however, Mann found more to deplore than to praise in foreign schools. The basic problem was European society itself, with its "foul and hideous forms of poverty, and wretchedness and crime," its domination by ecclesiastical and monarchical tyrants, and lack of a true system of popular education. Mann saw a direct relationship between the condition of society and the state of education in each nation visited by him. Britain was "tortured in all its vitals by the pangs of want and deadly wounds" caused by poor schools and the industrialists' exploitation of the lower classes; Ireland was handicapped by Catholicism and English persecution; the Scottish educational system was committed to "a wholly formal knowledge and an arbitrary application of the passages of the Bible"; Germany was divided by doctrinal differences; and educational practices in Italy and the Mediterranean countries were so bad that "no father would want his child to grow up there."

Horace Mann was adamantly opposed to corporal punishment in the schools, except under the most dire necessity. This was one aspect of the Prussian school system which particularly appealed to him. Of the thousands of children he had seen in classes there, he commented, *"I never saw one child undergoing punishment, or arraigned for misconduct. I never saw one child in tears from having been punished, or from fear of being punished."* (Mann's italics.) In contrast, Mann wondered "whether a visitor could spend six weeks in our own schools without ever hearing an angry word spoken, or seeing a blow struck, or witnessing the flow of tears."

This implied criticism of the schoolmasters of Massachusetts drew an immediate reaction. Thirty-one Boston schoolmasters issued a lengthy pamphlet entitled *Remarks on the Seventh Annual Report of Hon. Horace Mann,* condemning Mann as an academic and moral amateur totally unqualified to criticize experienced teachers and the historic educational system of Massachusetts. At the same time, an attempt was made to discredit the normal schools, libraries, methods, disciplines, and other reforms that had been introduced by Mann.

The schoolmasters' attack stung Mann into writing a *Reply,* which brought a *Rejoinder* by the schoolmasters and a second pamphlet, *Answer to a Rejoinder*, from Mann. The acrimonious dispute ended with strong popular support for Mann's position on the issues at stake.

Corporal punishment, the controversial matter which had set off the debate, was condemned by Mann in the strongest terms: "To thwack a child over the head because he doesn't get his lesson, is about as wise as it would be to rap a watch with a hammer because it does not keep good time. . . . You cannot open blossoms with a storm but under the genial influences of the sun. . . . The very blows which beat arithmetic and grammar in, beat confidence and manliness out. They lead to hatred, fraud, lying, revenge." As evidence of how prevalent the practice was in Mann's time, a survey found that floggings in a representative Boston school averaged sixty-five per day for four hundred children.

The minor war with the schoolmasters was but one of the battles which Mann had to fight, especially in the early years of his term as secretary. An enemy of public schools, Marcus Morton, was elected Governor of Massachusetts in 1839. One of his first moves was an attempt to fire Secretary Mann, "a reckless extravagance at a salary of fifteen hundred dollars a year." Prolonged debate in the legislature ended in a decisive defeat of the motion to abolish the Board of Education and Mann's position.

Another front was opened up by the ultraorthodox, the "sectarian preachers," as Mann called them, who as early as 1838 began to view with alarm the effect of the Board's policies on religious instruction in the schools. Religious bigots denounced Mann's efforts to ban the teaching of sectarianism in the common schools, berating him as an atheist, despite his strong support for Bible reading and the teaching of non-sectarian religion in the schools. Articles in the sectarian press charged that the system of education advocated by Mann would rob the people of their faith, and a diehard Calvinist minister, Reverend Matthew Hale Smith, preached a sensational sermon attributing the increase in sin in Boston to the malevolent policies of the Board of Education under Mann's influence. In his reply to Smith's violent attack, Mann pointed out that the Board had no control over the teaching of religion and the use of the Bible in the common schools; these were questions to be decided by the local school committees. He added, "The Bible was never so extensively used in our schools as at the present time; and its use has been constantly increasing ever since the influence of the Board was brought to bear on the subject."

What the conservative churchmen really wanted, Mann was certain, was a return to Puritan practices and principles and the teaching of sectarianism of their own particular brand. Such retrogression was neither practicable nor desirable, he knew, because the schools must serve the entire commonwealth, in which numerous sects were represented.

Under Mann's inspiring leadership, striking progress began to be evident in various phases of the schools' operations. As a practical reformer, he was greatly concerned with the dreary physical condition of schoolhouses, "to which the children should have been wooed by every attraction," but which had been "suffered to go where age and the elements would carry them." In his first report, Mann tried to arouse the public conscience by noting that children were being tortured by sitting six hours a day on benches without backs, built too high or too low from the ground. The buildings were often miserable shacks, with all classes in one room. Schoolhouses should be well constructed and sanitary, he maintained in one report after another, and went on to discuss the proper planning of rooms, ventilation, lighting, seating, and other features of a well-designed building.

Schools without books and libraries were anathema to Mann. His third report is devoted almost entirely to the subject and other references to the importance of books and reading are scattered throughout the series. Mann was shocked to discover that in the whole state of Massachusetts less than fifteen libraries were open to the public, thus "only a seventh part of the population was provided with opportunities for reading. . . . There are, moreover, in those libraries no books written for children." According to his goal, "every child ought to have a good library within half an hour's walk of his home." During his first year as secretary, Mann launched an ambitious plan for forming school libraries, prepared a list of approved books, and encouraged authors and publishers to produce books adapted to the child reader. He felt that children urgently needed a new literature written especially for them, and not for adults.

Mann also preached the extreme desirability of uniformity in school or text books. Here, he stated, "Uniformity and economy go hand in hand, while the evil of diversity brings with it the evil of a wasteful expenditure. The diversity of school books in the State, is also a serious inconvenience to teachers, and through them it reacts injuriously upon the schools."

In further pursuit of his continuous campaign for better teaching, Mann was a firm advocate of employing more women teachers. As he saw them, "Some of the arguments in favor of this change have been, the greater intensity of the parental instinct in the female sex, their natural love of the society of children, and the superior gentleness and forebearance of their dispositions,—all of which lead them to mildness rather than severity, to the use of hope rather than of fear as a motive of action, and to the various arts of encouragement rather than to annoyances and compulsion, in their management of the young." By the time of Mann's twelfth and last report, his hope had been substantially realized. In 1847–48, the ratio of women to men teachers in the Massachusetts schools was 5510 to 2424.

Salary levels were also rising. In 1838, Mann reported, "The average wages per month paid to male teachers throughout the state, inclusive of board, is twenty-five dollars and forty-four cents; and to female teachers, eleven dollars and thirty-eight cents." Exclusive of board, the average monthly wages of male teachers was $15.44, or $185.28 per year, and for female teachers, $5.38 a month, or $64.56 per year. About a decade later, the average wages of male teachers was $32.46, and of female teachers, $13.60, both inclusive of board. As Mann commented, "How inferior is the compensation paid to teachers, male and female, to what the dignity and importance of the vocation demands." He was particularly critical of "the grossly inadequate compensation made to female teachers," who could have earned six or seven times as much working in factories.

Nevertheless, financial support for public education was going up. In 1837, when Mann became secretary, town and city appropriations for common schools were estimated at $400,000. When he retired twelve years later, the total appropriations had reached about $750,000.

Two special problems associated with the schools, attendance and the length of the school year, occupied much of Mann's attention. Attendance he considered "deplorably low." In 1847, for example, 191,877 children of school age in Massachusetts were wholly or mainly dependent for their education upon the common schools. But of that number, 44,436 did not attend school during the summer term, and 29,196 failed to attend the winter term. Many others came irregularly. This unfortunate state of affairs was blamed by Mann on "the selfishness or cupidity" of parents or masters who were unwilling to spare the services of their children. For those children able and willing to attend, there was some gain in an extension of the school year from 100 to 115 days.

Following his twelve years of labor for education, Horace Mann re-entered politics, succeeding John Quincy Adams in the U.S. House of Representatives, where he joined the fight for the abolition of slavery. After two terms in Washington, he accepted the presidency of a new college, Antioch, in Yellow Springs, Ohio, and remained there until his death in 1859.

As an educational evangelist, Mann richly earned the reputation which later brought about his election to the Hall of Fame for Great Americans. The material achievements in Massachusetts schools during his time were notable, including the doubling of expenditures on free schools, better teachers' salaries, extension of the school term, vast improvements in buildings, libraries, textbooks, courses of study, and methods, and the inauguration of normal schools and teachers' institutes. Less tangible, but in the long run more important, is the idea deeply implanted by Mann that the common school is one of the supreme manifestations of the democratic faith, a concept which led to the universality of the free public school in America. An admonition in his final baccalaureate address at Antioch is a perfect expression of his social conscience: "Be ashamed to die until you have won some victory for humanity."

7–PROFESSIONAL HOMICIDE

OLIVER WENDELL HOLMES'
*The Contagiousness of Puerperal Fever Read
Before the Boston Society for Medical
Improvement and Published at the
Request of the Society*

THE CONDITIONS prevailing in early nineteenth-century hospitals, in Europe and America, can only be compared to a chamber of horrors. A pervading stench emanated from the saturation of wounds with pus. Four diseases took a heavy death toll: septicemia, a form of bood poisoning caused by pathogenic bacteria in the bloodstream; pyemia, with abscesses spread throughout the body; hospital gangrene, characterized by mortification of the tissues; and erysipelas, a contagious skin disease. The death rate from operations ranged from 25 to 40 per cent, and ran considerably higher for amputations.

The notable researches of Louis Pasteur on fermentation and applied bacteriology, of Joseph Lister on aseptic surgery, and Robert Koch's demonstrations that specific bacteria cause specific diseases all came after the middle of the century. Until then, few medical men suspected that lack of sanitation might be responsible for widespread infection and innumberable deaths. Surgical instruments were cleaned only casually; silk threads used for stitches were carried in the surgeon's lapel or pocket; when his hands were otherwise busy, the surgeon held the operating knife in his teeth; his coat, covered with stains and blood, was seldom if ever washed; and the surgeon did not trouble to wash his hands when going from one type of disease to another or from an autopsy to a living patient. Micro-organisms naturally flourished and multiplied.

Particularly perilous was childbirth in the hospitals—so hazardous indeed that it came near ruining the new science of obstetrics. When men doctors began to replace midwives, using forceps and making frequent examinations during labor, there was an immediate and rapid increase in "child-bed fever." The cases ordinarily began with a chill on the fourth day after the birth, fever rose, the abdomen became distended, and death nearly always followed. Autopsies revealed peritonitis and the formation of pus throughout the body.

Child-bed fever had long been known in the medical profession, but its causes remained a dark mystery. An English surgeon, Charles White, devoted the first chapter of his *Treatise on the Management of Pregnant and Lying-in Women* (1773) to "The Causes and Symptoms of the Puerperal or Child-bed Fever." The devastating plague was common throughout Europe. Dr. Logan Clendening cites a report of Paris' largest hospital, which lost more than half of the women in its maternity cases, and in Vienna in 1846 the First Clinic of the University lost from child-bed fever over 11 per cent of the 4010 patients it delivered.

A number of years earlier, alert observers among the doctors had begun to speculate on the reasons for the deadly infections. Alexander Gordon of Aberdeen published in 1795 *A Treatise on the Epidemic Puerperal Fever*, in which he states, "By observation, I plainly perceived the channel by which it was propagated, and I arrived at that certainty in the matter, *that I could venture to foretell that women would be affected with the disease upon hearing by what midwife they were to be delivered, or by what nurse they were to be attended, during their lying-in; and almost in every instance, my prediction was verified.*" Dr. Gordon confessed, "It is a disagreeable declaration for me to mention, that I, myself, was the means of carrying the infection to a great number of women." Many of the leading doctors, medical school teachers, and nurses of the period, on the other hand, ridiculed the notion that they might be guilty of transmitting the deadly disorder.

Child-bed fever was no less a curse in America than abroad. In the Boston area, puerperal fever became prevalent in the spring of 1842. At meetings of the Boston Society for Medical Improvement, of which Dr. Oliver Wendell Holmes, Professor of Anatomy at Harvard University, was a member, various physicians reported and discussed cases coming to their attention. Some fourteen or fifteen cases had occurred in Salem, and the disease was frequently seen on Cape Cod. There had been fifteen fatal cases of puerperal fever in Boston and vicinity within a period of about a month. New York was also suffering from an epidemic.

A shocking new turn of events came later in the year when several men contracted child-bed fever. A Dr. Whitney of Newton and two students, all of whom had lesions on their hands, did a postmortem examination on a woman dying of puerperal fever. The three became desperately ill, showing the usual symptoms of the disease, and a few days later died. A similar case was reported from Lynn, where a Dr. Barker made an examination of a patient who had died of puerperal fever. It was reported that "he had at the time several open sores on each hand, and pricked himself while sewing up the body." The following day he was ill and six days later was dead—doubtless not helped by the excessive bleeding which had been prescribed by the attending physician.

The cases thus reported to the Boston Society for Medical Improvement led to "animated discussion," and a question rose as to the contagion of puerperal fever and the possibility of physicians communicating it from one patient to another.

The suggestion that the disease was probably communicable struck a spark with Dr. Holmes and three weeks later, on February 13, 1843, he had a paper, revolutionary in its impact, ready to read to his fellow members. The title was "The Contagiousness of Puerperal Fever." By vote of the membership, the essay was published the following April in *The New England Quarterly Journal of Medicine and Surgery*.

Holmes was more celebrated in his own time and today as a literary light than as a man of medicine. Though presently little read except in textbook anthologies, devoted admirers of his light verse and essays among his contemporaries were numerous, especially in New England. In writing his utterly convincing argument against needless deaths in childbirth, Holmes' superb literary powers and his knowledge of medicine were combined in the most telling fashion.

Essentially, "The Contagiousness of Puerperal Fever" presents a long array of facts in support of the contention that the disease was contagious, was usually transmitted by the doctor or the nurse, and was due to a specific infection. Holmes opens with a declaration that every well-informed member of the medical profession realizes puerperal fever is sometimes passed on from one person to another. Anyone who thinks otherwise has not examined the evidence. "No negative facts, no opposing opinions," he writes, "be they what they may, or whose they may, can form any answer to the series of cases now within the reach of all who choose to explore the records of medical science."

To those who asserted that the case for contagion was not proven because not all exposed patients contracted child-bed fever, Holmes retorted, "Children that walk in calico before open fires are not always burned to death; the instances to the contrary may be worth recording; but by no means if they are to be used as arguments against woolen frocks and high fenders."

Illustrating the misinformation being disseminated by medical authorities, Holmes cites Dewees' standard *Treatise on the Diseases of Females,* which states unequivocally, "In this country, under no circumstances that puerperal fever has appeared hitherto, does it afford the slightest ground for the belief that it is contagious." On the contrary, Dr. Holmes was fully persuaded that "the disease known as Puerperal Fever is so far contagious as to be frequently carried from patient to patient by physicians and nurses."

Holmes concedes that little of a positive nature was known about how infection occurs, why some patients were susceptible and others escaped, how the disease is propagated, or why epidemics wax and wane. The clinching argument, in his view, was "that if it can be shown that great numbers of lives have been and are sacrificed to ignorance or blindness on this point, no other error of which physicians or nurses may be occasionally suspected will be alleged in palliation of this; but that whenever and wherever they can be shown to carry disease and death instead of health and safety, the common instincts of humanity will silence every attempt to explain away their responsibility."

Further reference was made to the 1795 treatise by Dr. Gordon of Aberdeen, who had observed that the only women who contracted puerperal fever were those who had been attended by a physician or nurse who had previously been in contact with patients suffering from the disease. According to Dr. Gordon, "the infection was as readily communicated as that of the small-pox or measles, and operated more speedily than any other infection with which I am acquainted."

Other citations to the professional literature on the subject, British and American, were offered by Dr. Holmes —all arriving at the same conclusion, that a direct relationship existed between the incidence of the disease and the doctor's or nurse's previous contacts with afflicted patients or postmortems. A Dr. Blundell, quoted by Holmes, was so discouraged "that in my own family I had rather that those I esteemed the most should be delivered, unaided, in a stable, by the manger-side, than that they should receive the best help, in the fairest apartment, but exposed to the vapors of this pitiless disease."

Based on numerous firsthand accounts, it is, said Holmes, "the plain conclusion that the physician and the disease entered, hand in hand, into the chamber of the unsuspecting patient."

After reviewing a "long catalogue of melancholy histories" of individual doctors and nurses responsible for multiple cases of puerperal fever, Holmes philosophizes on how much kinder nature unaided "deals with the parturient female, when she is not immersed in the virulent atmosphere of an impure lying-in hospital, or poisoned in her chamber by the unsuspected breath of contagion." Under other circumstances, the percentage of deaths from childbirth was extremely low.

Given the general atmosphere prevailing in the maternity hospitals of Holmes' time, there were long odds against a patient when she entered the doors. "Within the walls of lying-in hospitals," Holmes wrote, "there is often generated a miasm, palpable as the chlorine used to destroy it, tenacious so as in some cases almost to defy extirpation, deadly in some institutions as the plague . . . the loss of life occasioned by these institutions completely defeats the objects of their founders."

Near the conclusion of his paper, Holmes rises to a high point of eloquence in pleading his case:

It is as a lesson rather than as a reproach that I call up the memory of these irreparable errors and wrongs. No tongue can tell the heartbreaking calamities they have caused; they have closed the eyes just opened upon a new world of life and happiness; they have bowed the strength of manhood into the dust; they have cast the helplessness of infancy into the stranger's arms, or bequeathed it with less cruelty the death of its dying parent. There is no tone deep enough for record, and no voice loud enough for warning. The woman about to become a mother, or with her new-born infant upon her bosom, should be the object of trembling care and sympathy wherever she bears her tender burden, or stretches her aching limbs. The very outcast of the street has pity upon her sister in degradation when the seal of promised maternity is impressed upon her. The remorseless vengeance of the law brought down upon its victims by a machinery as sure as destiny, is arrested in its fall at a word which reveals her transient claims for mercy. The solemn prayer of the liturgy singles out her sorrows from the multiplied trials of life, to plead for her in the hour of peril. God forbid that any member of the profession to which she trusts her life, doubly precious at that eventful period, should regard it negligently, unadvisedly, or selfishly.

Eight conclusions were drawn by Holmes from his research and studies, all based upon practical experience and common sense. Among them were these: A physician engaged in the practice of obstetrics should not participate actively in the postmortem examination of cases of puerperal fever; if a physician is present at such autopsies, he should bathe thoroughly, change all his clothing, and allow twenty-four hours to pass before treating a patient; similar precautions should be taken in dealing with cases of erysipelas; a physician in whose practice a single case of puerperal fever has occurred "is bound to consider the next female he attends in labor" to prevent carrying the infection to her; if a physician has two cases of puerperal fever occurring within a short space of time, "he would do wisely to relinquish his obstetrical practice for at least one month," and try to rid himself of any contamination he may be carrying; if three closely connected cases occur in the practice of one individual, it "is *prima facie* evidence that he is the vehicle of contagion"; the physician should also take every precaution against nurses or other assistants transmitting the disease.

Holmes' eighth and last recommendation is so cogently expressed that it deserves to be quoted in full: "Whatever indulgence may be granted to those who have heretofore been the ignorant causes of so much misery, the time has come when the existence of a *private pestilence* in the sphere of a single physician should be looked upon, not as a misfortune, but as a crime; and in the knowledge of such occurrences the duties of the practitioner to his profession should give way to his paramount obligations to society."

Predictably, the conservatives and traditionalists reacted violently and adversely to the Holmes thesis. Such a forthright, forceful statement challenging fixed ideas was certain to arouse the antagonism of those whose teachings had been for years diametrically opposed to the concept of the contagiousness of puerperal fever. At the time, Philadelphia was the American center for the teaching of obstetrics, and two of the biggest guns in that city were wheeled out to demolish the upstart Holmes. Charles D. Meigs, Professor of Obstetrics at the Jefferson Medical College, and Hugh Lenox Hodge, Professor of Obstetrics and of the Diseases of Women and Children at the University of Pennsylvania, attacked Holmes vituperatively. Meigs pointed to the many cases of women during an epidemic of child-bed fever who did not contract the disease. "I prefer to attribute them [perpueral fever attacks] to accident, or Providence," he disclaimed, "of which I can form a conception, rather than to a contagion of which I cannot form any clear idea, at least as to this particular malady." In 1852 Hodge published an essay on the non-contagious character of puerperal fever, in which he asserted: "The result of the whole discussion will, I trust, serve, not to exalt your views of the value and dignity of our profession, but to divest your minds of the overpowering dread that you can ever become, especially to woman, under the extremely interesting circumstances of gestation and parturition, the minister of evil; that you can ever convey, in any possible manner, a horrible virus, so destructive in its effects, and so mysterious in its operations as that attributed to puerperal fever."

Undaunted, Holmes returned to the fray. In 1855 he reprinted his original essay unchanged in pamphlet form, in order to give it wider circulation, but retitled *Puerperal Fever as a Private Pestilence,* preceding it with a lengthy introduction, bringing his facts up to date. The introduction is prefaced with a quotation from the 1852 edition of Copland's *Medical Dictionary,* designed to put Drs. Hodge, Meigs, and their kind to shame:

Boards of health, if such exist, or, without them, the medical institutions of a country, should have the power of coercing, or of inflicting some kind of punishment on those who recklessly go from cases of puerperal fevers to parturient or puerperal females, without using due precaution; and who, having been shown the risk, criminally encounter it, and convey pestilence and death to the persons they are employed to aid in the most interesting and suffering period of female existence.

Point by point, Holmes replied to his critics, exposing the fallacies of their arguments. Referring to the strong and personal language used by Meigs, he says: "I take no offense and attempt no retort; no man makes a quarrel with me over the counterpane that covers a mother with her new-born infant at her breast." Holmes was especially concerned that medical students might be led astray by the statements of the two distinguished professors, which seemed to him to condone, if not actually encourage, professional homicide. One famous paragraph of the introduction, directed at students, suggests, "They naturally have faith in their instructors, turning to them for truth, and taking what they may choose to give them; babes in knowledge, not yet able to tell the breast from the bottle, pumping away for the truth at all that offers, were it nothing better than a professor's shrivelled forefinger."

Holmes concludes with a strong appeal to reasonable men: "The teachings of the two professors in the great schools of Philadelphia are sure to be listened to, not only by their immediate pupils, but by the profession at large. I am too much in earnest for either humility or vanity, but I do entreat those who hold the keys of life and death to listen to me also for this once. I ask no personal favor; but I beg to be heard in behalf of the women whose lives are at stake, until some stronger voice shall plead for them."

Dr. Holmes was being heard. The circulation of the *New England Quarterly Journal of Medicine and Surgery* was necessarily limited, but twelve years later, by the time the second edition of Holmes' work appeared, he could report, "I have abundant evidence that it has made many practitioners more cautious in their relations with puerperal females." His arguments had been prepared with such care that before long they became accepted facts among enlightened members of the medical profession. His essay undoubtedly saved many a mother from untimely death, or as a commentator for the Grolier Club's catalog of *One Hundred Influential American Books* phrased it, "No American publication in the nineteenth century saved more lives than this unassuming pamphlet, founded solely on the evidence of observed cases."

In his *The Professor at the Breakfast Table,* published some years later, Holmes indulged in reminiscences: "When, by the permission of Providence, I held up to the professional public the damnable facts connected with the conveyance of poison from one young mother's chamber to another's,—for doing which humble office I desire to be thankful that I have lived, though nothing else good should ever come of my life,—I had to bear the sneers of those whose position I had assailed, and, as I believe, have at last demolished, so that nothing but the ghosts of dead women stir among the ruins."

"At the time it was delivered," states the medical historian Dr. Henry R. Viets, "this paper was the most important contribution made in America to the advancement of medicine." The assertion may be questioned, if originality is the criterion, for William Beaumont's researches on the physiology of digestion were far more pioneering in character. As a matter of fact, Holmes laid no claim to great originality. Toward the end of a long life, he wrote that "others had cried out with all their might against the terrible evil, before I did, and I gave them full credit for it. But I think I shrieked my warning louder and longer than any of them, and I am pleased to remember that I took my ground on the existing evidence before the little army of microbes was marched up to support my position."

The story would not be complete without reference to a young Hungarian physician, Ignaz Philipp Semmelweis, a graduate of the University of Vienna's medical department. When Semmelweis became an assistant in the obstetrical clinic at Vienna, in 1848, he required students to wash their hands in chlorine water before entering the clinic. Later a solution of chloride of lime was used. Immediately there occurred a dramatic decrease in the previously high mortality rate from puerperal fever until it had almost vanished. Thereafter, Semmelweis continuously preached the doctrine that the obstetrician must come to his patients aseptically clean. Like Holmes, he was attacked viciously by the diehards, driven from one hospital to another, and eventually died insane. To Semmelweis, nevertheless, belongs the major credit for our first knowledge of the means to eliminate the horrible pestilence of puerperal fever.

8-STATE VERSUS INDIVIDUAL

HENRY DAVID THOREAU'S
Resistance to Civil Government

ONE OF THE STRANGEST PARADOXES in history is the inspiration for revolutionary movements furnished by a poet naturalist of mid-nineteenth-century New England. Henry David Thoreau, who worshiped nature in almost pagan fashion, a recluse who preferred his own company to that of others, who loved mankind but had little sympathy for man, and who thoroughly distrusted all forms of government—including democracy—was one of the great philosophical anarchists of all time. The influence of his writings has gone around the world.

Thoreau, a true eccentric, was a native of Concord, Massachusetts, of French-Scottish ancestry. The Thoreaus were simple artisans and the family existed barely above the poverty level. Henry graduated from Harvard at the age of twenty, after which he supported himself for a while by teaching, then by surveying, and finally by occasional manual labor. For two years he lived in Ralph Waldo Emerson's home, where he participated to a limited degree in the discussions of the transcendentalist circle. In the later years of his life, Thoreau was a general handyman in Concord, with few material needs or wants.

A turning point in Thoreau's life came in the summer of 1846. A war with Mexico was in progress—a war as unpopular with liberal American opinion as Vietnam later became. Objective evidence now appears to support the view that American troops were sent to the border on an expedition seeking trouble, preliminary to the annexation of Texas, though President Polk asserted that the first bloodshed was caused by a Mexican attack "on our own territory."

Even more unsettling was the chronic question of slavery, especially in New England, where the abolitionists kept the discussions in a constant state of ferment. Thoreau's sympathies were completely with the abolitionist cause, and he was aroused further by the persecution by state and local governments of his friends in the movement.

The crowning touch for Thoreau came with his own arrest for non-payment of poll taxes. For a year he had lived in a hut, built by himself, on Walden Pond, near Concord. Absorbed in the contemplation of nature, cut off from human companionship, he felt increasingly isolated from his neighbors. For several years he had refused to pay the poll tax, as a symbol of protest against a government that condoned slavery and waged war. The action emulated that of his fellow townsman Bronson Alcott, father of "Little Women," who had earlier announced his intention to pay no tax to support a government that aided slavery and who had been arrested and jailed for his defiance of the law.

One afternoon when Thoreau came into Concord from Walden Pond to pick up a pair of shoes which he had left to be repaired, an old friend, Samuel Staples, the local constable, approached him. Staples reminded Thoreau that his poll taxes were overdue and offered to lend him the money if he were short of cash. Thoreau explained that his refusal to pay was on moral grounds, not financial, whereupon Staples concluded that it was his duty to arrest him and lock him up in the village jail. Thoreau spent only one night in jail, for a heavily veiled woman called on Staples and paid the fine—much to Thoreau's displeasure. The identity of his liberator is unknown, but is believed to have been his Aunt Maria, who was shocked to find her nephew incarcerated. Thoreau was thus deprived of an opportunity to make a dramatic protest against the iniquities of government.

Nevertheless, Thoreau used the episode of his jailing as a point of departure for a work destined to be the most widely read and to have the greatest impact of anything that he ever wrote—his manifesto on civil disobedience. The original account was delivered, probably in 1848, as a lecture entitled "The Relation of the Individual to the State," and the following year published under the title of "Resistance to Civil Government" in Elizabeth Peabody's short-lived periodical *Aesthetic Papers*. Later the essay was renamed *Civil Disobedience* in Thoreau's collected works and under that title has been reprinted innumerable times.

Thoreau's neighbors were divided in their views on Thoreau's action in choosing to go to jail rather than to pay the tax. Bronson Alcott was immensely pleased, but Ralph Waldo Emerson thought that it was "mean, skulking, and in bad taste." According to a famous anecdote, possibly apocryphal, Emerson asked Thoreau what he was doing in jail. Thoreau, who was critical of Emerson for his refusal to take a strong stand against slavery, replied, "Why are you not here?"

Two main themes run through *Civil Disobedience:* contempt for the existing government and the supreme importance of the individual's own moral values. Thus the higher moral law, as interpreted by the individual conscience, it was held, should prevail against the dictates of government.

Thoreau begins by recalling Thomas Jefferson's declaration, "That government is best which governs least," and carries the conclusion a step further with the assertion, "That government is best which governs not at all." Thoreau continues:

> Government is at best but an expedient; but most governments are usually, and all governments are sometimes, inexpedient. The objections which have been brought against a standing army, and they are many and weighty, and deserve to prevail, may also at last be brought against a standing government. The standing army is only an arm of the standing government. The government itself, which is only the mode which the people have chosen to execute their will, is equally liable to be abused and perverted before the people can act through it.

The dead hand of the past was denounced by Thoreau in the actual administration of government. He saw the American Government, like others, as a tradition, "endeavoring to transmit itself unimpaired to posterity, but each instant losing some of its integrity." Under these circumstances, the government becomes inflexible, lacking in "the vitality and force of a single living man," incapable of stimulating fresh creative efforts, "a sort of wooden gun to the people themselves," the silent rule of the living by the dead.

The uselessness of government as it currently functioned was portrayed by Thoreau in these words:

> This government never of itself furthered any enterprise, but by the alacrity with which it got out of the way. *It* does not keep the country free. *It* does not settle the West. *It* does not educate. The character inherent in the American people has done all that has been accomplished; and it would have done somewhat more, if the government had not sometimes got in its way.

Thoreau soon makes a distinction, however, between himself and "those who call themselves no-government men." Recognizing that society is as yet unprepared to dispense with all government, he demands "not at once no government, but *at once* a better government." Even as matters stood, Thoreau acknowledged that "the Constitution, with all its faults, is very good, the law and the courts very respectable, even this State and this American government are, in many respects, very admirable and rare things to be thankful for." Furthermore, he differentiated between those functions of government of which he approved and those which he rejected: "I have never declined paying the highway tax, because I am as desirous of being a good neighbor as I am of being a bad subject; and as for supporting schools, I am doing my part to educate my fellow countrymen now."

Obviously, Thoreau's plea is for a distinction between bad government and good government, and for a corollary principle that it is the citizen's right and duty to resist evil in the state even to the point of open and deliberate disobedience to its laws.

The unbridled power of the majority is roundly condemned by Thoreau, thus repudiating a basic tenet of democracy. When power is in the hands of the people, it is the custom for a majority to rule, "not because they are most likely to be in the right, nor because this seems fairest to the minority, but because they are physically the strongest. . . . Must the citizen ever for a moment, or in the least degree, resign his conscience to the legislator? I think that we should be men first, and subjects afterward. . . . A wise man will not leave the right to the mercy of chance, nor wish it to prevail, through the power of the majority. . . . Moreover," maintains Thoreau, "any man more right than his neighbors constitutes a majority of one already."

Thoreau is especially critical of those citizens who "while they disapprove of the character and measures of a government, yield to it their allegiance and support," for those are "frequently the most serious obstacles to reform." He adds:

> Practically speaking, the opponents to a reform in Massachusetts are not a hundred thousand politicians at the South, but a hundred thousand merchants and farmers here, who are more interested in commerce and agriculture than they are in humanity, and are not prepared to do justice to the slave and to Mexico *cost what it may*. . . . There are thousands who are *in opinion* opposed to slavery and to the war, who yet in effect do nothing to put an end to them.

Thoreau's stand was uncompromising: "I cannot for an instant recognize that political organization as *my* government which is the *slave's* government also . . . when a sixth of the population of a nation which has undertaken to be the refuge of liberty are slaves, and a whole country [Mexico] is unjustly overrun and conquered by a foreign army, and subjected to military law, I think that it is not too soon for honest men to rebel and revolutionize."

Since the existence of unjust laws is undisputable, Thoreau states, the citizen has a choice among three types of action: obey them, obey them until they can be amended, or "transgress them at once." Some hold that resistance would be worse than the evil. Under an ideal government, Thoreau believes, citizens would be encouraged to point out its faults as a prelude to reforms. In practice, governments are hostile to reformers. "Why does its always crucify Christ, and excommunicate Copernicus and Luther, and pronounce Washington and Franklin rebels?"

Conceding that open obstruction of laws is likely to bring down the wrath of the state, Thoreau asserts, "Under a government which imprisons any unjustly, the true place for a just man is also a prison. . . . If any think that their influence would be lost there, and their voices no longer afflict the ear of the State, that they would not be as an enemy within its walls, they do not know by how much truth is stronger than error, nor how much more eloquently and effectively he can combat injustice who has experienced a little in his own person." If enough of its citizens are willing to defy unjust laws, the state will capitulate and change the laws. Referring to his own prison experience, Thoreau observes, "I saw that the state was half-witted, that it was timid as a lone woman with her silver spoons, and that it did not know its friends from its foes, and I lost all my remaining respect for it, and pitied it."

Thoreau's whole political philosophy unquestionably was based on the belief that the individual conscience is the only true criterion by which to judge what is right or wrong. To use the individual conscience as the sole valid guide for political action, on the other hand, is in direct conflict with the democratic principle of majority rule, as Thoreau recognized. In any case, to him, "There is but little virtue in the masses of men." One has to have faith in man, letting each man determine for himself what is right and just. In the final paragraph of *Civil Disobedience*, Thoreau describes his concept of a utopian government, where presumably no civil disobedience would be needed:

The progress from an absolute to a limited monarchy, from a limited monarch to a democracy, is a progress toward a true respect for the individual. Even the Chinese philosopher was wise enough to regard the individual as the basis of the empire. Is a democracy, such as we know it, the last improvement possible in government? Is it not possible to take a step further towards recognizing and organizing the rights of man? There will never be a really free and enlightened State, until the State comes to recognize the individual as a higher and independent power, from which all its own power and authority are derived, and treats him accordingly. I please myself with imagining a State at last which can afford to be just to all men, and to treat the individual with respect as a neighbor; which even would not think it inconsistent with its own repose, if a few were to live aloof from it, not meddling with it, nor embraced by it, who fulfilled all the duties of neighbors and fellow-men. A State which bore this kind of fruit, and suffered it to drop off as fast as it ripened, would prepare the way for a still more perfect and glorious State, which also I have imagined, but not yet anywhere seen.

It is easy to pick flaws in Thoreau's arguments for an anarchic society. A basic fallacy is the contention that mankind has no need for organized society or government and each man is able to provide for his own welfare in a complex world. A second error is the failure to recognize the nature of American democracy, which has never granted absolute authority to majority rule, but on the contrary contains numerous safeguards for minority opinion, no matter how small. In stating "the only obligation I have a right to assume is to do at any time what I think is right," and no government had "a pure right over my person or property but what I concede to it." Thoreau would have every citizen act as judge of the state and of his own behavior. The extreme liberalism personified by Thoreau glorifies individual free will, isolates the citizen from society, and frees him from all social and civic duties.

But on a higher plane, Thoreau's philosophy contains fundamental truth. It is the citizen's duty to fight injustice in society, to do his share to ensure that injustices are not perpetuated or created by the state. Under dictatorships, the problem becomes particularly acute, though even under democracies, as the state reaches out for constantly increasing power, the nature and extent of obedience to the state are matters of the most urgent concern to the individual. Perhaps there is little scope for individualism in an increasingly collective society. In any event, Thoreau's classic statement is an eloquent defense of and justification for making a place for the individual conscience.

The theory of civil disobedience is not original with Thoreau. Examples may be found in both the Old and New Testaments and in the writings of the third century B.C. Chinese philosopher Mencius and the fifth century A.D. Roman philosopher Boethius. Civil disobedience in American history has been an almost constant factor. Notable instances predating Thoreau are the actions of the Quakers in seventeenth-century New England, the Boston Tea Party, Shays' Rebellion, and the Declaration of Independence itself, wherein it is stated that "whenever any Form of Government becomes destructive of these ends [that is, life, liberty, and the pursuit of happiness] it is the Right of the People to alter it or to abolish it."

A century before Thoreau, the famous English jurist Sir William Blackstone laid down the dictum, "No laws are binding on the individual subject that assault his person or violate the conscience."

Nonetheless, the concept of civil disobedience was so effectively presented by Thoreau that he is now universally given credit for originating the theory.

For the remainder of his short life (he died in 1862 at the age of forty-five), Thoreau continued his attacks on the institution of slavery, supplementing *Civil Disobedience* with two fiery pamphlets entitled *Slavery in Massachusetts* and *Plea for Captain John Brown*.

A remarkable insight into Thoreau's character and personality comes from another great American, Walt Whitman, Thoreau's friend and contemporary:

> Thoreau was a surprising fellow—he is not easily grasped—is elusive: yet he is one of the native forces —stands for a fact, a movement, an upheaval: Thoreau belongs to America, to the transcendental, to the protestors: then he is an outdoor man: all outdoor men, everything being equal, appeal to me. Thoreau was not so precious, tender, a personality as Emerson: but he was a force—he looms up bigger and bigger . . . : every year has added to his fame. One thing about Thoreau keeps him very near to me: I refer to his lawlessness—his dissent—his going down his absolute road, let hell blaze as it chooses.

Historians are agreed that Thoreau's *Civil Disobedience* had little effect or influence during his own lifetime. Almost forty years were to pass before the worldwide repercussions of the essay began to be felt. Around 1900 the Russian novelist and philosopher Count Leo Tolstoy read the work and realized its implications for his own crusade to free the Russian serfs from near slavery under czarist rule.

Far more significant, however, was the discovery about 1907 of *Civil Disobedience* by a young Hindu lawyer, Mohandas Gandhi, then living in South Africa. In South Africa, Gandhi devoted himself mainly to violators of the discriminatory laws passed against members of the Hindu colony there. As Gandhi tells the story:

> My first introduction to Thoreau's writings was, I think, in 1907, or later, when I was in the thick of

the passive resistance struggle. A friend sent me the essay on "Civil Disobedience." It left a deep impression upon me. I translated a portion for the readers of "Indian Opinion in South Africa," which I was then editing, and I made copious extracts for the English part of that paper. The essay seemed to be so convincing and truthful that I felt the need of knowing more of Thoreau, and I came across . . . his *Walden,* and other shorter essays, all of which I read with great pleasure and equal profit.

Gandhi, who had been dissatisfied with the term first used to describe his movement, "passive resistance," but had found no acceptable substitute, at once adopted "civil disobedience" as his motto. Here was a statement of principle, he decided, that meant firmness without violence, and a devotion to truth and justice—a political policy completely in accord with Gandhi's philosophy. *Civil Disobedience* in the hands of Mahatma Gandhi became a bible of non-resistance. For his Hindu followers, Gandhi coined an equivalent, *Satyagraha,* a combination of two Sanskrit words, translated as "soul force" or "the force which is born of truth and love or non-violence."

Gandhi remained in South Africa through 1914, carrying on a running battle with government officials and gaining a number of important concessions for his race. Early in 1915 he returned to India. From then until his death at the hands of a Hindu assassin in 1948, Gandhi led the forces that eventually won independence for India and Pakistan. Civil disobedience was frequently used during those years and was sharpened by Gandhi into a weapon of remarkable effectiveness.

A leading authority on Thoreau's writings, Walter Harding, has traced editions of *Civil Disobedience* abroad, noting that "his works have been translated into virtually every major foreign language," including Czech, Danish, French, German, Spanish, Dutch, Swedish, Russian, Italian, Hebrew, Yiddish, and Japanese. The Fabians and early Labour Party members popularized Thoreau in England, distributing inexpensive paperbound editions of *Walden* and *Civil Disobedience,* with the Party's blessing. In Denmark, Harding reports, *"Civil Disobedience* was used as a manual of arms by the resistance movement against the Nazi invasion during World War II. It was circulated surreptitiously throughout the war years among the Danes as a means of encouraging them to further acts of resistance."

Back in the United States, *Civil Disobedience* has been an object of attack by conservative censors on a number of occasions. Upton Sinclair, Norman Thomas, and Emma Goldman were each arrested for reading Thoreau's essay from a public platform. In the 1950s during Senator Joseph McCarthy's purge of U.S. Information Libraries a copy of a standard text was removed from the shelves of each of the libraries because it contained *Civil Disobedience*.

The most striking application of Thoreau's ideas in America in recent years has been in the antisegregation movement, especially in the Southern states. Examples are the refusal of Negroes to ride segregated buses in Montgomery, Alabama; the boycotting by Negroes of segregated stores in Albany, Georgia; the kneel-ins of Negroes in the white churches of Nashville, Tennessee; and the Freedom Riders in Alabama and Mississippi. As much as a generation ago, one of the Negro leaders, James Robinson, in addressing a group which later became the Committee on Racial Equality (CORE), stated:

> Thoreau's *Civil Disobedience* was not much used by the Abolitionists for whom it was written; probably no one before Gandhi realized its significance for a new type of social movement based upon group discipline and personal conscience. As one reads this essay, it is impossible not to notice that almost every sentence is loaded with meaning for us today. . . . Substitute the economic, political, and social persecution of American Negroes today where Thoreau condemns Negro slavery—and you will scarcely find half a dozen sentences in the entire essay which you cannot apply to your own actions in the present crisis.

Dr. Martin Luther King, Jr., who achieved even greater fame in the civil rights movement, writes in his autobiography, *Stride Toward Freedom*:

> When I went to Atlanta's Morehouse College as a freshman in 1944 my concern for racial and economic justice was already substantial. During my student days at Morehouse I read Thoreau's "Essay on Civil

Disobedience" for the first time. Fascinated by the idea of refusing to cooperate with an evil system, I was so deeply moved that I reread the work several times. This was my first intellectual contact with the theory of nonviolent resistance.

Subsequently, discussing the boycott which he organized against segregated buses in Montgomery, King added:

At this point I began to think about Thoreau's "Essay on Civil Disobedience." I remembered how, as a college student, I had been moved when I first read this work. I became convinced that what we were preparing to do in Montgomery was related to what Thoreau had expressed. We were simply saying to the white community, "We can no longer lend our cooperation to an evil system."

Something began to say to me, "He who passively accepts evil is as much involved in it as he who helps to perpetuate it. He who accepts evil without protesting against it is really cooperating with it." When oppressed people willingly accept their oppression they only serve to give the oppressor a convenient justification for his acts. Often the oppressor goes along unaware of the evil involved in his oppression so long as the oppressed accepts it. So in order to be true to one's conscience and true to God, a righteous man has no alternative but to refuse to cooperate with an evil system. This I felt was the nature of our action. From this moment on I conceived of our movement as an act of massive non-cooperation.

The extreme hazards even of movements founded on principles of passive resistance and non-violence were tragically demonstrated in the assassinations of both Mahatma Gandhi and Martin Luther King, Jr.

Legal sanction for the doctrine of civil disobedience was given in a U.S. Supreme Court decision of 1945: "The victory for freedom of thought recorded in our Bill of Rights recognizes that in the domain of conscience there is a moral power higher than the State. Throughout the ages, men have suffered death rather than subordinate their allegiance to God to the authority of the State." This forthright statement reaffirmed William Blackstone's conclusion in his *Commentaries on the Laws of England,* nearly two centuries earlier.

The future will doubtless witness further use of the principles of civil disobedience, as conceived by Thoreau and perfected by Gandhi. The power of oppressed peoples everywhere, even in the ruthless dictatorships of modern times, can make itself felt through these devices. "Even the most despotic government," said Gandhi, "cannot stand except for the consent of the governed, which consent is often forcibly procured by the despot. Immediately the subject ceases to fear the despotic force, his power is gone." It must be conceded, nevertheless, that trends of government in the twentieth century show Thoreau's ideas and ideals fighting a losing battle.

"In Thoreau," wrote Vernon L. Parrington, American literary critic and historian, "the eighteenth-century philosophy of individualism, the potent liberalisms let loose on the world by Jean Jacques Rousseau, came to the fullest expression in New England. He was the completest embodiment of the *laissez-faire* reaction against a regimented social order, the severest critic of the lower economics that frustrate the dreams of human freedom. He was fortunate in dying before the age of exploitation had choked his river with its weeds; fortunate in not foreseeing how remote is that future of free men on which his hopes were fixed."

9–BLACK MAN'S ILIAD

HARRIET BEECHER STOWE'S
Uncle Tom's Cabin

WITHIN A DECADE after its publication *Uncle Tom's Cabin* had become the most popular novel ever written by an American. Sales had mounted into millions of copies, translations had appeared in dozens of languages, a score of dramatic versions were being presented by traveling theatrical troupes, and there is substantial evidence that the book precipitated the American Civil War.

The extraordinary vogue of *Uncle Tom's Cabin* can be attributed to several factors. First of all, it was a powerful story, full of memorable characters, told with passion and deep conviction. Fully as important is the novel's time-liness. A vast reading public was ready for it, prepared by the virulent political atmosphere in which slavery had become the dominant issue of American life. The bitter-ness of feeling in the North had been further intensified by passage of the Fugitive Slave Law in 1850. Lending force to the timely thesis and its dramatic narration is the religious element pervading *Uncle Tom's Cabin*, in a period when formal Christianity was most influential in American culture.

The author of *Uncle Tom's Cabin*, Harriet Beecher Stowe, was the daughter of a celebrated New England Presbyterian divine, Lyman Beecher. Of his thirteen sons and daughters, six, including the famous theologian Henry Ward Beecher, were clergymen. Harriet's education was overwhelmingly religious, though she was permitted by her father to read Sir Walter Scott's romances and Byron's poems, and their influence is obvious in her literary style. When Harriet was twenty-one, her father left Boston to become President of the Lane Theological Seminary in

Cincinnati. While in Cincinnati, Harriet married Professor Calvin Stowe, a minister, scholar, and pioneer advocate of publc education; the couple proceeded to produce seven children.

It was in Cincinnati that Harriet Beecher Stowe learned about slavery at first hand. On visits across the Ohio River in Kentucky she began to absorb impressions of the slave system in practice. She met abolitionists, runaway slaves, and Underground Railroad operators, became acquainted with colorful characters, and heard of lurid incidents relating to slavery—all of which were later woven into the fabric of her novel. Meanwhile, Harriet was conceiving a deep horror of the institution of slavery.

In 1850 Calvin Stowe was appointed to a professorship at Bowdoin College and he and his family moved to Brunswick, Maine. Previously, Harriet had demonstrated some writing ability through publication of a series of stories and sketches. Now, back in New England, she found herself caught up in the controversy created by the Fugitive Slave Act. A sister-in-law, Mrs. Edward Beecher, wrote to her, "Hattie, if I could use a pen as you can, I would write something that will make this whole nation feel what an accursed thing slavery is." Upon receiving the letter, Harriet exclaimed to her children, "I *will* write something, I will if I live."

Charles Edward Stowe's biography of his mother records the inspiration for a key incident in *Uncle Tom's Cabin*—the genesis of the novel. As reported, while Mrs. Stowe was seated at a communion table in the college church, "suddenly, like the unrolling of a picture, the scene of the death of Uncle Tom passed before her mind. So strongly was she affected that it was with difficulty she could keep from weeping aloud. Immediately on returning home she took pen and paper and wrote out the vision which had been as it were blown into her mind as by the rushing of a mighty wind."

Thus the first part of *Uncle Tom's Cabin* to be written was the conclusion. In January 1851 Mrs. Stowe began the transcription of the story of which she frequently remarked in later years, "The Lord Himself wrote it. I was but an instrument in His hand." Gamaliel Bailey, editor of the *National Era*, an antislavery paper of Washington, D.C., was approached about publication. Bailey had known the Beecher family in Cincinnati, where he edited another antislavery journal, the *Philanthropist,* until driven out by mob violence. Dr. Bailey accepted the manuscript and agreed to pay $300 for a work which Mrs. Stowe thought "may extend through three or four numbers." As described in advance by Mrs. Stowe in correspondence with Dr. Bailey, her story was "embracing a series of sketches which give the lights and shadows of the 'patriarchal institution,' written either from observation, incidents which have occurred in the sphere of my personal knowledge, or in the knowledge of my friends. I shall show the *best side* of the thing, and something *faintly approaching* the worst."

The "three or four" numbers of the *National Era* grew to forty—running from June 5, 1851, to April 1, 1852—before Mrs. Stowe's task was completed. At the end, the editor wrote, "Mrs. Stowe has at last brought her great work to a close. We do not recollect any production of an American writer that has excited more general and profound interest." The original honorarium of $300, however, was not increased.

Raw materials for the composition of *Uncle Tom's Cabin* were plentiful. Among the primary themes were the slave market, the forced separation of families, the contrast of plantation life in the slave's cabin and the master's mansion, immoral sexual behavior, and the problem of miscegenation. Mrs. Stowe drew inspiration and information from materials found in the antislavery reading rooms in Boston; by studying Theodore Weld's book, *American Slavery as It Is: Testimony of a Thousand Witnesses;* and from reading the narratives of fugitive slaves.

The first publisher approached about book-form publication of *Uncle Tom's Cabin* was the Boston firm of Phillips, Sampson and Company, who refused it for fear of offending their Southern customers—a classic instance of a publisher's misjudgment. A more adventuresome and enterprising publisher, John P. Jewett, agreed to take the book, though he, too, was skeptical of its sales possibilities. Accordingly, he suggested to the Stowes that they could either share the printing costs and profits with him equally or take a straight 10 per cent royalty. The Stowes were likewise unwilling to gamble and elected to receive a royalty—a costly decision on their part.

On March 20, 1852, shortly prior to the end of its serialization in the *National Era, Uncle Tom's Cabin,* subtitled *Life Among the Lowly,* appeared in two volumes, with a woodcut of a Negro cabin on the title page and cover. The original edition was five thousand copies, of which three thousand were sold the first day and the remainder the next day. A second edition was exhausted by the end of the month. Before the book was a year old more than three hundred thousand copies had been sold in the United States alone—an enormous total in relation to the population. Within five years, half a million copies of the novel had been bought in America and perhaps twice as many in the British Isles. More than twenty London editions appeared during 1852, of which only one paid royalties to the author. The rest were pirated, as were translations into French, German, Italian, Spanish, Russian, Danish, Flemish, Polish, Portuguese, Bohemian, Hungarian, and numerous more esoteric languages.

Equally unprofitable for Mrs. Stowe were various dramatizations of *Uncle Tom's Cabin*. She had refused to grant permission to dramatize the novel, because she disapproved of theatergoing, especially for the young. Without authorization from, or compensation to, the original author, therefore, the stage was soon crowded with commercially successful productions, generally totally lacking in literary merit. For generations, hundreds of "Tom" companies played and replayed every American town and city outside the South. The stage versions, featuring what one critic described as "an incalculably poisonous 'Topsy' and 'Uncle Tom' image of the American Negro," are responsible for the current detestation of these characters by Negroes and their use of "Uncle Tom" as an epithet.

The essential plot of *Uncle Tom's Cabin* is not complex, though it involves many characters. Actually, there are two plots. According to a common practice in Victorian fiction, the adventures of two groups of characters are alternated in the narrative. All commence as slaves in the border state of Kentucky. Thereafter, one plot revolves around Uncle Tom, a middle-aged, intelligent, and deeply religious black man; in the second plot, the central figure is Eliza, a young yellow-skinned matron, one of Tom's fellow slaves.

In the opening scene, a benevolent Kentucky slave owner, Mr. Shelby, in order to pay his debts, is compelled to sell some of his best slaves, including Uncle Tom, to a New Orleans slave dealer named Haley. Overhearing a conversation between Shelby and Haley, Eliza learns that her child Harry is also to be sold. During the night she flees with the boy across the frozen Ohio River, and seeks freedom in Canada. Her husband, George Harris, a slave on a nearby plantation, also escapes and follows her. Eventually, after many adventures with pursuing slave catchers, but aided by Quakers and other sympathetic whites along the way, they reach Canada and later Africa.

Uncle Tom is less fortunate. To avoid embarrassing his master, he refuses to run away, and is separated from his wife and children. On the trip down the Mississippi to New Orleans, Tom saves the life of little Eva by hauling her from the river, and in gratitude her father, St. Clare, buys him from the dealer. The next two years are pleasant ones for Tom as a servant in St. Clare's elegant New Orleans home, with the saintly child Eva, and her impish Negro companion, Topsy. Then Eva dies, and in her memory, St. Clare makes plans to free Tom and his other slaves. But St. Clare is accidentally killed trying to separate two quarreling men, and Mrs. St. Clare, a frivolous, heartless aristocrat, orders Tom sent to the slave market.

Tom is bought at public auction by a brutal, drunken Red River planter named Simon Legree, a native Vermonter. Despite impeccable behavior and all efforts to please his cruel master, Tom soon incurs Legree's hatred, and is frequently beaten. Two female slaves, Cassy and Emmeline, decide to make their escape from the plantation and go into hiding. Legree accuses Tom of aiding them, and he suspects Tom of knowing where they are hidden. When Tom refuses to reveal any information, Legree has him flogged into insensibility. Two days later, young George Shelby, son of Tom's former owner, arrives to redeem Tom. It is too late. The effects of his vicious beating are mortal and Tom dies. After knocking Legree down, George Shelby returns to Kentucky, frees all of his slaves in the name of Uncle Tom, and resolves to devote his future to the abolition cause.

As drawn by Mrs. Stowe, Uncle Tom becomes a Christlike figure. The ordeal of suffering inflicted upon him simply deepens his religious convictions. Tom endures gladly, sustained by a vision of the heavenly life to come. Before he loses consciousness he says to Legree, "I forgive ye, with all my soul." Tom is a black Christ sent to put a Yankee Satan to shame.

There is never any shrinking from stark realism on Mrs. Stowe's part. *Uncle Tom's Cabin*'s most shocking chapters are "Select Incidents of Lawful Trade," "The Slave Warehouse," and "The Martyr," but the entire book is a relentless, skillful depiction of the evils and horrors of slavery—a superb piece of propaganda.

It was Mrs. Stowe's intention to address her novel to Southern readers. She hoped to avert a war by reconciling the differences between the sections. The mission of *Uncle Tom's Cabin* was outlined by the author in a letter to a friend: "1st. To soften and moderate the bitterness of feeling in *extreme abolitionists*. 2nd. To convert to abolitionist views many whom this same bitterness had repelled. 3rd. To inspire the free colored people with self-respect, hope, and confidence. 4th. To inspire universally through the country a kindlier feeling toward the Negro race." Mrs. Stowe had attempted to be fair to the South. Both kind and cruel slave owners had been portrayed. Two of the meanest characters, Simon Legree and Marie St. Clare, were native New Englanders. Joel Chandler Harris concluded that despite herself Mrs. Stowe had found a certain charm in the slave system, for, he wrote, "all the worthy and beautiful characters in her book— Uncle Tom, little Eva, the beloved Master, and the rest— are the products of the system the text of the book is all the time condemning." Perhaps naïvely, Mrs. Stowe had expected that the principal objections to *Uncle Tom's Cabin* would come from abolitionists simply because she had represented *any* slave masters as good and kind.

Great were Mrs. Stowe's surprise and distress, therefore, when the South greeted her book with a hurricane of abuse. A flood of criticism, railing, and general denunciation was turned loose upon Mrs. Stowe by pro-slavery advocates in the North and South. Thousands of angry and vituperative letters poured in upon her. The *National Era* reported that some of the Southern courts were sentencing men to prison for long terms when the hated book was found in their possession. Southern magazine and newspaper reviewers denounced the novel for presenting an unfair picture of slavery, asserting that the author had spotlighted isolated, untypical instances of cruelty and mistreatment. Furthermore, they resented Mrs. Stowe's tone of righteous Puritan superiority, and maintained that she was meddling in matters of which she knew nothing. A South Carolina poet, William J. Grayson, put his seething sentiments into verse:

> A moral scavenger, with greedy eye . . .
> On fields where vice eludes the light of day,

She hunts up crimes as beagles hunt their prey;
Gleans every dirty nook—the felon's jail
And hangman's mem'ry, for detraction's tale,
Snuffs up pollution with a pious air,
Collects a rumor here; a slander there;
With hatred's ardor gathers Newgate spoils,
And trades for gold the garbage of her toils.

More reasonably, other Southern critics contended that no master with a thousand dollars invested in a slave would have permitted Uncle Tom or George Harris to be cruelly treated. They pointed out that Mrs. Stowe was ignorant of the laws governing the treatment of slaves and had no knowledge of Southern social customs. A great majority of the slaves, they insisted, were happy under the Southern patriarchal system. The most violent exception was taken to Mrs. Stowe's assumption that intellectually and morally the Negro was the equal of the white man.

Southern authors burst into print in great numbers in refutation of *Uncle Tom's Cabin*. At least thirty books, "anti-Uncle Toms," appeared prior to the Civil War, about half of them fictional, all supporting slavery and condemning abolitionism. Among the more widely read novels were Mary H. Eastman's *Aunt Phillis's Cabin; or, Southern Life As It Is* and J. W. Page's *Uncle Robin in His Cabin in Virginia and Tom Without One in Boston*. Another novel, *Liberia*, written by Sarah Josepha Hale, editor of *Godey's Lady's Book*, condoned slavery on the ground that Negroes lacked education for freedom.

Attacks came from as far away as London, where the *Times* ended its review with stern admonition, "Let us have no more 'Uncle Tom's Cabins' engendering ill will, keeping up bad blood and rendering well disposed, humane but critically placed men their own enemies, and the stumbling blocks to civilization and to the spread of the glad tidings from Heaven."

Uncle Tom's reception in the North was vastly different from that received below the Mason-Dixon Line. Abolitionists, churchmen, merchants, manufacturers, friends and admirers of Mrs. Stowe rushed to her defense. The week her book was issued, William Lloyd Garrison's *Liberator* predicted a "prodigious" effect "upon all intelligent and human minds," and the *Independent* declaimed, "Spread it round the world . . . thank God! it bids fair to become as familiar as household words." Henry W.

Longfellow wrote to the author, "I congratulate you most cordially upon the immense success and influence of *Uncle Tom's Cabin*. It is one of the greatest triumphs recorded in literary history, to say nothing of the higher triumph of its moral effect."

But more than the warm support of her friends was needed, Mrs. Stowe felt, to counteract the acrimonious assaults on *Uncle Tom's Cabin*. She feared that the powerful Southern propaganda, representing the book as a "tissue of lies," full of overdrawn characters, might weaken its influence. Accordingly, she set about the preparation of a strong counterattack, to be entitled *A Key to Uncle Tom's Cabin* (1853). The story was true, she insisted, though in fictional form. An array of facts drawn from laws, codes, court records, Southern newspapers, and private papers demonstrated that the statutes designed to protect the slave did not, in fact, protect him. The sources of the characters in *Uncle Tom's Cabin* are revealed to prove that they were not overdrawn. The experiences of individual slaves were related, showing that life could be more harrowing than fiction. The churches and the clergy were indicted for their failure to use their influence to put an end to slavery or even to mitigate its abuses. Describing the *Key* in a letter to an English friend, Mrs. Stowe wrote:

> It is made up of the facts, the documents, the things which my own eyes have looked upon and my hands have handled, that attest this awful indictment upon my country. I wrote it in the anguish of my soul, with tears and prayer, with sleepless nights and weary days. I bear testimony with a heavy heart as one who in court is forced by an awful oath to disclose the sins of those dearest.

The statement is hardly debatable that no other propaganda novel has ever made such a stir as did *Uncle Tom's Cabin*. As expressed by Charles Edward Stowe in the biography of his mother, "It was like the kindling of a mighty conflagration, the sky was all aglow with the resistless tide of emotion that swept all before it and even crossed the broad ocean, till it seemed as if the whole world scarcely thought or talked of anything else." The North came to recognize as never before the terrible evils of slavery and became violently hostile to the slave business. The book hastened, perhaps by years, the "irrepressible conflict" already threatening. No wonder that Abraham Lincoln greeted Mrs. Stowe on a visit to the White House as "the little woman who wrote the book that made this big war."

Whether *Uncle Tom's Cabin* actually caused the Civil War, as Lincoln intimated, is a matter for argument. The verdict of a loyal Southerner, Thomas Nelson Page, was as follows: "By arousing the general sentiment of the world against slavery, the novel contributed more than any other one thing to its abolition in that generation," and "did more than any one thing that ever occurred to precipitate the war."

How explain the phenomenal popularity of *Uncle Tom's Cabin?* The number of outright abolitionists and their sympathizers was small. Millions of people without strong political leanings and without any particular interest in the fate of the Negro, however, appear to have been irresistibly attracted to the Stowe novel. One analyst, Gorham Munson, in his *Twelve Decisive Battles of the Mind,* may have recognized the essence of the book's appeal:

> Not the least reason for its effectiveness is that consistently the author appealed to mankind's love of the fabulous. Eliza's leap and dash across the Ohio was fabulous. Readers loved it. Little Eva's perfection, Uncle Tom's humility, Legree's cruelty were fabulous. Eliminate the crude "impossibilities" from *Uncle Tom's Cabin,* and you have only a bad novel. It is the "impossibilities" that made it good propaganda.

The high emotional content of the book may have been an even more potent factor in gaining a vast circle of readers and at the same time implanting a deep hatred of the institution of slavery. The horrors that haunted Mrs. Stowe's mind had a similar impact on her readers—such episodes, for example, as those listed by another Stowe biographer, Catherine Gilbertson: "slave traders and bloodhounds pursuing Eliza; the woman whose child had been stolen, drowning herself in the Mississippi; old Prue dying in the cellar where 'the flies had got to her'; Rosa sent to the public whipping-house; Cassy's tale of atrocities; Emmeline and Lucy and Uncle Tom in the hands of Legree."

To these elements accounting for the book's immense

vogue could be added the skillful use of suspense in the plot's development; the humor, especially in the characters of Topsy, Sam, and Andy; the pathos in the case of Eva and several slaves; and the generally convincing character-izations.

The literary qualities of *Uncle Tom's Cabin* have been hotly disputed, though none question its effectiveness as propaganda. The book has been damned for too much preaching, and for being overly sentimental and melodra-matic. Critics have held that it is carelessly written, loosely constructed, and faulty in its English, and uses types for characters rather than actual personalities. The Negro dialect, they say, is more Yankee than Southern. But, paradoxically, for every critic who has attacked the novel there has always been another equally eminent who rises to defend it. The secret, Frank Luther Mott concluded, is that "it was a vital story, striking with extraordinary directness to the heart of fundamental human feelings and relationships." It is of interest to note the close parallels between *Uncle Tom's Cabin* and the twentieth-century novels of Erskine Caldwell, William Faulkner, and Lillian Smith. All have Southern locales and feature lust, illicit love, suicide, murder, and sadistic cruelty. Readers' tastes evidently continue to run to the elemental.

Harriet Beecher Stowe's career after *Unce Tom's Cabin* was in a sense anti-climactic. Only one other work on slavery came from her prolific pen. This was the novel *Dred, a Tale of the Great Dismal Swamp,* published in 1856. In four weeks 100,000 copies were sold, though *Dred* never approached the popularity of Uncle Tom. In *Dred,* the author's theme was the evil effects of the slave system upon the white man—both the owner and the poor white squatter. Miscegenation between the two races and its dire consequences for all the characters involved were dramatized. *Dred* is rich in sketches of poor whites, re-vivalist preachers, and plantation life, but there is no one central character, such as Uncle Tom, to win one's sympa-thy.

Henceforth, for the remainder of her long life of eighty-five years, Mrs. Stowe produced an endless flow of novels, stories, biographies, articles, and religious essays. For nearly thirty years she averaged a book annually, but the subject of slavery was largely abandoned. During the Civil War, her principal contribution was an open letter to the women of England, reminding them of their overwhelmingly favorable response to *Uncle Tom's Cabin* eight or nine years earlier, and reproaching them for pro-Southern sentiment and actions after the outbreak of the war. As a result, mass meetings were held throughout the British Isles, helping to change English ruling opinion toward the Union cause. Hence, Mrs. Stowe's letter may have played an important part in preventing English interference at a time when it could have endangered the Northern side.

10–AMERICAN UTOPIA

EDWARD BELLAMY'S
Looking Backward, 2000-1887

"HOPE SPRINGS eternal in the human breast," wrote Alexander Pope, "Man never is, but always to be, blest." The concept of paradises, celestial and terrestrial, is of remote antiquity and has inspired a vast literature. Most celebrated of the classical imaginary earthly gardens of Eden are those described in Plato's *Republic* and Sir Thomas More's *Utopia*.

Of many modern utopias, the most successful, by all odds, is Edward Bellamy's *Looking Backward* (1888). Within a decade after its publication, a million copies had been distributed and translations had appeared in virtually every important language. At least a hundred other utopian works tried to emulate the best-selling Bellamy novel. Simultaneously, the book was giving a tremendous boost to an American brand of socialism. Over the past eighty years, the social and political influence of *Looking Backward* has been incalculable.

The mood of the people of the late nineteenth century was ripe for Bellamy's book—a fact which contributed immensely to the phenomenal reception which it received. Widespread discontent was being created by panics, depressions, and bitter conflicts between capital and labor. Two current ideals, laissez-faire and free competition, were in the saddle and riding high. The centralization of economic power which developed after the Civil War had led to a breakdown of ethical standards. The middle class was being crowded from the business world by large corporations and monopolies, thereby diminishing opportunities for the individual. Farmers and laborers were forming organizations to protect themselves against what they considered oppressive conditions and forces. There was even a feeling on the part of some Americans that the democratic system itself had broken down, and perhaps an alternative should be sought.

The word "socialism," however, has always been deeply suspect in the American mind, tainted with its association with European radicalism, and any system of reform involving co-operative production and distribution, if it were to be acceptable to an American audience, would have to be adapted to national ideas and principles—with emphasis on the practical. This was Edward Bellamy's great achievement in *Looking Backward*.

One fundamental difference is apparent between the utopias of classical writers and Bellamy's. Plato's *Republic* presumed that men must become godlike in nature and More's *Utopia* is based upon the assumption that all men will be pure, honest, and imbued with a love of humanity. In contrast, Bellamy proposed to found an *ideal state* rather than attempt to create an ideal man. Under Bellamy's regime, human nature remains the same, but the environment is changed. There was a profound conviction, eloquently expressed in *Looking Backward*, that if human nature could be placed in a great environment, it would react nobly.

His early years were an important influence in shaping Bellamy's social thought. A native of Chicopee Falls, Massachusetts, born in 1850, he remained throughout his life essentially a villager in outlook and sympathies. His father was a Baptist minister for many years, and the atmosphere of the home naturally inculcated idealism and puritanism. Young Bellamy grew up eager to promote justice and to mitigate poverty and suffering in the world. While rejecting the formal theology of his church, he retained its belief in democracy, its social sympathies, and its humanitarianism. At the impressionable age of eighteen, he accompanied a wealthy cousin on visits to several European countries, where his dissatisfaction with the existing social order was deepened by observing the destitution and drabness of the Old World slums. "It was in the great cities of Europe," Bellamy wrote, "that my eyes were first fully opened to the extent and consequences of man's inhumanity to man."

After his return home, the youthful Bellamy studied law for a short period, and spent several years in newspaper work. His ambition, however, was for a literary career.

Several early novels and short stories were well received. One, *The Duke of Stockbridge: A Romance of Shays' Rebellion,* marked an evolution in Bellamy's social philosophy; the author's sympathies throughout are clearly on the side of the defeated villagers and backcountry farmers, instead of for the victorious forces of law and order. Here, too, Bellamy showed a keen understanding of the interrelation of economic and political forces.

Nearly ten years were to pass before Bellamy's social conscience impelled him to launch another crusading novel, but during that period he had matured, had studied and thought much about the industrial problems of the era, and had developed an effective writing style. The fruit of the preparatory process was *Looking Backward, 2000–1887.* In a later postscript to the book, Bellamy writes:

> *Looking Backward,* although in form a fanciful romance, is intended, in all seriousness, as a forecast, in accordance with the principles of evolution, of the next stage in industrial and social development of humanity, especially in this country; and no part of it is believed by the author to be better supported by the indications of probability than the implied prediction that the dawn of the new era is already near at hand, and that the full day will swiftly follow.

Bellamy's famous book begins as a simple fantasy but its theme is gradually transformed into a minute description of a brave new world of the future, a view of the state of society existing in the United States in the year 2000. The hero and presumed author is Julian West, a well-to-do thirty-year-old Bostonian, engaged to the charming Edith Bartlett. West suffered from insomnia and had an underground chamber specially constructed so that he could sleep without being disturbed by the noise of the town. In addition, he used the services of a doctor who put him into a hypnotic sleep.

On the night of May 30, 1887, West's house was burned, and no one knew of his underground chamber except his doctor, who had left town, and his valet, who perished in the fire. Thus West was left to lie in his hypnotic state until the year 2000, when he was discovered in the course of some excavation work—setting a sleeping record well in excess of Rip van Winkle's. A Dr. Leete, who now occupied the property with his wife and

daughter Edith, awoke him. From here on, the tale is concerned with Julian West's reactions to the amazing world of the twenty-first century and his romance with the young and beautiful Edith, who, through a happy coincidence, turns out to be a great-granddaughter of West's nineteenth-century love.

From conversations with Dr. Leete, West hears the history of the transition from the old to the new civilization. In 1887 giant trusts in commerce and industry were monopolizing power and wealth. The concentration of business in the hands of fewer and fewer great capitalists convinced the people that they must take strong measures to protect themselves against exploitation. But instead of abolishing the huge trusts and returning to small-scale enterprises, the decision was made to become even larger. In short, government would take over the control of industry and commerce and administer them for the welfare of all the people. In Dr. Leete's words:

> Early in the last century the evolution was completed by the final consolidation of the entire capital of the nation. The industry and commerce of the country, ceasing to be conducted by a set of irresponsible corporations and syndicates of private persons at their caprice and for their profit, were intrusted to a single syndicate representing the people, to be conducted in the common interest for the common profit.

Under the plan for nationalization of industry, all citizens between the ages of twenty-one and forty-five are required to serve in an industrial army. The nation became the sole employer and workers were distributed according to the needs of industry. The industrial army is divided into ten departments covering all branches of industry, headed by lieutenant generals. Each general was elected by the retired members of his department, rather than by the active workers. The commander in chief was the President of the United States, who was elected by all the men in the nation not connected with the industrial army, that is, the retired citizens.

There was no child labor. All citizens attended school until the age of twenty-one. On October 15 each year all those who had reached twenty-one were enrolled in the industrial army and those who had reached forty-five were retired. For the first three years the young men and women served in the general army. Afterward they were allowed a certain choice of occupation or profession, depending upon ability and the requirements of the economy. To prevent overstaffing or understaffing, the hours in different occupations varied. Thus the workers in some industries might be required to put in half as many hours as in more attractive pursuits.

Dr. Leete and his daughter take West for a tour of the city, which had become completely transformed. Beautiful buildings were set in the midst of pleasant, restful squares, planted with trees, flowers, and grass. The people were well dressed and happy. Nowhere was there any evidence of poverty, dirt, or squalor. There were no shops, but each section of the city had a large, handsome store, where samples and specimens were displayed. Attendants took orders and the items desired were dispatched from a central warehouse.

Money had long since been abolished, though values were still stated in terms of dollars. Instead of cash rewards, every citizen over twenty-one was entitled each year to an equal share of the nation's products. There was an overflowing abundance of goods of every kind and all of first quality, since no justification existed for producing inferior articles. A wife received as much compensation as her husband and an allowance was made for minor children. Consequently, families were economically comfortable. Every person held a card crediting him with a specified number of monetary units each year, and as purchases were made, the appropriate sum was deducted. The credits could be used for any purpose desired, including such luxury goods as fur coats, silverware, and works of art. The industrial leaders were expected to produce whatever the consumers demanded. Prices were set according to the amount of labor needed to produce the various articles.

Bellamy calculated that the labor of the citizens from twenty-one to forty-five produced an annual equivalent of $2500 (at least $8000 in terms of purchasing power in 1968) for each one because of the enormous savings effected. Military forces were abolished. Crime was reduced to a minimum, because there was no longer any incentive to steal; consequently, police forces were drastically cut and prisons were nearly empty. There was no interest on a national debt, no taxes or tax collectors, no bankers, no insurance agents, no lawyers, and no advertising. Wastes characteristic of private industry were eliminated, unproductive activities ceased, and unemployment was non-existent.

Even the weather is controlled. When a shower of rain comes, huge awnings unfold overhead and keep the city dry. Music is distributed by telephone to all houses; the turn of a dial will produce a light or classical program. Meals can be taken at home or in a public restaurant. If in the latter, a family can arrange to have a private room reserved for its permanent and exclusive use. People may spend their allowances in travel aboard, if they wish, for Europe, Australia, Mexico, and parts of South America have become industrial republics also and accept American credit cards on an international account. Family life has been improved, since economic pressures no longer exist, and the race has grown stronger eugenically as young women had become more selective in choosing husbands and the number of mental defectives had declined.

Bellamy's ideal world of the year 2000 was not without its compulsions. The system of state socialism permitted a considerable degree of personal freedom, but if a man refused to recognize the authority of the state and declined to serve in the industrial army, he lost all his rights. There was no room for conscientious objectors. A man able to work and persistently refusing was sentenced to solitary confinement on bread and water until he had a change of heart. As Dr. Leete phrased the matter, "To speak of service being compulsory would be a weak way to state its absolute inevitableness. Our entire social order is so wholly based upon and deduced from it that if it were conceivable that a man could escape it, he would be left with no possible way to provide for his existence. He would have excluded himself from the world, cut himself off from his kind, in a word, committed suicide."

The system had special rewards, however, for the ambitious, diligent, and most able citizens. A strong incentive was promotion into the managerial class through a series of steps: a foremanship, a superintendency, generalship of a guild, chief of one of the ten major departments (groups of allied trades), and, finally, the presidency. Each level corresponded to a military rank from lieutenant to general-in-chief. Furthermore, "Apart from the grand incentive to endeavour, afforded by the fact that the high places in the nation are open only to the highest class men, various incitements of a minor, but perhaps equally effective, sort are provided in the form of special privileges and immunities in the way of discipline, which the superior class men enjoy."

Special provision was made also for artists and authors. A man who wrote books or painted pictures could devote his whole time to such an occupation, if his royalties were sufficient to compensate the state for loss of his services from the industrial army. He was therefore under a certain constraint to produce books or art works that would sell. Ministers and students for the priesthood, too, were excused from service in the industrial army, if members of the church provided enough credits to support them.

Outside the industrial army, incentives are provided in the form of decorations: "The highest of all honors in the nation, higher than the presidency, which calls merely for good sense and devotion to duty, is the red ribbon awarded by vote of the people to the great authors, artists, engineers, physicians, and inventors of the generation. Not over one hundred wear it at any one time, though every bright young fellow in the country loses innumerable nights' sleep dreaming of it."

Bellamy had almost unlimited faith in technology and scientific and technical progress. The machine, to him, becomes the key to social advancement. In *Looking Backward*, therefore, we find devices which are the equivalent of radio and television, the airplane, power-drawn plows to till the farms, and giant mills—airy, cheerful, and all but noiseless—to manufacture goods. Unlike some other utopian writers, who sought to flee back to the handicraft age, Bellamy believed that the machine is not the enemy but the potential servant of mankind. As visualized by him, the mechanical conquest of nature, with its vast economies in the use of human energy, has, through social control, finally placed the human race by the year 2000 in a secure world, surrounded by plenty. Bellamy's exposition of the benefits of science and invention, a belief almost universally shared by his fellow Americans, helped to make real his concept of a utopia based on efficiency and doubtless contributed to its appeal for millions of readers.

It is, in fact, the atmosphere of realism surrounding Bellamy's world of the twenty-first century which lends credibility to the story and added immensely to its popularity. Like Daniel Defoe's *Robinson Crusoe*, detail is piled

upon detail in such fashion that we come fully to accept
the actual existence of the places described.

The effectiveness of the novel is enhanced also by a
dramatic conclusion. In a hideous nightmare, Julian West
finds himself back in the benighted nineteenth century. He
walks through the city and sees the pitiful sights of poverty and squalor, crime and human misery. He enters the
home of his betrothed for the marriage supper, but is so
depressed by the suffering and horrors just observed that
he launches into a speech urging his friends to become
aware of the terrible conditions of their time:

> With fervency I spoke of that new world, blessed
> with plenty, purified by justice and sweetened by
> brotherly kindness, the world of which I had indeed
> but dreamed, but which might so easily be made real.
> But when I had expected now surely the faces around
> me to light up with emotions akin to mine, they grew
> ever more dark, angry, and scornful. Instead of en-
> thusiasm, the ladies showed only aversion and dread,
> while the men interrupted me with shouts of
> reprobation and contempt.

As his erstwhile friends kick him into the street, Julian
West awakes; 1887 had been the dream and 2000 the
reality, and he was back with his beloved Edith.

In a striking parable, the virtues of his ideal republic
are contrasted by Bellamy with the absurdities of the
economic system prevailing in 1887:

> By way of attempting to give the reader some gener-
> al impression of the way people lived . . . I cannot do
> better than compare society . . . to a prodigious coach
> which the masses of humanity were harnessed to and
> dragged toilsomely along a very hilly and sandy road.
> The driver was hungry and permitted no lagging.
> . . . Despite the difficulty of drawing the coach at all
> along so hard a road, the top was covered with
> passengers who never got down, even at the steepest
> ascents. These seats on top were very breezy and
> comfortable. Well up out of the dust, their occupants
> could enjoy the scenery at their leisure, or critically
> discuss the merits of the straining team. Naturally
> such places were in great demand and the competition
> for them was keen, every one seeking as the first end

in life to secure a seat on the coach for himself and to leave it to his child after him.

Critics of *Looking Backward* pick flaws in Bellamy's millennium. They fear the corporate or fascist features of his organization of society and see threats to popular liberties in the creation of ten great guilds and election of the President and other top officials by veterans of the industrial army. They suggest further that bigness can be inefficient and there are potentialities for maladministration in a huge bureaucracy. Experience with industrial conscription has not been happy, and the rigid regimentation of men's lives prescribed by Bellamy fails to take into account psychological differences among individuals.

On the other hand, Bellamy did not worship size for its own sake nor did he desire to suppress the individual. Though the new industrial society was to be controlled centrally, the country was divided into a series of self-sufficient areas in each of which "all the important arts and occupations" were represented. Thus a person attached to one locality could remain there among his friends, and retain the advantages of decentralized government. In fact, he was expected to share responsibility for the management of his own community. As expressed by Daniel Aaron, in his *Men Of Good Hope*, "Bellamy belongs among the first of the planners who wanted to ruralize the city and urbanize the country, to stop the unwholesome exodus from the farm and preserve the regional outlook."

Bellamy had no idea of starting a social revolution when he wrote *Looking Backward*. His readers, however, regarded his plan for a reorganized society as a vision of hope and a rational program of reform. The popularity of the work and the seriousness with shich people accepted the ideas therein inspired the author to limited political activity. The *Nationalist* (later *The New Nation*) was founded as the organ of the new movement. Nationalist or Bellamy clubs were started in Boston and soon spread throughout the country; by 1891, there were 162 such clubs in the United States—all dedicated to the promotion of the Bellamy principles. Bellamy himself developed into a nationally and internationally known lecturer and publicist, and the closing years of his short life (he died at forty-eight) were devoted to efforts to translate the dream of *Looking Backward* into realistic social and political action. Shortly before his death, he published another work, *Equality*, designed to provide detailed, systematic economic data in support of his original theme.

A host of influential contemporary writers and thinkers endorsed and promoted Bellamy's general philosophy, among them William Dean Howells, Mark Twain, Thorstein Veblen, Frances Willard, Margaret Fuller, Ida M. Tarbell, Samuel Gompers, Clarence Darrow, John Dewey, William Allen White, Heywood Broun, Norman Thomas, and, in England, Bernard Shaw and Sidney Webb. Bellamy's immense impact on other countries is traced at length in Sylvia E. Bowman's *Edward Bellamy Abroad: An American Prophet's Influence*, in which it is demonstrated that *Looking Backward* had, and to some extent retains, a worldwide audience.

In his *Economic Novel in America*, Walter Fuller Taylor presents an able summing up of the historical significance of Bellamy's work:

> He was an extraordinarily gifted author and thinker, who, in many ways, gave completest voice to the American middle-class protest against plutocracy. Like many of his middle-class contemporaries, he brought to bear on the social problems of our Gilded Age, the culture of our Golden Day. Like most of his contemporaries, he assumed the rightness of democracy, opportunity for the personal growth of the individual, and progress; and when these values were threatened by corrupt business practices and the rule of the rich, he rebelled. Like the average American citizen, he desired economic security, abundance, and the personal development in which a moderate prosperity is almost prerequisite.

In seeking a collectivist society as a solution to economic problems, Taylor continues, Bellamy was probably speaking for a minority of his fellow Americans. Nevertheless, he had an acute understanding of middle-class aims and values, and was able to dramatize them effectively.

Many of the evils of Bellamy's day have been eliminated or mitigated in the eighty years since he wrote *Looking Backward*, and reforms which he advocated have been incorporated into the nation's laws. The closest modern equivalent in organization to the state-controlled society proposed by Bellamy is Soviet Russia, where numerous obstacles have stood in the way of a fair test. In any event, it can be asserted with confidence that society's advances have come largely through new social ideas dreamed up by such reformers as Bellamy.

11—RULING THE WAVES

ALFRED T. MAHAN'S
The Influence of Sea Power upon History, 1660-1783

THE MAN who did more to shape the modern navies of the world than any other individual never rose above the rank of captain while in active service and became a rear admiral only when he retired. Eighty years ago, Alfred Thayer Mahan discovered that sea power has always been a deciding factor in world dominion. His extensive writings, demonstrating and substantiating this central theme, became required reading in every great navy in the world. Through all Mahan's sea-power volumes runs one precept: Without command of the sea, no nation can attain the fullest measure of internal well-being or of influence in international affairs.

Mahan was age fifty when he entered the hall of fame. Nothing in his undistinguished naval career, extending over thirty years, had given evidence of unusual talent, either as writer or naval strategist. His opportunity came in 1886, when he was asked to join the staff of the newly established naval war college at Newport as a lecturer on naval history and tactics. Mahan prepared himself for the assignment by an intensive period of reading and thinking. An inspiration came to him through a study of Mommsen's historical writings, and particularly through Mommsen's failure to recognize the all-important influence of sea power upon Hannibal's career. As Mahan wrote later, "how different things might have been could Hannibal have invaded Italy by sea, as the Romans often had Africa, instead of by the long land route; or could he, after arrival, have been in free communication with Carthage by water."

For the next four years, Mahan developed and polished

a series of lectures upon the "effect of naval power upon history." From the lectures emerged, in 1890, an epoch-making work, *The Influence of Sea Power upon History, 1660–1783*. The title was chosen with premeditation. Mahan picked the phrase "sea power," as he stated subsequently, "to compel attention and to receive currency. . . . I deliberately discarded the adjective 'maritime' as being too smooth to arrest men's attention or stick in their minds." The word "sea" is more romantic than "maritime" and the term "power" suited the age of steam and electricity and power politics.

Mahan's aim was to investigate general and naval history from the middle of the seventeenth century to the close of the Napoleonic Wars. The period from 1660 to 1783, the golden age of sea power, was selected because it marked the rise of modern European states and their struggle for existence and supremacy. From his intensive study of the era, Mahan concluded that there had been a continuing rivalry for control of the seas and that control of the pathways of seaborne commerce was, and likely would always be, the key to world power.

As between sea power and land power, Mahan set out to prove, a relentless sea blockade has always proved more decisive than an invincible land army. As an example, he analyzed the war between England and France, which "nearly ruined Great Britain, but entirely ruined Napoleon." The effects of a sea blockade, Mahan showed, were slow and unspectacular, but inexorable. "Those far distant storm-beaten ships, upon which the Grand Army never looked, stood between it and the dominion of the world"; eventually the unseen force brought about France's economic strangulation.

A clear distinction was drawn by Mahan between sea power and naval power. Sea power includes not only military strength to rule the sea, but, equally important, "the peaceful commerce and shipping from which alone a military fleet naturally and healthfully springs, and on which it securely rests." An expanding foreign commerce is essential to national power and prosperity, according to Mahan's thesis, and in order to compete successfully in the worldwide struggle for markets, a nation must have a strong merchant marine. Furthermore, the merchant vessels must have safe ports at the end of their destinations and protection throughout their voyages. To provide secure ports and overseas markets, a nation requires colonies, while to ensure safe passage a powerful navy is essential. The navy also provides protection for the colonies and naval bases.

Thus, though Mahan asserts, "The history of sea power, while embracing in its broad sweep all that tends to make a people great upon the sea or by the sea, is largely a military history," he continually reminds his readers that navies, campaigns, and battles are only means to other ends. A definition of sea power, therefore, includes military navies and naval bases around the world, plus merchant shipping and seaborne trade. A strong navy can hardly exist without a flourishing merchant shipping fleet. A merchant marine ensures both national prosperity and a reservoir of skilled seamen in time of war. Accordingly, as seen by Mahan, there are three basic elements constituting a nation's sea power: capacity for manufacturing production, its own merchant shipping with a navy sufficient to protect it, and colonies to absorb the surplus products.

For the period so searchingly analyzed by Mahan, England possessed all the requisites of sea power: a navy strong enough to protect her commerce, and colonies and naval bases scattered around the globe. Because England cultivated sea power while her opponents neglected it, she became arbiter of world affairs, was able to thwart the ambitions of Louis XIV and Napoleon, and thereby, Mahan believed, to save civilization.

France, in striking contrast, while her material resources were adequate to acquire sea power, failed to develop maritime might because her rulers were mainly preoccupied with pursuing territorial and dynastic ambitions on the continent of Europe. Throughout the period under review, French naval power was hopelessly inferior to the British.

The greater portion of *The Influence of Sea Power upon History* was devoted to a naval history of the years 1660–1783. Here are recorded the many wars in which England was engaged with the Dutch, Spanish, and French during the time when she was consolidating her colonial empire in North America and India. In the first eighty-nine pages of his narrative, however, Mahan discussed the conditions or general principles which have most directly affected the sea power of nations. These are six in number: (1) geographical position, (2) physical conformation, (3) extent of territory, (4) number of population, (5) character of the people, (6) character of the government.

Of prime importance is *geographical position,* for "if a nation be so situated that it is neither forced to defend itself by land nor induced to seek extension of its territory by way of the land, it has, by the very unity of its aim directed upon the sea, an advantage as compared with a people one of whose boundaries is continental." Thus England has a great advantage over France and Holland as a sea power. A nation located upon two bodies of water, e.g., France and the United States, tends to disperse rather than to concentrate its naval force—the reason why the United States Navy was centered by a policy decision in the Atlantic prior to the construction of the Panama Canal. Further, a central position, with ports near major trade routes and a strong base for hostile operation against possible enemies, is of great strategic advantage. In England's case, such a position gave her control of the Channel and North Sea trade routes, through which the trade of Holland, Sweden, Russia, Denmark, and much of Germany had to pass.

In reviewing the second of his six elements, *physical conformation,* Mahan points out, "The seaboard of a country is one of its frontiers; and the easier the access offered by the frontier to the region beyond, in this case the sea, the greater will be the tendency of a people toward intercourse with the rest of the world by it." Numerous and deep harbors, especially if they are outlets of navigable streams, are a source of strength and wealth, though "they become a source of weakness in war, if not properly defended." Mahan's explanation for France's relative weakness in sea power, despite her possession of these natural resources, was "the physical conditions which have made France a pleasant land, with a delightful climate, producing within itself more than its people needed." England, less richly endowed, was drawn naturally to maritime enterprises, and her sea power was developed by merchants and colonists, manufacturers and producers. Even more urgently, Holland was driven to the sea to survive.

The third and last of the geographical conditions affecting the evolution of a nation as a sea power, as distinguished from its inhabitants, is *extent of territory.* Here, Mahan notes, "it is not the total number of square miles which a country contains, but the length of its coast-line and the character of its harbors that are to be considered." Given geographical and physical factors, the extent of seacoast may be a source of weakness or strength, depending upon whether the population is large or small. An example offered is the Southern states during the American Civil War. The whole Southern coast was effectively blockaded because of the comparatively small population, further handicapped by the great length of the coast and its numerous inlets.

Following an examination of natural conditions, Mahan turns to an analysis of population as it affects the development of sea power. First is the *number of population*, but "it is not only the grand total, but the number following the sea, or at least readily available for employment on ship-board and for the creation of naval material, that must be counted." Here again France is used as an illustration: "The population of France was much greater than that of England; but in respect of sea power in general, peaceful commerce as well as military efficiency, France was much inferior to England." Also significant is reserve strength—organized reserve forces, reserve of seafaring population, reserve of mechanical skill, and reserve of wealth, in all of which England excelled.

Next considered by Mahan is the effect of the *character of the people* in its relation to sea power. "Almost without exception," he wrote, history shows that "aptitude for commercial pursuits must be a distinguishing feature of the nations that have at one time or another been great upon the sea." Though the English and the Dutch were often contemptuously dismissed as "nations of shopkeepers," their maritime trade was built upon far more solid bases than was that of the Spanish and Portuguese, greedy for gold, or the thrifty, hoarding French, unwilling to risk investments in foreign commerce. "The tendency to trade," comments Mahan, "involving of necessity the production of something to trade with, is the national characteristic most important to the development of sea power."

Closely related is colonizing ability. National genius is exhibited in the capacity for planting healthy colonies. Colonization, it is observed, "is most healthy when it is most natural. Therefore colonies that spring from the felt wants and natural impulses of a whole people will have the most solid foundations; and their subsequent growth will be surest when they are least trammeled from home, if the people have the genius for independent action"—a lesson learned from the American Revolution. England's record as a great colonizing nation, it was noted, has been uniquely successful.

Finally, Mahan inspects the *character of the government* and its institutions in relation to the growth of sea power. Particular forms of government and the character of rulers, it is found, "have exercised a very marked influence upon the development of sea power." Actually, great sea powers have been created under both democracies and despotisms, though those which grow up under free governments are most likely to survive for long periods: "Despotic power, wielded with judgement and consistency, has created at times a great sea commerce and a brilliant navy with greater directness than can be reached by the slower processes of a free people. The difficulty in the former case is to insure perseverance after the death of a particular despot."

Since England had reached, and held over an extended period, first rank as a sea power, Mahan examined in particular detail the governmental policies responsible for her achievement. With considerable consistency, he discovered, English policy and action throughout several centuries had been directed toward control of the sea. Without regard to what king was on the throne or which political party was dominant, the English had recognized the basic importance to the nation of the maintenance of naval supremacy.

At the time when he was writing, however, Mahan wondered whether the English will to remain a great sea power still prevailed:

> Whether a democratic government will have the foresight, the keen sensitiveness to national position and credit, the willingness to insure its prosperity by adequate outpouring of money in times of peace, all which are necessary for military preparation, is yet an open question. Popular governments are not generally favorable to military expenditure, however necessary, and there are signs that England tends to drop behind.

After an extended historical review of the actions of various governments in relation to the sea careers of their people, Mahan decided that government influence works in two ways. First, in times of peace:

The government by its policy can favor the natural growth of a people's industries and its tendencies to seek adventure and gain by way of the sea; or it can try to develop such industries and such seagoing bent, when they do not naturally exist; or, on the other hand, the government may by mistaken action check and fetter the progress which the people left to themselves would make.

Second, in time of war, sea power is determined by the attitude of the government toward creating, equipping, and adequately maintaining "an armed navy, of a size commensurate with the growth of its shipping and the importance of the interests connected with it." Equally essential was "the maintenance of suitable naval stations, in those distant parts of the world to which the armed shipping must follow the peaceful vessels of commerce."

Thus having examined and reflected upon the six basic conditions affecting sea power, Mahan was prepared to undertake a detailed analysis of European naval wars of the period from 1660 to 1783. The remainder of *The Influence of Sea Power upon History* is devoted to this historical review. For background, Mahan describes the general conditions prevailing in Europe in the late seventeenth century, with particular attention to Spain, France, Holland, and England—the nations that were to be principally involved in future struggles for sea power. As Mahan viewed it, the history of Europe during the tumultuous years that followed was largely a contest among the western powers for control of the sea. Beginning his survey with the Dutch War of Charles II, he emphasized the extent to which England's commercial interests were involved in the War of the Spanish Succession, from which England emerged as a Mediterranean power, holding Gibraltar and Port Mahon. In the Seven Years' War, Wolfe's success was made possible by the fleet, which opened the St. Lawrence and prevented the arrival of reinforcements from France. The fundamental meaning of sea power was demonstrated again during the American Revolution, when England, with divided naval forces, was unable to cope with the combined might of France and Spain, and the American colonies were therefore able to win their freedom.

Constant reference is made by Mahan to the American situation and special consideration given to the potentialities of the United States as a sea power. An analogy was drawn between the Mediterranean Sea and the Caribbean. The latter "will be still closer if a Panama Canal route ever be completed." In that event, our weakest frontier, the Pacific, would no longer be remote from the most dangerous of possible enemies. Americans were reminded of the key part played by the Union Navy in the defeat of the Confederacy. Now the United States needed a navy which could at least prevent a European fleet from establishing a blockade of its Atlantic seaboard. Indeed, Mahan's book had as its principal purpose the awakening of American opinion to the need for a great navy. The point is stressed by Mahan's biographer, Captain Puleston:

> Mahan had written his book . . . to rekindle among his own countrymen their former interest in sea power. He believed Americans had been so engrossed in developing the interior of the country that they had unnecessarily thrown away a great heritage. He did not want his country to follow the example of France under Louis XIV and become primarily a land power.

As a dedicated believer in maritime might, Mahan had just cause for concern when he viewed his native land. The United States had no navy worth the name in 1890. The powerful British fleet ruled the Atlantic and protected America against possible European aggression. No threat existed from any other direction. The pride of the U.S. Navy in the eighteen eighties was the White Squadron, composed of three small cruisers and a dispatch boat. The first American battleship was not constructed until 1889.

American indifference to sea power was doubtless accounted for in large measure by the fact that the nation possessed neither colonies nor large merchant marine— two of Mahan's chief justifications for the maintenance of a strong navy. Even so, Mahan held, the United States should have a navy, including a fleet of capital ships to ensure foreign neutral shipping access to its ports whenever the nation was engaged in war.

Mahan's sea-power concept fitted perfectly the bellicose mood of the era in which it was first stated; it fell at once upon fertile soil. Already in the air was an awakening to the importance of sea power, not only in Britain, where it was supported by long tradition, but in Germany, Japan, and, to a somewhat lesser extent, the United States. A renewed competition in navies had begun and imperialistic nations were reaching out to grab colonial possessions around the world. As one British writer commented, Mahan's teaching "was as oil to the flame of colonial expansion everywhere leaping into life." Puleston remarked that "it might have been written to order for the British Cabinet, so clearly did it support all their contentions"; the French naval leaders of the period "passionately lamented the downfall of French sea power that Mahan so aptly described"; and Kaiser Wilhelm II of Germany quoted Mahan's book "to justify his conviction that Germany's future lay upon the sea."

Within a short time, translations of *The Influence of Sea Power upon History* were available in German, Japanese, French, Italian, Russian, and Spanish. In Britain, critics hailed the book as "the gospel of England's greatness." One admiral asserted that for the improved position of the British Navy after 1900, "we have not to thank either Conservatives or Liberals, but Mahan and no one else."

Such comments are more readily appreciated and understood when it is realized that at the time Mahan was writing the English Navy had experienced a lengthy period of financial starvation, its personnel had been reduced to a skeleton force, and its might was being rapidly outstripped by more modern French and Italian ships. Britain's navy was described by one seaman as "a menagerie of unruly and curiously assorted ships," over two thirds unarmed. Mahan's support for a modernized, powerful English fleet was therefore extremely timely, and greatly accelerated the movement for naval reorganization and strengthening.

English admiration and esteem for Mahan were demonstrated during two visits which he paid to Britain in 1893 and 1904. He was a guest of honor at state dinners given by Queen Victoria and the Prime Minister, the first foreign guest of honor ever entertained by the Army and Navy Club, and both Oxford and Cambridge awarded him honorary degrees within a week's time. What Admiral Mahan had done, in effect, was to interpret English history to Englishmen. They had performed great deeds and he was the first to make them understand the full significance of what they had done.

But since *The Influence of Sea Power upon History* was not, as one critic suggested it should have been, published in a language intelligible only to Americans and English-men, its impact on Germans and Japanese was as forceful as on the British. Wilhelm II reported, "I am just now not reading but devouring Captain Mahan's book." The Kaiser ordered a copy placed in the library of every German warship, and all German naval officers were ordered to read and study it. The work was instrumental in persuading the Kaiser that "our future lies upon the water; the trident must be in our fist." There is evidence that in the last months of his life, following the outbreak of World War I, Mahan suffered much mental distress because of the role he had thus unintentionally played in stimulating the growth of the German Navy.

Similarly in Japan, every captain of a Japanese ship of war was served out a copy of Mahan's book as part of his equipment. Mahan himself noted that more of his voluminous writings were translated into Japanese than into any other language. The Japanese were eager to learn Western ways, and began an extensive correspondence with Mahan on the building of navies, the size of guns, and other naval matters. Mahan declined, however, an invitation from the Japanese to become their official naval adviser. Nevertheless, taking their cue from him, the Japanese proceeded to become the supreme naval power of the Far East. That they learned their lesson well was first convincingly demonstrated in the 1904–5 war with Russia.

Among the leading countries, only the United States, which Mahan was most anxious to influence, was slow to accept his teachings. Several years before the Spanish-American War, Mahan urged the annexation of Hawaii, to be defended in future by a big navy. He maintained that world markets should be developed for American goods, with naval support, and that the United States should take over and govern backward people for their own good.

Mahan's arguments made two converts in key positions: Theodore Roosevelt in the White House and Henry Cabot Lodge, a leader in the Senate, both of whom became advocates of a great American navy. Roosevelt found a perfect expression of his philosophy of the Big Stick in Mahan's writings, and he used the sea power theories to help win American public opinion to a policy of expansion across the seas. Both the direct and indirect influence of Mahan on the huge program of naval expansion in the

United States, beginning in the eighteen nineties, is clear and marked.

Following his first great popular success, Mahan's prolific pen poured forth a flood of books and magazine articles. Some twenty volumes of books and collected essays were supplemented by scores of periodical contributions. Most significant were additions to the "sea-power series," notably *The Influence of Sea Power upon the French Revolution and Empire, 1793–1812*, regarded by critics as a more thorough and carefully documented work than *The Influence of Sea Power upon History;* biographies of Nelson and Farragut; and *Sea Power in Its Relations to the War of 1812.*

Mahan laid no claim to originality in his concept of control of the sea as a major force in the destiny of nations. "Not to mention other predecessors," he stated, "with the full roll of whose names I am even now unacquainted, Bacon and Raleigh, three centuries before, had epitomized in a few words the theme on which I was to write volumes." Mahan pointed out correctly, however, "that no one since those two great Englishmen had undertaken to demonstrate their thesis by an analysis of history, attempting to show from current events, through a long series of years, precisely what influence the command of the sea had upon definite issues. . . . This field had been left vacant, yielding me my opportunity." Mahan's view of history was narrow, as various commentators have suggested, and many vital factors were ignored, but unquestionably he provided new outlooks on politics and economics.

In the judgment of scholars, Mahan's permanent rank as a historian will not be on a par with his contemporary fame. His pre-eminent success was as a propagandist. By the time of his death the United States had reached most of the goals he had set for it: the building of a great navy, the construction of the Panama Canal, and the acquisition of bases in the Caribbean and Pacific. Perhaps his philosophy that "whoever rules the waves rules the world" had been too successful, for the major nations had become engaged in a mad competition for supremacy on the sea. A French naval expert declared that Mahan "profoundly modified in his own lifetime the history of the age in which he lived." Among his obituaries was a tribute that would have delighted Mahan: "The super-dreadnoughts are his children, the roar of the 16-inch guns are but the echoes of his voice."

Granting that Mahan's doctrines were substantially valid for his own time and for the preceding centuries, a legitimate question is whether they have been made obsolete by technological advances of the twentieth century. In particular, has the advent of air power, A-bombs and H-bombs, intermediate and intercontinental ballistic missiles superseded sea power in today's world? In World War II, sea power played an outstanding part, but it had to be closely co-ordinated with air power, for ships unprotected from the air were highly vulnerable. The postwar development of superbombs has cast a shadow over the future of navies. One such bomb could conceivably incapacitate an entire fleet. The development by the United States and the Soviet Union of great fleets of nuclear-powered submarines, on the other hand, furnishes evidence that sea power may still have a place, even in an atomic age.

12–THE RECEDING FRONTIER

FREDERICK JACKSON TURNER'S
The Significance of the Frontier in American History

THE MOST striking characteristic of American history from the beginning of the colonial era to the present has been the irresistible westward movement of the American people. Certainly, for the first three centuries the existence of a great frontier to the west was one of the dominating facts in American life.

Starting with the foundation at Jamestown in 1607, a great land, comprising more than three million square miles, was conquered, fierce nomadic Indian tribes were defeated, and innumerable natural obstacles were overcome.

The importance of the frontier was recognized as early as the seventeenth century by such writers as William Byrd, William Bradford, and John Winthrop, at a time when the frontier did not extend beyond the New England coast and the Carolina hills. Later, in his *Letters from an American Farmer*, Crèvecoeur in 1793 reported that on the American frontier "individuals of all nations are melted into a new race of men." Novelists and poets, such as James Fenimore Cooper, Washington Irving, Longfellow, and Whittier, in the early nineteenth century had begun to mine the romantic treasure-house which was the West. One of our most perceptive statesmen, Thomas Jefferson, wrote in 1824:

Let a philosophic observer commence a journey from the savages of the Rocky Mountains eastwardly toward our seacoast. The Indians he would observe in the earliest stage of association living under no law but that of nature, subsisting and covering themselves with the flesh and skins of wild beasts. He would next find these on our frontiers in the pastoral state, raising domestic animals to supply the defects of hunting. Then succeed to our own semibarbarous citizens, the pioneers of the advance of civilization, and so in his progress he would meet the gradual shades of an improving man until he would reach his, as yet, most improved state in our seaport towns.

Jefferson himself expanded the frontier with the Louisiana Purchase; our first log-cabin president, Andrew Jackson, represented the frontier mentality; and Abraham Lincoln drew inspiration from his pioneer beginnings. In the late eighteen eighties, Theodore Roosevelt focused attention on western themes with his notable work *The Winning of the West*.

Thus, though the concept of a vast American frontier had long since become soundly established in the popular mind, Frederick Jackson Turner was the first American historian to assert that the frontier was a major—if not the chief—explanation for American culture and civilization. Turner's conclusion was that the nation's history had been shaped by the "ever retreating frontier of free land," a fact which he saw as "the key to American development." Immigrants had come from many different European lands and the frontier environment had blended them into an American "composite nationality." The new Americans formed strong individualisms and a distinctive democracy. In a sense, Turner saw in the story of the frontier the history of mankind evolving gradually from the most primitive to the most cultured stage.

The Turner hypothesis was first completely stated in a paper entitled "The Significance of the Frontier in American History," presented before a session of the American Historical Association in Chicago, July 12, 1893. Turner, a native of Portage, Wisconsin, was himself a product of the frontier, born in 1861 on the edge of the wilderness, and in frequent touch with Indians, fur traders, and loggers, as well as with people of varied national ancestries.

Turner's development as historian of the westward movement was in the nature of a revolt against the prevailing—in his eyes, sterile—methods of teaching the nation's history. Until his appearance, American historians were preoccupied with politics and constitutional problems. The widely held "germ theory" taught that American institutions were simply a continuation of European beginnings. Slight attention was paid to economic, social, and geographic factors. Turner's view was different. In the words of a leading historian, Avery Craven, "Because he had been part of a rapidly changing order, he saw American history as a huge stage on which men, in close contact with raw nature, were ever engaged in the evolution of society from simple beginnings to complex ends." The time had come, Turner believed, to de-emphasize the pre-Revolutionary era and the professional historians' obsession with colonial and New England history.

The immediate inspiration for Turner's famous essay was a statement appearing in a bulletin issued by the Superintendent of the Census for 1890: "Up to and including 1880 the country had a frontier of settlement, but at present the unsettled area has been so broken into by isolated bodies of settlement that there can hardly be said to be a frontier line. In the discussion of its extent, its westward movement, etc., it can not, therefore, any longer have a place in the census reports." Here Turner discerned the close of a great historical epoch, the end of a four-hundred-year period of continuous westward advance and settlement. Until then, he asserted, "American history has been in a large degree the history of the colonization of the Great West. The existence of an area of free land, its continuous recession, and the advance of American settlement westward, explain American development."

The impact on the pioneer as he penetrated the continent was dramatic and highly conducive to "rapid and effective Americanization." Turner continues:

The wilderness masters the colonist. It finds him a European in dress, industries, tools, modes of travel and thought. It takes him from the railroad car and puts him in the birch canoe. It strips off the garments of civilization and arrays him in the hunting shirt and the moccasin. . . . Little by little he transforms the wilderness, but the outcome is not the old Europe. . . . The fact is, that here is a new product that is American. . . . Thus the advance of the frontier has meant a steady movement away from the influence of Europe, a steady growth of independence on American lines. And to study this advance, the men who grew up under these conditions, and the political, economic and social results of it, is to study the really American part of our history.

Critics have frequently asked exactly what Turner meant by the term "frontier." Apparently, he used different definitions for different purposes. In various contexts, as the western historian Billington points out, the frontier was "the meeting ground between savagery and civilization," or the "temporary boundary of an expanding society at the edge of substantially free lands," or "a migrating region," a "form of society," a "state of mind," a "stage of society rather than place," a "process," "the hither edge of free land," the "line of most rapid and effective Americanization," the "region whose social conditions resulted from the application of older institutions and ideas to the transforming influences of free land," or "the graphic line which records the expanding energies of the people behind it." Also acceptable to Turner was the Census Bureau's definition based on population—less than two people per square mile being considered empty.

Judging from his diverse interpretations, Turner regarded the frontier as advancing through various stages: the explorer's frontier; the frontier of the hunter, the trapper, the fur trader, and the miner; the frontier of the plantation owner and pioneer farmer; and, finally, the frontier of trade, of manufacture, and of organized government. Broadly speaking, Turner saw the frontier in two ways: as "a geographic region adjacent to the unsettled portions of the continent, in which a low man-land ratio and unusually abundant natural resources provided an exceptional opportunity for the small-propertied individual to advance himself economically and socially"; and, second, as "the process through which individuals and their institutions were altered by contact with a social environment which provided unique opportunity for self-advancement through the exploitation of relatively unused natural resources."

Turner describes in inspiring fashion the succession of American frontiersmen who, over a period of several generations, followed on each other's heels, one after another:

> Stand at Cumberland Gap and watch the procession
> of civilization, marching single file—the buffalo fol-
> lowing the trail to the salt springs, the Indian, the
> fur-trader and hunter, the cattle raiser, the pioneer

farmer—and the frontier has passed by. Stand at the South Pass in the Rockies a century later and see the same procession with wider intervals between. The unequal rate of advance compels us to distinguish the frontier into the trader's frontier, the rancher's frontier, or the miner's frontier, and the farmer's frontier. When the mines and the cow pens were still near the fall line the traders' pack trains were tinkling across the Alleghanies [sic], and the French on the Great Lakes were fortifying their posts, alarmed by the British trader's birch canoe. When the trappers scaled the Rockies, the farmer was still near the mouth of the Missouri.

The frontier as a great "safety valve" intrigued Turner's imagination, as it had earlier Benjamin Franklin's and Thomas Jefferson's. According to the concept, free land was available as a refuge for the depressed and unhappy, the adventurers, and the economic failures from the East. Social conflicts and industrial strife were thereby alleviated. "Men would not accept inferior wages and a permanent position of social subordination," states Turner, "when this promised land of freedom and equality was theirs for the asking. . . . The wilderness ever opened the gate to escape to the poor, the discontented and oppressed. If social conditions tended to crystallize in the East, beyond the Alleghenies there was freedom," where "free lands promoted individualism, economic equality, freedom to rise, democracy."

An essential corollary of the safety-valve theory was the presumed availability of an almost unlimited supply of cheap farmland. Later historians have tended to reject Turner's assumption of "free land," i.e., that the public domain was open to all after the Homestead Act was passed in 1862, and had previously been sold for $1.25 per acre. The spoiler of this beautiful dream was the land speculator, who was always just ahead of the farmers in the advance westward, buying up the best farmlands and most likely town sites. The settler then had the alternative of paying the speculator's price or taking inferior land. "As a result," Billington notes, "for every newcomer who obtained a homestead from the government, six or seven purchased farms from speculators."

In addition to the land cost, furthermore, machinery, animals, and housing needed to start a farm in the mid-nineteenth century came to a minimum of $1000, while travel rates from east to west were high in relation to prevailing wages. Thus, a majority of factory workers and Eastern farmers were simply priced out of the market. In the post-Civil War era, the population shifts in the East were predominantly from country to city, from farm to factory. Turner himself later modified his safety-valve theory by conceding that the "distance and cost of migration to the interior" kept labor in the East. Actually, few workers from Eastern factories moved west and those who did migrated in periods of prosperity rather than depression.

Nevertheless, while Western lands were seldom free, they were substantially cheaper than those in Europe or the East, encouraging migration and serving as an indirect safety valve for Eastern farmers, no longer able to make a living on their exhausted land, who would otherwise have moved to industrial centers. Not to be overlooked, too, was a psychological factor acting as a safety valve: Laborers in the East *believed* that they could escape to the frontier, if conditions became sufficiently unsatisfactory, even though in actuality they could not or did not. Foreseeing possible future wealth and social status for themselves, therefore, radical social movements held little appeal for them.

Another prime Turner contention was that American democracy was a product of the forest environment. "American democracy was born of no theorist's dream," he asserts. "It came stark and strong and full of life out of the American forest and it gained new strength each time it touched a new frontier." The statement has been vigorously attacked and defended. Critics have maintained that such democratic institutions as manhood suffrage, popular legislative representation, and legislative power over the executive evolved through centuries of time and came to the American colonies primarily through England. Apparently Turner was misunderstood; he did not intend to deny these ancient origins, for in a later clarification of the point he wrote that "the history of our institutions, our democracy, is not a history of imitation, or simple borrowing; it is the history of the evolution and adaptation of organs in response to changed environment, a history of the origin of new political species." In short, American democracy derived from European democracy, but in the process had undergone changes sufficiently great to be considered a new species. Recent studies of pioneer communities have demonstrated that the frontier did, indeed, have an impact on the unique American brand of democracy. Democratic institutions imported from England in the frontier environment became even more democratic. Among the reasons were the widespread ownership of land, which gave everyone a desire to participate in government; the fact that all the people were on a common economic and social level; and the citizens' experience in drafting state constitutions, as organized government proceeded westward.

Also valid is Turner's view that the frontier accentuated the spirit of nationalism and individualism in the United States. All the states except the original thirteen were created by the Union and as a consequence their citizens were more national- than state-conscious. The special problems of the frontier, such as need for land, transportation, and markets, and protection against enemies could often be resolved more effectively by the national than by state or local governments. "The economic and social characteristics of the frontier worked against sectionalism," Turner wrote, and "the mobility of population was death to localism." It was observed also that the West had a "growing tendency to call to its assistance the powerful arm of national authority." Turner concludes, "It was this nationalizing tendency of the West that transformed the democracy of Jefferson into the national republicanism of Monroe and the democracy of Andrew Jackson."

The impact of the frontier in shaping the American character was one of Turner's favorite themes. Under the influence of pioneer conditions, he saw the settlers as developing highly distinctive individual traits:

> The result is that to the frontier the American intellect owes its striking characteristics. That coarseness and strength combined with acuteness and inquisitiveness; that practical, inventive turn of mind, quick to find expedients; that masterful grasp of material things, lacking in the artistic but powerful to effect great ends; that restless, nervous energy; that dominant individualism, working for good and for evil, and withal that buoyancy and exuberance which comes with freedom—these are traits of the frontier, or traits called out elsewhere because of the existence of the frontier.

Criticisms of certain aspects of the Turner frontier theory have been previously indicated. Most frequently attacked are the arguments that the frontier had served as a safety valve for the East's discontented, or that it had been the source of American democracy. Recent historians have objected, too, to Turner's contention that America's development was primarily a product of the frontier, and it is claimed that he ignored such vital forces as the class struggle, industrialization, urbanization, and the growth of transportation systems. The charge is unjust, though Turner may have exaggerated the importance of the frontier. He did not see the frontier as the sole explanation of American history. "In truth," he said, "there is no single key to American history. In history, as in science, we are learning that a complex result is the outcome of the interplay of many forces. Simple explanations fail to meet the case." Thus, while it is erroneous to attribute American historical development to any single cause, one of the great molding forces during the eighteenth and nineteenth centuries unquestionably was the nation's westward expansion, symbolized by the frontier.

It has been said of Frederick Jackson Turner that he wrote less and influenced his own generation more than any other historian. One critic concluded that for forty years Turner "has so completely dominated American historical writing that hardly a single production of that time has failed to show the marks of his influence," and another observed that "American history has been reinterpreted and rewritten because of him." One of the most esteemed of American historians, Charles A. Beard, concluded that the Turner paper "was destined to have a more profound influence on thought about American history than any other essay or volume ever written on the subject."

Turner's message had an impact far beyond academic circles. There is evidence that he had a direct effect upon the ideas and political policies of Woodrow Wilson and Theodore Roosevelt. When Franklin D. Roosevelt was campaigning for the presidency in 1932, he obviously drew on Turner in the following statement:

Our last frontier has long since been reached, and there is practically no more free land. More than half of our people do not live on the farms or on lands and cannot derive a living by cultivating their own property. There is no safety valve in the form of a western prairie to which those thrown out of work by the eastern economic machines can go for a new start.

The concept of the frontier as a central theme in national history was also referred to in addresses by John F. Kennedy, who adopted the "New Frontier" as the battle cry for his administration. In his acceptance speech at the Democratic National Convention at Los Angeles in 1960 Kennedy said:

> I stand tonight facing west on what was once the last frontier. From the lands that stretch 3,000 miles behind me, the pioners of old gave up their safety, their comfort, and sometimes their lives to build a new world here in the West . . . we stand today on a new frontier—the frontier of the 1960s—a frontier of unknown opportunities and perils—a frontier of unfulfilled hopes and threats.

Wide agreement exists today that Frederick Jackson Turner and Francis Parkman have been the two greatest interpreters of the American scene. The frontier theory itself has continued to be a pervasive idea in American historical writing, influencing all our thinking, popular and scholarly, about the growth of the American nation.

Other nations and continents, it has been noted, have had frontiers in their historical backgrounds, notably Africa, Latin America, Canada, and Russia. The Turner hypothesis has been applied to those areas, but with indifferent or inconclusive results. If the frontier experience had, in fact, so profoundly affected American democracy, nationalism, and individualism, why had not the same phenomena been observed elsewhere? The answer appears to be that the American frontier was unique. Nowhere else was a comparable combination of circumstances to be found. As stated by Billington, "Where autocratic governments controlled population movements, where resources were lacking, or where conditions prohibited ordinary individuals from exploiting nature's riches, a frontier in the Turnerian sense could not be said to exist."

A new dimension was added to the frontier concept by Walter Prescott Webb, in his book *The Great Frontier* (1952), who concludes that the history of the modern world can be most rationally explained by the hypothesis. Until 1492, Webb holds, the social pattern of Europe had for centuries remained virtually unchanged. Then came the Age of Discovery and soon the Great Frontier was opened to the civilized world. For the next four centuries practically the entire earth—"three new continents, a large part of a fourth, and thousands of islands"—was Europe's frontier. A great empty area became available to Europe's crowded and impoverished people, and they swarmed out over the globe to reap the harvest of land, precious metals, and other natural resources. The new riches inspired drastic changes in government and society: Serfdom was replaced by capitalistic free enterprise, democracy challenged autocracy, religious freedom succeeded religious authoritarianism, and justice for the individual under law became a firmly established practice. But like the American, the Great Frontier has come to an end, Webb believes, as the freedom of the individual has become increasingly restricted, free enterprise is eliminated by totalitarian governments, and the welfare-state principle assumes responsibility for the lives of all citizens. Frontier democracy and individualism in such societies are doomed to extinction.

13–MUNICIPAL MUCKRAKER

LINCOLN STEFFENS'
The Shame of the Cities

CITIES HAVE BEEN TORMENTED by sin and corruption at least since the time of Sodom and Gomorrah. Municipal misgovernment is not an American invention, therefore, though it reached a high state of perfection here under the Tweed Ring in New York, Matt Quay and Boies Penrose in Pennsylvania, and such lesser, but equally notorious, political figures as Crump in Memphis, Hague in Jersey City, and Pendergast in Kansas City. The almost insoluble problems of the large urban area—e.g., New York City has been called "ungovernable"—aid and abet dishonesty, crime, malfeasance in office, and a general breakdown of orderly government. A recognition of the virulence of the malady was the establishment of a cabinet-level agency, the U.S. Department of Housing and Urban Development, in 1965.

The first major exposé of the corruption existing behind the façade of representative government in our cities was the work of Lincoln Steffens, who was tagged, around the turn of the century, by Theodore Roosevelt, along with Ida Tarbell, Ray Stannard Baker, and others, as a "muckracker." Steffens himself claimed the honor of being "the first muckraker," because his series of articles revealing the sordid operations of crooked politicians in American cities began a month before Ida Tarbell's equally startling exposure of the iniquitous activities of John D. Rockefeller's Standard Oil Company. Actually, both had been preceded by other writers who can properly be classified as muckrakers, notably Mark Sullivan on Pennsylvania's morals, Ray Stannard Baker on railroads and corporations, Finley Peter Dunne (speaking through

"Mr. Dooley") on trusts and government, Ernest Poole on slum conditions, Frank Norris on railroads and stock exchanges, and David Graham Phillips on social and ethical problems.

A true muckraker was concerned not only with bringing to light the rascality of governments and corporations—a negative or destructive approach—but with finding constructive solutions to the evil conditions revealed by their investigations. They were reformers at heart. In the first decade of the twentieth century, muckraking became a national movement which roused public opinion and brought about numerous salutary changes. One of the most influential products of the muckraker school was Lincoln Steffens' *The Shame of the Cities*.

Steffens' muckraking activities began more or less by accident. A native of California, he had completed his formal education in Germany and France, and returned home, in 1892, to become a newspaper reporter on the New York *Evening Post*. His reporting assignments included Wall Street, where he covered the Panic of 1893, and the police department, where he collected his first evidence of a police-criminal tie-up. The latter beat brought Steffens into touch with Theodore Roosevelt, new commissioner of police. After four years as city editor of the *Commercial Advertiser*, 1897–1901, Steffens accepted an invitation to join the staff of *McClure's Magazine*.

Steffens thus became part of a publishing revolution which was rapidly changing the reading habits and ideas of the American public. S. S. McClure's magazines were setting new styles in low prices, lively formats, and controversial content, and his stable of writers was among the nation's most widely read. Steffens' original appointment as managing editor, for which he showed slight talent, was soon superseded by a roving assignment—to go out and search for suitable material.

From a tip picked up in Chicago, Steffens learned of the aggressive campaign being carried on by Joseph Wingate Folk, circuit attorney, against municipal corruption in St. Louis. Folk was a successful young attorney who had been chosen by the local bosses to run as attorney for the circuit, under the misapprehension that he could be managed. Apparently Folk did not realize, prior to his election, the nature of the machine with which he was to be associated—the intricate network of crime, shady deals, buying of legislators, looting of public funds,

and general state of corruption which held the city in its
grip. This was the story which Steffens told in two articles
for *McClure's Magazine*, "Tweed Days in St. Louis"
(written in collaboration with a local journalist, Claude H.
Wetmore) and a sequel, "The Shamelessness of St. Louis,"
published the following year.

In the late 1890s, St. Louis was under the administration of Mayor Ziegenhein and boodling became the only
real business of the city government. There were "combines" of municipal legislators who sold rights, privileges,
and public franchises for their own individual profit. The
St. Louis charter gave legislative power to a Municipal
Assembly, composed of a Council and a House of Delegates, a number of whose delegates were illiterate. The
votes of all were strictly controlled by the machine, and
money collected for valuable privileges and franchises was
distributed among the members—after the bosses had
skimmed off a lion's share. Franchises worth millions were
granted without payment of a cent to the city, payrolls
were padded with the names of non-existent persons, and
funds intended for public improvements went to the
boodlers. Men paid thousands of dollars for election to the
Assembly, anticipating huge dividends on their investment.

The corruption of St. Louis, Circuit Attorney Folk was
shocked to discover, came from the top. Behind the
looters were the best citizens, merchants and financiers,
men of wealth and social standing, who because of special
privileges granted them, supported and defended the
crooked politicians. Men of supposedly high integrity,
church members and Bible class teachers, contributed to
the support of the syndicate, fearing that otherwise they
would face financial ruin.

Immediately after his election, Joseph Folk set out to
clean up the city. A number of ward heelers and party
workers were soon behind bars for illegal registrations and
other election frauds. A newspaper reporter informed Folk
that a large sum of money had been placed in a bank for
the purpose of bribing certain assemblymen to vote for
passage of a street railroad ordinance. Prompt and courageous action by Folk uncovered deposits, amounting to
$135,000, in two of St. Louis' largest banking institutions,
and any payments by them were legally estopped until the
courts had acted.

Consternation spread rapidly among the conspirators.
Representatives of the House and Council combines were

arrested and placed under heavy bonds. Prominent businessmen were charged with bribery and perjury. Some took flight to other states or to foreign countries. All the power and wealth of the bribe givers and bribe takers were brought to bear on Folk to force him to drop the investigation. Statesmen, lawyers, merchants, clubmen, and churchmen called on him to cease such activities against his fellow citizens. Though he stood practically alone, Folk was undaunted and continued his relentless pressure on the malefactors. Other instances of corruption dating back a decade were uncovered. In the ensuing trials, the ringleaders who had not fled the city were convicted and received prison terms.

The tale of the "master boodler," the boss of St. Louis, Colonel Edward R. Butler, is related in the second article, "The Shamelessness of St. Louis." A master horseshoer by trade, Butler had begun his political career as boss of a tough ward. Gradually his power increased until he had bipartisan control of both the Democratic and Republican Parties in St. Louis, was ruling the city with an iron hand, and had accumulated a fortune of several million dollars through bribes and blackmail. To break up the ring, Folk realized that he had to catch the boss. Butler was indicted for bribery. On a change of venue order, the hearing was held in Columbia, Missouri; there, after a spectacular trial, the jury returned a verdict, "Guilty: three years."

Steffens is strongly critical of the "supineness" of the people: "In the midst of all these sensations, and this obvious, obstinate political rottenness, the innocent citizens, who must be at least a decisive majority, did not register last fall." Pessimistically, therefore, he concluded that the ring was still in control and was only waiting for Folk's retirement to resume its old practices.

In a third article, "The Shame of Minneapolis," subtitled "The Rescue and Redemption of a City that was Sold Out," Steffens' views were more hopeful. Contrasting with St. Louis' predominantly German population, Minneapolis had been settled by New Englanders, Norwegians, and Swedes. Too occupied with their own affairs to find time for public business, the citizens had allowed "the loafers, saloon keepers, gamblers, criminals, and the thriftless poor of all nationalities" to take over the municipal government. The boss of the odoriferous aggregation was a popular doctor, Albert Alonzo Ames, four times elected mayor of Minneapolis and head of a system of robbery, blackmail, and plunder conducted by professional criminals under police direction.

In his fourth and last term as mayor, Ames outdid himself, aided and abetted by his brother Fred as chief of police; Norman W. King, a professional gambler, as liaison man with Minneapolis thieves, confidence men, pickpockets, and gamblers; Irwin A. Gardner, who collected tribute from houses of prostitution; "Coffee John" Fitchette, who sold positions on the police force; and detective captain Norbeck, who was assigned the duty of "throwing scares into trimmed suckers." Of 225 men in the police force, 107 were dismissed, because the gang suspected that they were too honest, and the others were charged a price for their retention. With this auspicious beginning, thieves in the local jail were turned loose on the city, with instructions to hand over their loot to the detectives in charge. Gambling went on openly, and disorderly houses multiplied; auction frauds were instituted; opium joints and unlicensed saloons were protected; burglaries were common. The ring's revenue from these varied illicit sources was enormous.

Then the thieves began to fall out among themselves and the system became demoralized. In the midst of it all, a grand jury was convened in 1902 for the summer term, and a successful businessman, Hovey C. Clarke, was selected as foreman. Clarke decided that the time had come to rip up the Ames gang. Private detectives were employed by the jury to collect evidence, aggrieved jailbirds were encouraged to turn against their former partners in crime, and indictments began to be handed down against Fred Ames, Gardner, Norbeck, and many lesser members of the gang. Finally, Mayor Ames, under indictment and heavy bonds for extortion, conspiracy, and bribery, left the state on a night train. Policemen who had been removed by Ames were reappointed to the force. Criminal elements continued to fight the reform administration which had taken over the city government, but after four months of the emergency administration, Steffens' judgment was that "Minneapolis should be clean and sweet for a little while at least, and the new administration should begin with a clear deck."

As in St. Louis, the Minneapolis grand jury was startled by the character of the citizens who opposed its work and who came to the defense of the corrupt leaders. Steffens' comment was, "No reform I ever studied has failed to bring out this phenomenon of virtuous cowardice, the baseness of the decent citizen."

After St. Louis and Minneapolis, Steffens' next target was Pittsburgh, Pennsylvania. His opening observation was that "Minneapolis was an example of police corruption; St. Louis of financial corruption. Pittsburgh is an example of both police and financial corruption." Whereas St. Louis and Minneapolis had found public-spirited officials who exposed and rectified the wretched state of municipal affairs, Pittsburgh had had no such good fortune. It was not from indifference, however, for "angry and ashamed, Pittsburgh is a type of the city that has tried to be free and failed."

The railroads, according to Steffens, began Pittsburgh's corruption. The early railroads were helped by municipal bonds, and then proceeded to repudiate the bonds and to go into politics. New railroads purchased their rights of way by outbribing the older roads. As corporations multiplied and capital branched out, corruption increased.

Pittsburgh's boss was Christopher L. Magee. In Pittsburgh, Magee found a community perfectly adapted to the boss system: a growing town too busy for self-government; two parties about equal in strength, neither well organized; unsystematic boodling; and councils holding legislative, administrative, and executive powers that could be easily manipulated. As a partner, Magee took in William Flinn, an Irish contractor and natural politician. As long as Magee lived, the combination was unbeatable.

The first step in Magee's strategy was to seize control of the city councils. This he did by running relatives and friends for councilmen, and then bartenders, saloonkeepers, liquor dealers, and others with a close tie-up to the vices. Further to strengthen his grip, Magee took over Allegheny County, in which Pittsburgh is located, making the county part of the city government. Though Magee was a Republican, he won Democratic support by sharing patronage. Nearly one fourth of the places on the payroll were held by Democrats.

From building a dominant political machine, Magee moved on to form close working relations with banks, trust companies, and brokers, who shared in the city's business. The manufacturers and merchants were kept in line by small municipal grants and privileges. In Steffens' opinion, "The business man, the typical American merchant everywhere, cares no more for his city's interest than the politician does."

Magee needed only the state to make his rule absolute. A deal was arranged with Senator Matthew S. Quay, political boss of Pennsylvania, whereby it was agreed that the Magee machine would support Quay for his business in the state, in return for which Quay would surrender to Magee the state's function of legislation for the city of Pittsburgh. Magee and Quay quarreled constantly over the division of powers and spoils, both being strong and inordinately ambitious, but practically the compact held together at first.

With their control of Pittsburgh assured beyond dispute, Magee and his lieutenant Flinn proceeded to exploit the city for their private gain. Magee took over the financial and corporate side, dictating the use of streets, handling franchises, and building and running railways. Flinn's province was public contracts for his own firm and he grabbed a monopoly of such business as repairing old streets and laying out new ones, renovating districts, creating parks, building bridges, and erecting municipal buildings. All attempts by outsiders to break the monopoly were repulsed.

The looting of Pittsburgh by the Magee-Flinn ring went on for a quarter of a century. Throughout the period, however, a few upright citizens fought the combine, joining to form the Municipal League. A break between Quay and Magee seemed to give the League its opportunity. After an acrimonious fight in 1856–96, Magee and Flinn and Boss Martin of Philadelphia determined to kill Quay politically. To save his skin, Quay ran upon a reform platform. Pittsburgh was promised a new charter, but the charter never got through the legislature, for suddenly Quay made a deal with the city bosses in order to be re-elected to the United States Senate, and the ring was left in control of Pittsburgh.

Subsequently, Magee's health failed and Flinn was unable to hold the ruling machine together. A Citizens' Party was organized and in the February 1902 election beat the ring. The celebrating reformers were soon astonished to discover, however, that a new political boss, Tom Bigelow, had taken over the Citizens' Party, and was applying regular machine methods. The grafters, the corporations, and the railroads came to terms with the "reform" administration and proceeded to operate as before. The situation as stated by one citizen was: "We have smashed a ring and we have wound another around us. Now we have got to smash that."

To complement the Pittsburgh story, Steffens turned his attention to another Pennsylvania city, Philadelphia, characterized as "corrupt and contented," and "the worst governed city in the country." Philadelphia had gone through reforms—for example, breaking up the "Gas Gang," headed by Boss James McManes, which had flourished during the late sixties and seventies. A good charter adopted in 1885 had seemed to promise sound government.

But then the citizens had relaxed, having faith that their new charter, the "Bullitt Law," would ensure sound government. The Bullitt Law concentrated in the mayor executive and political power and complete responsibility. The first two mayors elected after that law went into effect in 1887 were estimable businessmen, totally unfamiliar with the game of politics as played by the professionals. Under them the foundation was laid for the take-over of the city government by a corrupt political machine. The honest citizens of Philadelphia were effectively disfranchised and election frauds were practiced on a grand scale. In a typical election the number of fraudulent or stolen votes was estimated between forty and eighty thousand, always with a generous margin for keeping the ring in power. Philadelphians, Steffens discovered, "have no more rights at the polls than the Negroes down South." At the same time that their ballots became valueless, the bosses took away their choice of parties by gaining control of the Republican and Democratic organizations, as had been done in Pittsburgh, sharing federal and county patronage.

To make graft safe, Boss David Martin recognized that the people must gain sufficient benefits from their municipal government to keep them quiet—good water, good light, clean streets well paved, fair transportation, not too much vice, public order and safety, and no open corruption. These things Martin gave them—at a price. Through his hands passed all public franchises, public works, and public contracts, from each of which a toll was taken. Nevertheless, all the city's business was given at least a semblance of legality, and the citizens were getting something for their money, a return of perhaps as much as 75 per cent.

Martin's downfall came not from any uprising of Philadelphia citizens but as punishment for insubordination, because he refused to follow Boss Quay's order to nominate Boies Penrose as mayor. Martin teamed up with Chris Magee of Pittsburgh to beat Quay, but Quay beat them both on his "reform" platform. Quay's man, Samuel H. Ashbridge, was elected mayor of Philadelphia and another disciple, Penrose, became a U.S. senator. The principle of moderate grafting followed by Martin was promptly tossed overboard by Ashbridge, who entered the office of mayor in debt and emerged a wealthy man. As summed up by the Municipal League:

> The four years of the Ashbridge administration have passed into history, leaving behind them a scar on the fame and reputation of our city which will be a long time healing. Never before, and let us hope never again, will there be such brazen defiance of public opinion, such flagrant disregard of public interest, such abuse of powers and responsibilities for private ends.

Instances of the Ashbridge machine's "brazen abuse of power" were the increase of protected vice, the importation from New York of the white slavery system of prostitution, and the spread of gambling and policy making. Corruption reached even into the public schools, where the teachers had to purchase their jobs and to pay a percentage of their salaries for election expenses.

And "What did the Philadelphians do?" asked Steffens, replying "Nothing." The people, he went on to charge, "seem to prefer to be ruled by a known thief than an ambitious reformer." Any popular revolt against the venal system, however, was hamstrung in advance by disfranchisement and the taking away of any choice of parties. As Steffens was writing, Philadelphia was making one more effort at reform under a new mayor, John Weaver, a native Englishman.

From Philadelphia, Steffens moved on to Chicago. Reminiscent of Carl Sandburg's poem "Chicago" is his description of the city: "First in violence, deepest in dirt; loud, lawless, unlovely, ill-smelling, irreverent, new; an overgrown gawk of a village, the tough among cities, a spectacle for the nations;—I give Chicago no quarter and Chicago asks for none."

Steffens subtitled his Chicago article "Half Free and

Fighting On." Apparently to his surprise, he found that Chicago had no political boss, no one owned the mayor, and the City Council was controlled by the Voters' League, a reform organization. The League was fighting, as its immediate goal, for representative government rather than for good government. The city government was still riddled with police graft; there were dealings with criminals, gamblers, prostitutes, liquor dealers, thieves, and even murderers; and the streets of Chicago were dangerous for any citizen abroad after dark. On the other hand, the worst of the city aldermen had been defeated for re-election, and the board of aldermen was now protecting the city's interests in awarding franchises and privileges generally.

There was much about the Chicago reforms, Steffens suggested, that other cities could emulate to their advantage. About thirty years later, in his famous *Autobiography,* Steffens expressed disappointment and disillusionment. The reform movement in Chicago had failed and the blame was placed squarely on the businessmen who "hated and fought and clamored and wriggled and bribed out of their contracts with the practical, honest, fair 'reform' government of Chicago. And finally they killed it as literally as the gunmen of Chicago now kill one another, and as safely. Why? They said (to me) that what they wanted was, not this so-called representative, but good government."

For his sixth and last city on which to perform a muckraking operation, Steffens chose New York, where he found "a good government, or, to be more precise, it has a good administration." The anti-Tammany forces had elected as Mayor Seth Low, a successful businessman who had given the city an honest, efficient administration, one of the best in the country, but who was disliked by many New Yorkers because of his cold personality. The alternative to Low's reform regime was a restoration of Tammany corruption.

Tammany's brand of corruption was based upon the corruption of the people. Steffens found that "its grafting system is one in which more people share than any I have studied." The people's votes came cheap, "bought up by kindnesses and petty privileges." The big graft went to the leaders. Not even Tammany knew how rich police corruption was until the Lexow Committee, a legislative investigating body, exposed the facts. When in power, Tammany not only received "rake-offs" on all the city's expenditures, but collected millions from business, industry, and other non-official sources.

Near the time Steffens' article appeared, New York's mayoralty election was held, and Seth Low's administration was campaigning for re-election. Low was defeated, and Tammany was triumphantly restored to office. The downfall of honest government was accomplished through the votes of the people and heavy contributions made by business interests to the Tammany election expenses. With such an outcome, Steffens comments in his *Autobiography,* "it seems rational to conclude that business men do not want good government much more than they want a representative democracy, that the people do not like good men and good government, or, let us say, professionally good men in office and unyielding good government. They both prefer 'bad' government."

Once when a clergyman in a lecture audience asked Steffens what lay at the root of corruption, Steffens replied: "Most people, you know, say it was Adam. But Adam, you remember, he said that it was Eve, the woman she did it. And Eve said no, no, it wasn't she; it was the serpent. And that's where you clergy have stuck ever since. You blame that serpent, Satan. Now I come and I am trying to show you that it was, it is, the apple."

In each of the half-dozen cities he had investigated, Steffens discovered the same pattern: an alliance between "respectable" businessmen and disreputable gang politicians to rob the taxpayers. For every dollar spent for public improvements, another went to the thieves. Slums, firetraps, and brothels continued to exist because law enforcement officers had been bribed, frequently by landlords who posed as churchmen and pillars of the community. The process of corruption, Steffens contended, was universal and uniform. Further, "no one class is at fault, nor any breed, nor any particular interest or group, or party. The misgovernment of the American people is misgovernment by the American people . . . the people are corrupt in small ways as their leaders are in big ways."

Steffens became increasingly skeptical of the value of mere exposure of corruption and of reform movements. Muckraking, he felt, only "improved the graft system." He saw reforms as spasmodic efforts to punish bad rulers which were soon over. The people avoid self-government. "A self-acting form of government is an ancient superstition. We are an inventive people and we all think that we shall devise some day a legal machine that will turn out good government automatically."

The Shame of the Cities exerted a wide influence and resulted in an immense amount of cleaning up of the conditions which Steffens had described so vividly, in such minute detail, and with such startling skill. *The Shame of the Cities* constitutes a primary source on American city government. In Max Lerner's judgment, "if we valued our historical figures according to their usefulness in creating a richer and healthier American culture, men like Lincoln Steffens would be heroes to be celebrated in every school and college."

14—HORRORS OF THE STOCKYARDS

UPTON SINCLAIR'S *The Jungle**

THE PALM for achieving foremost rank among modern American propagandist novelists is readily carried off by Upton Sinclair. Simultaneously, he was one of the most prolific writers in the nation's literary history, and is probably the most widely read abroad of all American authors; according to a recent count, there are 772 translations of his books in forty-seven languages and in thirty-nine countries, with the totals continuing to mount.

Sinclair has been aptly compared to another great propagandist, Thomas Paine. Like Paine, he attacked with burning indignation and reckless courage every variety of social abuse and injustice. The appellations "a pamphleteer for righteousness" and "the last of the muckrakers" are apt descriptions of Sinclair's stormy literary career.

When Sinclair died in 1968, at the age of ninety, he could view in retrospect a lifetime devoted to crusades: smiting labor spies, the meat-packing industry, a corrupt press, Wall Street speculators, New York society, alcoholism, the murderers of Sacco and Vanzetti, Tom Mooney's persecution, bourgeois morality, coal-mine conditions, popular evangelism, secondary and higher education, the oil industry, the evils of war. As Robert Cantwell ably summed up the case: "Few American public figures, let alone American inspirational novelists, have written so many books, delivered so many lectures, covered so much territory, advocated so many causes or composed so many letters to the editor, got mixed up in so many scandals, been so insulted, ridiculed, spied on, tricked and left

*Revision of the "Afterword" from the Signet edition, reprinted by permission of The New American Library, Inc.

holding the bag—few, in short, have jumped so nimbly from so many frying pans into so many fires, and none has ever managed to keep so sunny and buoyant while the flames were leaping around him."

Sinclair was an early convert to Socialism, though frequently failing to follow orthodox party lines. His propagandistic efforts carry a constant refrain: the theme of the capitalist as a heartless scoundrel and the workingman as an oppressed hero. In the midst of the depressed thirties, he narrowly missed an opportunity to put into practice his Socialistic theories when, as Democratic nominee for Governor of California, he conducted a spectacular campaign on the EPIC platform—"End Poverty in California." The bitter and determined opposition of the state's powerful business interests cost him the election.

Sinclair's leap from obscurity to fame was sudden. In his early twenties he had made up his mind to become a successful writer or to starve in the attempt. He came extremely close to the latter before accomplishing the former: His first five novels, published from 1901 to 1906, produced altogether less than a thousand dollars in royalties.

The turning point was *The Jungle*, in 1906, the most popular and most influential of all Sinclair's numerous novels. This savage indictment of labor and sanitary conditions in the Chicago stockyards first appeared serially in *The Appeal to Reason*, a Socialist weekly, when the author was a mere twenty-seven.

The times were ripe for *The Jungle*. Still fresh in the public's memory was the "embalmed beef" scandal of the Spanish-American War. Theodore Roosevelt, hero of the battle of San Juan Hill, had testified before a Senate investigating committee that he would just as soon have eaten his old hat as the canned food that, under a government contract, had been shipped to the soldiers in Cuba. Languishing in Congress as Sinclair was composing his celebrated exposé was a bill prepared by Dr. Harvey W. Wiley, "Father of the Pure Food and Drug Act," to tighten the laws and to protect consumers against unscrupulous manufacturing and business practices.

Also helping to set the scene for *The Jungle* was the whole school of "muckrakers"—Roosevelt's epithet for the journalists and reformers who, during the first decade of the present century, were busily investigating and exposing political misrule and business avarice. Among the highlights of the genre, previously noted, were Lincoln Steffens' articles on municipal graft, Ida M. Tarbell's *The History of the Standard Oil Company,* Ray Stannard Baker on the railroads, Thomas W. Lawton on contemporary financiers, Charles Edward Russell on the beef trust, and Samuel Hopkins Adams' sensational series of articles on patent medicines and the press. As revealed by the muckrakers, wholesale corruption permeated the nation's life, and their charges were buttressed with stories of stolen franchises, payroll padding, fraudulent letting of contracts, alliances of police with vice, foul slum dwellings, poverty in the cities, worthless stock schemes, dishonest insurance companies, and thieving monopolies.

It is doubtful, however, whether any of the previous muckraking jobs had the terrific impact on public consciousness of Upton Sinclair's *The Jungle,* partly perhaps because of its popular fictional form, but more likely because it hit people where they were most sensitive—in the stomachs. *The Appeal to Reason,* with a circulation of half a million, mainly in working-class districts, offered Sinclair five hundred dollars for subsistence while he investigated the lives of the Packingtown workers. For seven weeks Sinclair lived with the underprivileged, wretched aliens in the Chicago stockyards, and then returned to his home in New Jersey to write about what he had seen, heard, and smelled. According to the author, *"The Jungle* was written in a board cabin, eight feet by ten, set on a hillside north of Princeton, New Jersey,"* in a period of about nine months.

Even before serialization of the novel was completed, word began to spread outside its proletarian audience. Calls for back issues were reaching the magazine in considerable numbers. Nevertheless, the first five book publishers approached by Sinclair rejected his manuscript, afraid that the book contained too much dynamite. Finally, the impatient author solicited readers of *The Appeal to Reason* to ensure publication by ordering copies and paying in advance. Twelve thousand orders poured in and the book was set up in type. At that point, Doubleday, Page and Company stepped in with an offer to publish the book, provided they could verify its essential truth. The Doubleday editor, Isaac F. Marcosson, went to Chicago and interviewed Dr. W. K. Jaques, formerly head of meat inspection at the stockyards, who had been fired because of his insistence upon a drastic scrutiny and condemnation of diseased meat. Dr. Jaques testified that *The Jungle* contained no serious exaggerations or misstatements.

Furthermore, Marcosson reported, "I was able to get a Meat Inspector's badge, which gave me access to the secret confines of the meat empire. Day and night I prowled over its foul-smelling domain and I was able to see with my own eyes much that Sinclair had never even heard about."

The Jungle appeared under the Doubleday imprint and immediately created a sensation at home and abroad. Advance proofs had been sent to the leading American newspapers, and on the release date, January 25, 1906, the story exploded on front pages from coast to coast. Additional publicity was assured by sending a special advance copy to the current occupant of the White House, Theodore Roosevelt, "the master press agent of all time." So impressed was Roosevelt with *The Jungle's* revelations that he wired Sinclair to visit him at once to discuss the matter.

The foremost social critic of the period, Finley Peter Dunne's "Mr. Dooley," thus described the Rooseveltian reaction to *The Jungle*:

Tiddy was toying with a light breakfast an' idly turnin' over th' pages iv th' new book with both hands. Suddenly he rose fr'm th' table, an' cryin': "I'm pizened," begun throwin' sausages out iv th' window. Th' ninth wan sthruck Sinitor Biv'ridge on th' head an' made him a blond. It bounced off, exploded, an' blew a leg off a secret-service agent, an' th' scatthred fragmints desthroyed a handsome row iv ol' oak-trees. Sinitor Biv'ridge rushed in, thinkin' that th' Prisidint was bein' assassynated be his devoted followers in th' Sinit, an' discovered Tiddy engaged in a hand-to-hand conflict with a potted ham. Th' Sinitor fr'm Injyanny, with a few well-directed wurruds, put out th' fuse an' rendered th' missile harmless. Since thin th' Prisidint, like th' rest iv us, has become a viggytaryan. . . .

The Jungle has been compared to the writings of Leo Tolstoy and other nineteenth-century Russian novelists and to such French naturalists as Zola in its complete pessimism, its mood of black despair, and its unrelieved tragedy. The setting is the stockyards and slums of Chicago. A succession of races—the Germans, the Irish, the Bohemians, the Poles, the Lithuanians, the Slovaks—had followed each other as stockyard workers, lured from their Old World villages to America by agents of the packers with promises of phenomenal wages.

In *The Jungle* is told the epic tragedy of Jurgis Rudkus, a Lithuanian peasant, and a group of his relatives and friends, immigrants all, who lived, worked, and died in the stockyards district. There, in Packingtown (as Sinclair called the stockyards), the immigrants encountered virtually every evil to be found in American industry, politics, and society. Unable to speak English, they were easily exploited and victimized by those in power—the packers and their foremen, the police, the political bosses, real estate dealers, and all the rest of the "upper class." Jurgis has to pay graft to get and to keep his job; the real estate man cheats him by selling him a house on the installment plan with hidden clauses the Lithuanian cannot read, and which eventually cause him to lose his home; he is unmercifully speeded up on the job and suffers injuries; he and his family are afflicted by horrible diseases; he is laid off and blacklisted, and goes to jail unjustly for smashing the face of a brutal boss. One by one, Jurgis and his group are crushed: The old men are thrown on the scrap heap to starve, the women turn to prostitution to live, Jurgis' wife, attended in childbirth by an ignorant midwife, dies from lack of proper care, and his infant son is drowned in one of the stinking pools of green water around his wretched shack. Nowhere does Sinclair spare the squeamish reader in his realistic portrayal of the filth, the stench, and cruelty of the stockyards. Finally, Jurgis, physically broken and alone, is left to wander until he becomes convinced that only Socialism can remake and save this hideous world.

The powerful meat-packing industry did not propose to submit meekly to Sinclair's accusations, nor to tight government regulation of its operations. On the contrary, it was prepared to fight them with every weapon at its command. A commission sent to Chicago by the Secretary of Agriculture to investigate conditions in Packingtown was persuaded by the "Beef Trust" that *The Jungle* was the product of a disordered and sensation-seeking mind. A series of articles in *The Saturday Evening Post,* purportedly written by J. Ogden Armour, actually ghostwritten, denied unequivocally the exposés by Sinclair and others.

Such influential newspapers as the Chicago *Tribune* and the Boston *Transcript* rallied to the defense and attacked Sinclair in editorials and news stories. Large sums were spent by the meat packing industry for advertisements attempting to counteract in the public mind the revolting picture of the stockyards presented in *The Jungle*. Equally significant, relentless pressure was brought on Congress to prevent or to emasculate any legislation aiming at federal control or regulation of the industry.

Meanwhile, Roosevelt decided to send to Chicago another commission composed of two New York social workers, Charles P. Neill, then Labor Commissioner, and James B. Reynolds. The commission returned from Chicago with a scathing report, confirming the main charges of *The Jungle* and adding their personal observations on the prevailing conditions. Roosevelt withheld release of the report temporarily, retaining it instead as a club to hold over the meat packers. He hoped that by threatening to publicize the report's findings, he could curb the packers' violent opposition to the Beveridge amendment to the Agricultural Appropriation Bill. This bill, introduced with the President's approval, provided for the extension of genuine government inspection to all the processes of preparing meat.

When the packers remained stubborn and unyielding in their opposition, Roosevelt sent a message to the House strongly urging the passage of the Beveridge amendment (already adopted by the Senate without a dissenting vote), and released the first part of the Neill-Reynolds report. The country was swept by a storm of indignation as it began to realize that the canned goods and other meats it consumed were prepared among filth and degradation. A familiar rhyme was parodied in the press:

> Mary had a little lamb,
> And when she saw it sicken,
> She shipped it off to Packingtown,
> And now it's labeled chicken.

Though continuing vigorous denials of the charges against them, the packers were making frantic efforts to clean up the packing plants. The argument which finally convinced them that some kind of legislation was necessary was the hard fact that, as one packing-house executive stated, "The sale of meat and meat products has been more than cut in two." After further bitter debate, both the Pure Food and Drug Act and the Beef Inspection Act were passed in modified form and became laws of the land—less than six months after the appearance in book form of *The Jungle*.

The results were described by President Roosevelt in a message to Congress on December 3, 1907: "The pure-food law was opposed so violently that its passage was delayed for a decade; yet it has worked unmixed and immediate good. The meat-inspection law was even more violently assailed. . . . Two years have not elapsed, and already it has become evident that the great benefit the law confers upon the public is accompanied by an equal benefit to the reputable packing establishments. The latter are better off under the law than they were without it."

The most extraordinary aspect of the national furor over *The Jungle*, with its international repercussions, was that public attention was concentrated almost exclusively upon material regarded by Sinclair as incidental, mere background and local color for his major theme, which was the oppression of the Packingtown workers. Scarcely a dozen pages out of 308 were concerned with the gruesome details of meat production: grinding up of poisoned rats, hogs dead of cholera used for a fancy grade of lard, the sale to food markets of the carcasses of steers condemned as tubercular by government inspectors, and, most dramatic of all, the folklore about men who served in the cooking rooms and occasionally fell into the boiling vats, ultimately going out to the world as Durham's Pure Leaf Lard! But it was these casual references to the food they were buying and eating that excited and angered the people and created irresistible demands for reform.

Sinclair had a larger purpose in writing *The Jungle*. The novel was intended first of all as an appeal for Socialism and as a protest against "wage slavery." This aim was recognized by a fellow Socialist, Jack London, who hailed the book with unrestrained enthusiasm: "It will open countless ears that have been deaf to Socialism. It will make thousands of converts to our cause. It depicts what our country really is, the home of oppression and injustice, a nightmare of misery, an inferno of suffering, a human hell, a jungle of wild beasts. . . . What 'Uncle Tom's Cabin' did for the black slaves 'The Jungle' has a large chance to do for the white slaves of today."

Ironically and to Sinclair's keen disappointment, as he

wrote, "I aimed at the public heart and by accident I hit it in the stomach." The Socialist vote in America did not increase, nor did the social revolution appear to be any closer. There was only a prodigious commotion about beef and pork. With this and the fame and fortune which the book brought him, the author had to be content. After all, it was an important fact that *The Jungle* had, as Marcosson pointed out, "achieved a permanent and constructive reform in an industry that touches and affects every human being."

And yet, perhaps even more had been gained. By the contrast which Sinclair emphasized between wealth and poverty in the American scene, by his attacks on organized greed, his condemnation of man's inhumanity to man, and the "lyrical emotion" of *The Jungle,* he has been a moving force in awakening the nation's conscience and bringing about drastic changes in the organization of society. Only the wholly callous, insensitive person could remain indifferent to Sinclair's eloquent plea for an end to the cruelties and injustices of exploitation of the workers and to his hope for a peaceful solution of the class struggle.

Upton Sinclair won his crusade for federal legislation and inspection, but the war for clean meat was far from over. As late as 1967, more than sixty years later, there were shocking revelations concerning unsanitary conditions in intrastate slaughterhouses, not subject to federal laws because their products were not shipped across state lines. Some 15 per cent of the slaughtered animals and 25 per cent of the processed meat thus escaped federal regulation. Policing this meat was left to the individual states. Only twenty-nine states had meat inspection laws, however, and most of those were judged to be inadequate by the U. S. Department of Agriculture.

Despite the meat industry's strong resistance and reluctance in Washington to take action, national protests forced Congress to enact legislation requiring the states to meet federal standards. Most fittingly, President Lyndon B. Johnson invited Upton Sinclair to the White House to witness the signing of the Wholesale Meat Act, on December 16, 1967.

15-REVOLUTION IN MEDICAL SCHOOLS

ABRAHAM FLEXNER'S
Medical Education in the United States and Canada

IF A LAYMAN were asked today what profession exemplifies the highest ethical standards and the most rigorous training for its practitioners, he would undoubtedly answer medicine. The long and arduous trail leading to a Doctor of Medicine degree and a license to practice is presently marked by extended periods spent in general education, in medical education, clinical training, internship, and hospital residency, and in meeting the requirements of state and national examining boards.

It was not always thus, as Abraham Flexner discovered in the first decade of the present century. Complaints of the low standards prevailing in the field of medical education had been heard before, but no one fully realized how incredibly bad conditions were until the Flexner investigation, the findings of which were published in 1910.

The origin of the Flexner bombshell was an interview between its author and Henry Pritchett, President of the Carnegie Foundation for the Advancement of Teaching. Pritchett asked that Flexner undertake a survey of American medical schools. Flexner's training was in the classics and at the time he was head of a leading preparatory school. The proposal came as a complete surprise to him, and he suggested that Pritchett must have him confused with his brother, Simon Flexner, the brilliant director of the Rockefeller Medical Institute. He himself was not a medical man and had never set foot in a medical school.

Pritchett's reply was, "That is precisely what I want. I think these professional schools should be studied not from the point of view of the practitioner but from the standpoint of the educator. . . . This is a layman's job, not a job for a medical man." Flexner agreed to undertake the task.

Flexner's landmark survey of medical education in the United States and Canada began on December 1, 1908. In preparation for the undertaking, Flexner read everything that he could find on the history of medical education in Europe and America. The most important and stimulating volume, he noted, was a German work, Billroth's *The Medical Sciences in the German Universities*. His second step was a visit to Chicago, where he interviewed officials of the American Medical Association and read the "creditable and painstaking," but "extremely diplomatic" reports in the AMA files on the country's medical schools. Finally, Flexner went to Baltimore to talk with distinguished members of the Medical Department of Johns Hopkins University (Flexner was a Johns Hopkins graduate), to try to find out what a medical school ought to be. Only the Hopkins school then had standards comparable to the best European centers for medical education.

With the preliminary period of careful study and preparation behind him, Flexner proceeded on a swift tour of the 155 medical schools in the United States and Canada. He had no fixed pattern and used no questionnaire in his investigation. In each instance, however, he went and saw every one of the 155 schools and talked with medical school faculty members and their students. Flexner soon came to realize that five points were conclusive in judging the quality and value of a medical school:

First, the entrance requirements. What were they? Were they enforced?

Second, the size and training of the faculty.

Third, the sum available from endowment and fees for the support of the institution, and what became of it.

Fourth, the quality and adequacy of the laboratories provided for the instruction of the first two years and the qualifications and training of the teachers of the so-called preclinical branches.

Fifth, the relation between medical schools and hospitals, including particularly freedom of access to beds and freedom in the appointment by the school of the hospital physicians and surgeons who automatically should become clinical teachers.

Given this outline of what to look for, Flexner found

that he could quickly sample student records to determine whether the standards, high or low, stated in the school catalog were being enforced or evaded; whether the faculty was composed of local doctors or of full-time teachers trained elsewhere; and the amount of the school's income. "A stroll through the laboratories disclosed the presence or absence of apparatus, museum specimens, library, and students; and a whiff told the inside story regarding the manner in which anatomy was cultivated." Other questions elicited information about clinical facilities, that is, the extent to which the school enjoyed rights or merely courtesies in the local hospitals.

Amusing incidents in the course of Flexner's travels were frequent. On one occasion, he visited an osteopathic school in Des Moines and found every door locked, though each was labeled: ANATOMY, PHYSIOLOGY, PATHOLOGY, etc. The janitor could not be found. In the evening, Flexner returned to the school, found the janitor, gave him five dollars, in return for which he opened every door. The equipment in each of the rooms was identical, consisting of a desk, a small blackboard, and chairs; there were no charts or apparatus.

The conditions uncovered by Flexner were shocking and he pulled no punches in applying such words as "disgraceful" and "shameful." The city of Chicago with its fourteen medical schools was described as "the plague spot of the country." It was found that entrance requirements were enforced in only ten of the medical schools in the United States. Libraries were inadequate or non-existent in 140 of the schools, and laboratory courses for the first and second years were deplorably equipped and poorly conducted in 139 of the schools.

Simon Flexner, Abraham's brother, once described the first medical school he attended in 1887 as "a school in which the lecture was everything. Within the brief compass of four winter months, the whole medical lore was unfolded in discourses following one another in bewildering sequence . . . and lest the wisdom imparted should exceed the student's power of retention, the lectures were repeated precisely during the second year at the end of which graduation with the degree of Doctor of Medicine was all but automatic."

The situation had changed little two decades later, when Abraham Flexner began his study. The methods of instruction were mainly didactic, i.e., lectures, rather than laboratory experiments and observation. For the past twenty-five years there had been an enormous overproduction of uneducated and poorly trained medical practitioners, in complete disregard of the public welfare. Physicians in the United States were four or five times as numerous in proportion to population as in older countries like Germany. The mass production of ill-trained men was due to the existence of a large number of commercial schools, whose blatant advertising attracted unprepared youth to go from being store clerks and factory workers into the study of medicine. Cutthroat competition for students was unbounded.

The proprietary or commercial schools investigated by Flexner were profitable businesses, paying large dividends to their owners and stockholders. Not only were laboratories lacking, but many medical schools provided no hospital facilities whatever. For the sake of respectabiliy, a number of schools had allied themselves to universities, but the universities failed to make themselves responsible for the standards of the schools or for their support. Nearly one half of the medical schools had incomes below $10,000 per year.

The existence of many of the unnecessary and inadequate medical schools was defended by the argument that a poor medical school was justified in the interest of the poor boy, because he could not afford to go to a more expensive school. Flexner's retort was that the poor boy had no right to go into such a life-or-death profession as medicine, if he was unwilling or unable to obtain suitable preparation. Furthermore, the argument was generally insincere, being put forward to save the poor medical school rather than from any genuine desire to help the poor boy.

Another major conclusion reached by Flexner was that a hospital under complete educational control is as necessary to a medical school as a laboratory of chemistry or pathology. For that reason, Flexner urged hospital trustees to open hospital wards to teaching and for the universities to appoint to their staffs teachers who were devoted to clinical science.

At the end of his nearly two years of firsthand study, Flexner's report was issued by the Carnegie Foundation as its "Bulletin Number Four." The opening chapter of *Medical Education in the United States and Canada* is a historical and general review. In a little more than a century, the United States and Canada had started 457 medical schools, many of them short-lived or stillborn. Laboratory equipment generally consisted of a skeleton or a few bones. The schools were essentially private ventures, moneymaking in spirit and object. "A school that began in October would graduate a class the next spring." The lecturers simply divided a rich harvest, and "chairs" on the faculty were valuable pieces of property. All applicants who could pay their fees were accepted, failures were rare, and the school's diploma constituted a license to practice. State boards of examiners had not yet been created.

Medical schools affiliated with universities were scarcely better than the proprietary institutions. Flexner notes that until well into the eighties the medical schools of Harvard, Yale, and Pennsylvania had been virtually independent of their parent universities. They managed their own affairs, disposed of professorships by common agreement, and segregated and divided fees. An increasing knowledge of chemical, biological, and physical sciences was little utilized in the training process for physicians. The stethoscope had been in use for more than thirty years before adoption in the Harvard Medical School, and a microscope in the school's list of equipment was mentioned for the first time a year later.

A few schools, however, had begun to work toward higher standards. The first was Johns Hopkins, established in 1893, which was the first American medical school of genuine university caliber, requiring a Bachelor's degree for admission, supported by an endowment, maintaining well-equipped laboratories, and with its own hospital. Harvard followed in 1901, under the leadership of President Charles Eliot, with a series of reforms, ending with the requirement of an academic degree for admission. Fourteen other schools specified two or more years of college work as a prerequisite, and about a dozen were satisfied with high school graduation. The remainder "ask little or nothing more than the rudiments or the recollection of a common school education."

On the basis of his first quick overview, Flexner concluded that the country needed fewer and better doctors and the way to get them was to produce fewer. "To support all or most present schools at the higher level would be wasteful, even if it were not impracticable," he declared, "for they cannot be manned."

Flexner was particularly outspoken in his condemnation

of the commercial exploitation of medical education. He reported that "the advertising methods of the commercially successful schools are amazing. Not infrequently advertising costs more than laboratories. The school catalogues abound in exaggeration, misstatement, and half-truths. The deans of these institutions occasionally know more about modern advertising than about modern medical teaching."

Nearly one half of Flexner's report is devoted to the medical school's course of study in its various aspects. Traditionally, he points out, medical teaching had evolved through three stages. The first, lasting for many centuries, was the era of dogma, when the writings of Hippocrates and Galen were handed down as a sacred canon. The second era was the empiric, beginning in the sixteenth century with the study of anatomy; the empiric method was ignorant of causes, classified totally unlike diseases together on the basis of superficial symptomatic resemblance, and prescribed treatments, such as bleeding, as apt to kill as cure. Medical students were passive listeners, studied anatomy by watching a teacher dissect, and learned therapeutics by taking the word of the lecturer or of the textbook.

Going on to the most recent stage, Flexner states:

> The third era is dominated by the knowledge that medicine is part and parcel of modern science. The human body belongs to the animal world. It is put together of tissues and organs, in their structure, origin, and development not essentially unlike what the biologist is otherwise familiar with; it grows, reproduces itself, decays, according to general laws. It is liable to attack by hostile physical and biological agencies; now struck with a weapon, again ravaged by parasites. The normal course of bodily activity is a matter of observation and experience; the best methods of combating interference must be learned in much the same way. Gratuitous speculation is at every stage foreign to the scientific attitude of mind.

The teaching of modern medicine, like all scientific teaching, is characterized by activity, Flexner comments. Instead of merely watching, listening, and memorizing, the student *does* something, usually in the laboratory or in the clinic. He must learn know-how, as well as theory. At the time that Flexner was writing, the curriculum of the best medical schools had already fallen into the pattern familiar today: the first two years devoted mainly to laboratory sciences—anatomy, physiology, pharmacology, pathology—and the last two to clinical work in medicine, surgery, and obstetrics. After examining the state of the art in all its branches, Flexner concludes: "One closes a brief review of the medical sciences with a feeling akin to dismay. So much remains to find out, so much is already known,—how futile to orient the student from either standpoint! Practically, however, there is no ground for despair. . . . After a strenuous laboratory discipline, the student will still be ignorant of many things, but at any rate he will respect facts: he will have learned how to obtain them and what to do with them when he has them."

In 1910, sixteen medical schools qualified for Flexner's first division, requiring for entrance two or more years of college work.* All these were organic parts of full-fledged universities; their medical courses were based upon adequate premedical scientific training; their laboratories met university standards in equipment, management, and appearance; and as a rule there were separate laboratories for anatomy, physiology and biochemistry, pharmacology, pathology and bacteriology. The curriculum was heavily loaded, in part to compensate for the deficiences of premedical education. Higher standards in high school and college, Flexner suggests, would relieve the congestion.

The schools of the second division, requiring for admission high school graduation or the "equivalent," are further divided by Flexner into three groups. The first is a small minority, "straining hard to get from the high school to the college basis." The best of the lot, considering the quality of the student body, the number of full-time faculty members, and the adequacy of laboratories, museum, and library, were judged to be New York University, Syracuse, Northwestern, Jefferson Medical College, Tulane, St. Louis University, Texas, McGill, and Toronto. All were handicapped by having to rely entirely or mainly on student fees and by the poor preliminary preparation of their students.

A second variety of schools basing their programs on high school graduates included "those that, content to

* Johns Hopkins, Harvard, Western Reserve, Rush (University of Chicago), Cornell, Stanford, Wake Forest (N.C.), Yale, and the state Universities of California, Minnesota, North Dakota, Wisconsin, Michigan, Kansas, Nebraska, and South Dakota.

operate on a lower plane, are still commercially effective." Here "the atmosphere is at best that of a successful factory," lacking scientific spirit; the schools rarely carried on any research, and their faculties were generally composed of active practitioners, without modern training. Their "laboratories are often slovenly and, except during class hours, entirely abandoned." In general, no funds were set aside for books and "the school grind is merrily independent of medical literature."

The worst of the three kinds of schools operating on a high school or equivalent basis was described by Flexner as "basely mercenary." They were mainly "cramming establishments"; the students did not even own textbooks; teaching accessories, such as books, museum, modern charts, or models, were absent; and the effective teaching of any of the laboratory sciences was impossible. Flexner demanded the application of "all the force that law and public opinion can wield to crush out the mercenary concerns that trade on ignorance and disease."

The importance of a teaching hospital was strongly stressed by Flexner. Without it, "the school cannot even organize a clinical faculty in any proper sense of the term." Furthermore, control of the hospital should be under the medical school and appointments to its staff made on the basis of fitness, eminence, and skill. The medical field, Flexner remarked, "abounds in questions for which the university hospital with its laboratories is the right place."

A good number of the schools investigated by Flexner possessed absolutely no dispensary provision at all," and some were "destitute of hospital facilities."

Flexner summed up the overall situation in American medical education, as he found it, in the following hard-hitting statement:

As a matter of fact, many of the schools mentioned in the course of this recital are probably without redeeming features of any kind. Their general squalor consorts well with their clinical poverty: the classrooms are bare, save for chairs, a desk, and an occasional blackboard; the windows streaked with dust and soot. In wretched amphitheaters students wait in vain for "professors," tardy or absent, amusing the interval with ribald jest or song. The teaching is an uninstructive rehearsal of text-book or quiz-compend: one encounters surgery taught without patient, instrument, model, or drawing; recitations in obstetrics without a manikin in sight,—often without one in the building. Third and fourth year men are frequently huddled together in the same classes.

The fundamental blame for the sad state of affairs described in the foregoing paragraph was placed by Flexner on finances. He emphasized that proper medical education cannot be conducted at a profit, or even at cost. The best medical schools were far from self-supporting. Unless aided by large endowments, they "burden seriously the general resources of their respective universities"— as true today as when Flexner was writing. Of the 155 medical schools visited, Flexner noted that more than 120 depended on fees alone. Of this group, the better institutions used fees to equip and maintain laboratories; the others assigned only a small part to pedagogical purposes, and distributed the rest among the teachers, who in such cases were always practicing physicians.

Lack of direct responsibility on the part of the parent universities accounted in part for the bad conditions found by Flexner. A university which took a medical school under its wing, he declared, had three duties: the definition and enforcement of entrance standards, the upholding of scientific ideals, and responsibility for adequate support. Among the 155 medical schools examined by Flexner, eighty-two were university departments, though often only nominally.

A revealing section of the Flexner report, especially as to specific detail, is "Part II, Medical Schools of the United States and Canada Arranged Alphabetically by States and Provinces and Separately Characterized." Following is a sampling of some of Flexner's salty evaluations:

Birmingham (Ala.) Medical College—"The hospital is largely given over to surgical patients,—gunshot and other wounds being decidedly abundant."

University of Arkansas Medical Department (*not* affiliated with the University) and College of Pysicians and Surgeons, both in Little Rock—"Neither has a single redeeming feature."

California Medical College (Los Angeles)—"This school

has led a roving and precarious existence . . . a disgrace to the state whose laws permit its existence."

Denver and Gross College of Medicine—"There is a total absence of scientific activity. A few cases of books are found in the college office behind the counter."

Georgetown University School of Medicine—"There is no library accessible to students, no museum, and no pharmacological laboratory."

Georgia College of Eclectic Medicine and Surgery (Atlanta)—"Its anatomy room, containing a single cadaver, is indescribably foul. . . . Nothing more disgraceful calling itself a medical school can be found anywhere."

Kansas Medical College (Topeka)—"The dissecting room is indescribably filthy; it contained, in addition to necessary tables, a single, badly hacked cadaver and was simultaneously used as a chicken yard."

Maryland Medical College (Baltimore)—"The school building is wretchedly dirty . . . one neglected and filthy room is set aside for bacteriology, pathology, and histology: a few dirty test-tubes stand around in pans and old cigar-boxes."

St. Louis College of Physicians and Surgeons—"The school is one of the worst in the country."

Pulte Medical College (Cincinnati)—"Anything more woe-begone than the laboratories of this institution would be difficult to imagine. The dissecting room is a dark apartment in the basement."

Chattanooga (Tenn.) Medical College—"This is a typical example of the schools that claim to exist for the sake of the poor boy and the back country."

In a chapter on "Medical Sects," Flexner pays his respects in no uncertain terms to dissenting faiths among the American medical schools. He found no sectarian institutions in Canada, but thirty-two in the United States, divided among homeopathic, eclectic, physiomedical, and osteopathic. Standards for them all were almost invariably low. The homeopathic schools, in Flexner's view, furnished "a striking demonstration of the incompatibility of science and dogma," while "the eight osteopathic schools fairly reek with commercialism. Their catalogues are a mass of hysterical exaggerations, alike of the earning and

of the curative power of osteopathy." To control the
medical dissenter, Flexner recommends that all practitioners of the healing art be required by law to meet a rigidly
enforced preliminary educational standard; that every
school possess requisite facilities; and every licensed physician demonstrate a practical knowledge of the body and
its afflictions.

Flexner's mission, as he conceived it, was by no means
limited to destructive criticism of existing medical education. He was anxious to find remedies, to point toward the
road for reconstruction. The first essential, Flexner believed, was to reduce the number of medical schools and
to improve their product. Several principles should govern
such a reorganization and reconstitution: (1) A medical
school should be a department of a university, preferably
located in a large city, in order to procure clinical material; (2) it is possible, however, even in small communities
to develop superior medical schools, if high scientific ideals
are maintained, the university control is real, and strong
financial support is provided; (3) there should be only one
school to a single community, to avoid needless expense,
eliminate competition for students, to recruit one strong
faculty, and to assure adequate hospital facilities; (4)
since students tend to study medicine in their own state,
the schools should be well distributed geographically.

To make his recommendation specific and graphic,
Flexner included a map showing the suggested number,
location, and distribution of medical schools. His proposal,
in brief, was to reduce the 155 existing schools to thirty-
one, a step which "would deprive of a medical school no
section that is now capable of maintaining one," and
would provide a system actually able to produce twice as
many doctors as the country needed.

The right and duty of the state to regulate medical
education are emphasized by Flexner. "The physician is a
social instrument," he notes, and further, "practically the
medical school is a public service corporation. It is char-
tered by the state; it utilizes public hospitals on the ground
of the social nature of its service. The medical school
cannot then escape social criticism and regulation." To the
argument that state control impairs individual freedom,
Flexner replies, "Society forbids a company of physicians
to pour out upon the community a horde of ill trained
physicians . . . restriction put upon the liberty, so-called, of

a dozen doctors increases the effectual liberty of all other citizens."

In his autobiography, *I Remember*, published thirty years later, Flexner recounts the reaction to his report:

> It produced an immediate and profound sensation, "making," as we say nowadays, "the front page." The medical profession and the faculties of the medical schools, as well as the state boards of examiners, were absolutely flabbergasted by the pitiless exposure. We were threatened with lawsuits, and in one instance actually sued for libel for $150,000. I received anonymous letters warning me that I should be shot if I showed myself in Chicago, whereupon I went there to make a speech before a meeting called by the Council on Medical Education and returned unharmed.

State boards of examiners accepted the report and the press spread its findings among the general public. Medical schools which had been operated mainly for profit went out of business. A number of schools pooled their resources to survive and independent schools sought university connections. Seven schools in Louisville, Kentucky, became one. Fifteen in Chicago were shortly consolidated into three. Writing in 1924, fifteen years after his original investigation, Flexner reported that the number of schools had been cut in half, weak schools had been almost wholly eliminated, matriculation requirements had been tightened, everywhere equipment and facilities had been improved, and laboratory subjects were being taught by full-time, specially trained teachers.

Following completion of his study, Flexner was asked by the Rockefeller Foundation: What amount of money spent on what project would result in the greatest initial reform in medical education? The most needed reform, responded Flexner, was to pay clinical professors full salaries to free them from the necessity of outside practice. On his recommendation, the Rockefeller Foundation gave Johns Hopkins one and a half million dollars to endow professorial chairs in medicine, surgery, obstetrics, and pediatrics. Subsequently, Flexner influenced Rockefeller to grant $50,000,000 to the General Education Board for medical research. Matching funds multiplied the original a dozen times, adding some $600,000,000 to the

endowment of American medical schools. George Eastman was persuaded to donate $5,000,000 for the Roches-
ter Medical School, the beginning of that institution's
distinguished reputation.

Flexner, who was in his early forties when he finished
his survey of American medical education, lived to the
ripe age of ninety-two. His highly productive career in
later years was marked by a study of medical education in
Europe; an inquiry, for the Rockefeller Foundation, into
prostitution in Europe, inspired by a grand jury investigation of prostitution, white slavery, and corrupt police
organization that had rocked New York; service with the
General Education Board to uplift education in the South;
the writing of another highly influential book, *Universities: American, English, German;* and the creation and
directorship of the Institute for Advanced Study at Princeton.

16–AMERICA'S MOST USEFUL CITIZEN

JANE ADDAMS' *Twenty Years at Hull-House*

WHEN JANE ADDAMS founded Hull House in 1889, there were no trained social workers in America and not until several years later a department of sociology in an American university. In no city in the nation, however, was there a more crying need for social-minded citizens than in Chicago toward the end of the nineteenth century.

In approximately a half century, Chicago had grown from a trading post mired down in mud to a roaring commercial city of a million inhabitants, second largest in the land. Two thirds of the population was foreign-born and a high proportion of the remainder was second-generation Irish or German. The greater part of Chicago was a jungle of ramshackle wooden tenements and unpaved streets. As described by Jane Addams in her famous autobiography, *Twenty Years at Hull-House,* "The streets are inexpressibly dirty, the number of schools inadequate, sanitary legislation unenforced, the street lighting bad, the paving miserable and altogether lacking in the alleys and smaller streets, and the stables foul beyond description. . . . Rear tenements flourish; many houses have no water supply save the faucet in the back yard, there are no fire-escapes, the garbage and ashes are placed in wooden boxes which are fastened to the street pavement."

Into this great melting pot swarmed thousands of immigrant people, a world in miniature, drawn from every quarter of the globe—Italians, Russians, Jews, Germans, Negroes, Greeks, Poles, French Canadians, and dozens of other nationalities—lured from their homes by tales of America's wealth and now predominantly trapped in Chicago's sweatshops. The poor were further handicapped, in most instances, by their ability to speak only foreign languages, by remaining wedded to Old World customs, by illiteracy, and by lack of skilled training.

Jane Addams followed a circuitous route on her way to Hull House. Born in 1860 in the town of Cedarville, Illinois, to well-to-do Quaker parents, she suffered in her early years from curvature of the spine, eventually corrected by an operation. After graduation from Rockford Seminary, she entered the Women's Medical College of Philadelphia, but within a few months the spinal difficulty sent her to a hospital for a prolonged stay. Following recovery, on her physician's advice she dropped her ambition to study medicine and spent the next two years touring Europe.

In the course of her travels abroad, Jane Addams' future career began to take shape. She was profoundly shocked by the London slums, where she "received an ineradicable impression of the wretchedness of East London," and the terribly overcrowded quarters of the poor, where she saw "huge masses of ill-clad people clamoring around hucksters' carts," bidding for decaying vegetables and fruit. The beginnings of her lifetime interest in the labor movement came with attendance at a meeting of the London match girls, who were on strike against low wages.

"It is hard to tell," wrote Jane Addams, "just when the very simple plan which afterward developed into the Settlement began to form itself in my mind . . . but I gradually became convinced that it would be a good thing to rent a house in a part of the city where many primitive and actual needs are found." The brutalities of a Spanish bullfight which she witnessed in Madrid apparently influenced further her desire to eliminate cruelty and suffering from the world.

The plan which a year later led to the creation of the Hull House settlement was broached to an old-time school friend and traveling companion, Ellen Gates Starr, who enthusiastically agreed to join her in the venture.

For a model, Jane Addams decided to emulate Toynbee Hall in London, the world's first social settlement, founded four years earlier by a group of Oxford University students who were dedicated to improving conditions in the poorest districts. Here in the heart of the Whitechapel district, the most evil and unhappy section of London's East End, a number of intensely social-minded young men

had come to live and work. The London experiment
provided Jane Addams with a vital clue in her ambition to
bring American college women closer to the harsh realities
of life. Without the example of Toynbee Hall, Hull House
may never have been established. Jane Addams was influenced during her London sojourn, too, by the socialistic
thought of William Morris, the Webbs, and young George
Bernard Shaw.

Following her return to the United States, Jane Addams
spent several months searching the slums of Chicago for a
suitable home for the new settlement. The quest ended,
she writes, when one "Sunday afternoon in the early
spring, on the way to a Bohemian mission in the carriage
of one of its founders, we passed a fine old house standing
well back from the street, surrounded on three sides by a
broad piazza which was supported by wooden pillars of
exceptionally pure Corinthian design and proportion." The
house was located at the junction of Blue Island Avenue
and Halstead and Harrison Streets. It had been built in
1856 by a pioneer citizen, Charles J. Hull, long before the
area became overrun by teeming thousands of immigrants, who now existed mainly in dirty, overcrowded
shacks. In the interim, Hull House had been used as a
factory, furniture warehouse, and home for the aged. Its
immediate neighbors were a saloon and an undertaker's
establishment.

To Jane Addams, the Hull House district constituted an
ideal area in which to apply her ambitious designs. The
streets were deep in mud, three or four families shared a
spigot in the yard, there were only three bathtubs for the
jam-packed thousands in a radius of a third of a mile,
dirty children crawled up and down rickety stairways and
out over the gutters, housewives in strange headdresses
threw slops into the streets, garbage was rarely collected
and rank odors came from stables and poor sewage disposal. It was a society in which the strong and the ruthless
forged ahead and the weak and the helpless were doomed
to defeat. Social welfare as a function of government was
virtually non-existent.

Hull House was the beginning of what was to become a
major movement to ameliorate the condition of the very
poor in America, the settlement house idea, the original
concept of social work. The aim of Hull House, as stated
in the papers for its incorporation, was "to provide a
center for a higher social life; to institute and maintain

educational and philanthropic enterprises, and to investi
gate and improve the conditions in the industrial districts
of Chicago."

The first and abiding concern of Jane Addams, Ellen
Starr, and some twenty volunteers when Hull House
opened its doors was children. Babies were dying by the
hundreds because of dirt, ignorance, and malnutrition.
Mothers were invited to bring their babies in for baths; a
public playground for children, the first in Chicago, was
laid out on the site of some demolished houses donated by
a wealthy young man, William Kent; a kindergarten was
organized to care for the young children of the numerous
working mothers in the area—children who had previously
roamed the streets unprotected or had remained locked up
in their tenement rooms all day. The cost in human terms
of forced parental neglect was poignantly described by
Jane Addams in the cases of three crippled children
brought to the house:

> One had fallen out of a third-storey window, another
> had been burned, and the third had a curved spine
> due to the fact that for three years he had been tied
> all day long to the leg of the kitchen table, only
> released at noon by his older brother who hastily ran
> in from a neighboring factory to share his lunch with
> him.

Illinois had no child labor law except for children employed in mines, and consequently children as young as
four were cruelly exploited under sweatshop conditions,
coming home with pennies earned at the rate of four cents
an hour. The parents were frequently to blame, Jane
Addams notes, for working children contributed to their
support and the "parents gradually found it easy to live
upon their earnings."

In the needle trades, expensive garments were cut in
unsafe factories, then sewed together at home by women
and children. Jane Addams demanded factory safety laws
and the prohibition of child labor. A "Jane Club" was
founded in 1891 for the benefit of factory girls, a boarding
club to provide mutual support. Other groups were organizing themselves into the first large-scale women's labor
unions. In 1904, Jane Addams was elected vice-president
of the National Women's Trade Union League. As she
observed some years later, "even in the very first years of

Hull House we began to discover that our activities were gradually extending from the settlement to a participation in city and national undertakings."

A lively campaign carried on by Jane Addams and her associates led to an investigation, by a special committee of the Illinois legislature, of sweatshop conditions in Chicago, and later to the first factory law in Illinois, regulating sanitary conditions and fixing fourteen as the age at which a child might be employed.

Until the agitation for labor legislation began, Hull House had been non-controversial. Now there were protests that it was fostering radicalism. Employers, politicians, and slum parents banded together "to run Jane Addams out of town." She was interfering with business and must be stopped. One manufacturer offered $50,000 to support Hull House, if Jane Addams would cease her lobbying for safety laws and "drop all this nonsense about a sweat-shop bill of which she knew nothing."

Jane Addams' efforts to have better sewers built and to improve garbage collection were violently objected to by grafting ward politicians. The women of the neighborhood were sent out in pairs to find and report violations of the sanitary code. The reports were ignored by the City Council until the newspapers began to play them up. By now, the mayor was sufficiently impressed to appoint Jane Addams to the "political plum" of garbage inspector for her ward, at a salary of a thousand dollars a year. The job was no sinecure. She was up at six in the morning to see that the men were early at work, and followed the loaded wagons, "uneasily dropping their contents at intervals, to their dreary destination at the dump"; she forced the contractor to increase the number of wagons from nine to seventeen, took careless landlords into court because they would not provide proper garbage receptacles, and arrested tenants who tried to make the garbage wagons carry away the contents of their stables. Three years in the job were enough to stir up the city and to start Chicago on the way toward cleaning itself up.

Some battles were won and then temporarily lost. An eight-hour-day law for women in factories and workshops was declared unconstitutional by the State Supreme Court, and some years passed before adequate child labor laws were enacted and enforced in Illinois.

At times the warfare was bitter. Governor Altgeld had used all the powers of his office to support Jane Addams and her associates in their fight for humane laws to protect women and children and had backed the radical eight-hour-day proposal. But Altgeld signed his own political death warrant in pardoning three anarchists accused of participating in the Haymarket Riot of 1886. When "Viper" Altgeld, as he was referred to by the Chicago *Tribune,* died in 1902, the only speakers at his funeral were his law partner Clarence Darrow and Jane Addams.

One reason for Hull House being under frequent suspicion and attack was its sponsorship of the Working People's Social Science Club. Once weekly for seven years the club met to hear the airing of various shades of political, economic, and social opinion. Speakers included anarchists, socialists, and other varieties of radicals. "Visitors refused to distinguish," wrote Jane Addams, "between the sentiments expressed by its members in the heat of discussion and the opinions held by the residents themselves." She added, "During this decade Chicago seemed divided into two classes; those who held that 'business is business' and who were therefore annoyed at the very notion of social control, and the radicals, who claimed that nothing could be done to really moralize the industrial situation until society should be reorganized."

Archibald MacLeish, on the occasion of the one-hundredth-anniversary observance of the birth of Jane Addams, viewed the controversies in which she was involved as follows:

The decent and responsible opinion of her time was either against her or indifferent to the issue she raised. It was not a crank who said that Jane Addams ought to be hanged to the nearest lamp post: it was a solid citizen who, like other solid citizens, regarded any legislation aimed at the protection of children in factories as an attack on his right, as a citizen of a free country, to do as he pleased. And it was not an irresponsible newspaper which hounded her as a radical: it was a newspaper most of the responsible people of the city read.

On the political front, Jane Addams was unaffiliated, convinced as she was that "the Settlement cannot limit its friends to any one political party or economic school" if its civic ideals were to be attained. The only political campaign in which she took part was in support of Theodore Roosevelt's Progressive Party in 1912. It was Roosevelt who characterized her as "America's most useful citizen."

Undaunted by her traducers, Jane Addams continued to direct Hull House in a multifarious program of social betterment. Within the Settlement itself, one building after another was added, to provide a gymnasium for boys; a coffee house where people could get hot drinks and good food without going to saloon bars; studio, art museum, music room, and theater; bedrooms and clubrooms for working girls. Hull House expanded until in time it grew into a kind of community center for all Chicago. Immigrants came for Americanization lessons, to sing folk songs, to hear discussions, practice such arts and crafts as painting, drawing, pottery, carving, spinning, and weaving, and to act in plays. Children came to play, young people to dance. In the constant procession, numbering tens of thousands each year, also were girls in trouble who had been turned out of their homes; men out of jobs or in trouble with the law; and multitudes of other sick, tired, or lonely people seeking help. Hull House thus evolved into a clearinghouse for every kind of social service, acting as an experimental laboratory for social reform.

Hull House research helped substantially to lift the burden of disease and bad housing from its neighborhood. By 1898, the ward's mortality rate fell from third to seventh in the city. A model Tenement House Ordinance was passed in 1901; a bacteriological study by Dr. Alice Hamilton, following a typhoid epidemic, led to the dismissal for incompetence of eleven out of twenty-four employees of the Sanitary Bureau; a new law regulating the sale of narcotics was enacted in 1907. Other investigations were undertaken of impure milk supplies, the qualifications of midwives, and occupational diseases—all inspired or supported by the Hull House experience.

A frequent misconception is that "Saint Jane" gave up comfort, ease, and all the amenities of life to share in the poverty of Chicago's needy. In actuality, she had no desire to sink to the poverty level. On the contrary, her purpose was to raise the level of all those about her. Under her direction, Hull House was a place to encourage beauty and to obtain maximum enjoyment from widely diversified interests and activities—music, art, literature, theater and dance, education, intellectual discussion, physical health—in short, to develop the whole person. Public and social agencies, to justify their existence, Jane Addams believed, must promote everyone's health and happiness. She was not, as she remarked on numerous occasions, a reformer. She wanted to establish a place in and around which a fuller life might grow for others *and for herself:* "The good we secure for ourselves is precarious and uncertain until it is secured for all of us and incorporated into *our common life.*"

A new dimension was added to Jane Addams' life with the outbreak of World War I. Here her Quaker background came strongly to the fore. Before 1914, as she wrote later,

> my temperament and habit had always kept me rather in the middle of the road; in politics as well as social reform I had been for 'the best possible.' But now I was pushed far toward the left on the subject of the war and I became gradually convinced that in order to make the position of the pacifist clear it was perhaps necessary that at least a small number of us should be forced into an unequivocal position.

The story of those years is told by Jane Addams in volume two of her memoirs, *The Second Twenty Years at Hull-House.* The position occupied by pacifists and war opponents was a lonely one. As expressed by Jane Addams, "no one knew better than we how feeble and futile we were against the impregnable weight of public opinion, the appalling imperviousness, the coagulation of motives, the univeral confusion of a world at war."

Jane Addams' opposition to war was related closely to her lifetime concern with equal rights for women. A world which still resorted to violence to settle its disputes would always give women lower status, penalizing them for their inferior strength. The place of women throughout the world, Jane Addams was certain, was threatened by the coming of World War I. In one of her most bitterly attacked speeches, she declared that war was an old men's game inflicted on the young, who had little enthusiasm for fighting as a method of settling disputes.

Before America's entry into the war, Jane Addams had organized an American Women's Peace Party, which by 1916 had a membership of forty thousand. She also helped to establish the Women's International League for Peace and Freedom in 1915 and served as its president for fourteen years. When in 1931 she received the Nobel Prize for Peace, the entire award, amounting to $16,000, was donated to the Women's International League.

Fortunately for Jane Addams, in the midst of this crisis in her life she received an invitation from Herbert Hoover to assist him in the Department of Food Administration, of which he had been made director in May 1917. A perfect outlet for her humanitarian inclinations was provided by the huge task of distributing supplies for the relief of starving populations in the allied and neutral countries of Europe.

Even after the war, however, Jane Addams remained a controversial figure. Her earlier activities in support of slum clearance and labor legislation had aroused the suspicion and hostility of businessmen and conservative politicians. Now her campaign against war and for peace brought her the hatred of the professional patriots. She was denounced as un-American by the American Legion, and the Daughters of the American Revolution condemned her as "a factor in a movement to destroy civilization and Christianity." Because of her uncompromising stand for peace, her popularity suffered enormously and until the coming of the Great Depression her leadership of welfare and charitable movements was questioned. During that period, she writes, "there is little doubt that social workers exhibited many symptoms of this panic and with a kind of protective instinct carefully avoided any identification with the phraseology of social reform."

The advent of the Depression and the New Deal reinstated Jane Addams as a national heroine. Many of her former associates became directly involved with the New Deal's relief, social security, and public housing measures and their administration. Shortly before Jane Addams' death in 1935, she was feted in Washington on the occasion of her seventy-fifth birthday as no woman had been before. In national and international circles she gained the kind of high esteem later accorded Eleanor Roosevelt.

Long before the end of her career, however, Jane Addams had begun to experience a certain amount of disillusionment with Hull House and what it and like institutions could accomplish. "One of the first lessons we learned at Hull House," she wrote, "was that private beneficence is totally inadequate to deal with the vast numbers of the city's disinherited." As early as 1894, in another period of depression, her doubts had been expressed: "In the face of desperate hunger and need, these activities could not but seem futile and superficial." Despite Hull House and similar settlements in other cities, that is, in the face of all the ameliorative activities in progress, poverty, the slums, crime and vice, misgovernment, illiteracy, and exploitation of human beings remained. After nearly fifty years of valiant effort, Hull House was still surrounded by slums, merely an island in a sea of human misery. Only the municipal, state, and federal governments, obviously, possessed resources adequate to solve the tremendous problems—if they were capable of solution.

It is a curious phenomenon that Jane Addams should be so much better remembered than a number of her contemporaries whose achievements in public life were of comparable importance. Jill Conway, writing in the anthology *The Woman in America*, points out that Lillian Wald in New York began settlement work at approximately the same time, was instrumental in establishing nursing as a career for women and in founding the Federal Children's Bureau; Mary Richmond was outstanding as a social worker; Florence Sabin and Alice Hamilton had notable careers of public service in the medical profession; Florence Kelley directed the National Consumers' League in its campaigns for social reform and social legislation; Julia Lathrop's work as head of the Federal Children's Bureau was highly constructive; and Grace and Edith Abbott made significant contributions as guardians of immigrant groups. The explantion for the difference, Miss Conway decides, is Jane Addams' "charismatic personality," her exceptional intellectual endowment, and her own very real achievements in public life. Her prolific writings, especially *Twenty Years at Hull-House* and *The Second Twenty Years at Hull-House*, also helped to spread her fame and gain general recognition.

Nearly all of the forlorn causes for which Jane Addams fought were in time won and even her most controversial ideas obtained wide public acceptance. Before she died, most of the states had enacted child labor laws and safety regulations for men and women in industry were well established, as were programs of adult education, public playgrounds, day nurseries, and sanitary codes. Another cherished ideal, woman suffrage, for which she had long campaigned, was achieved in 1920, when the Nineteenth

Amendment extended the franchise to women in all states of the Union.

The British labor leader John Burns once commented that Jane Addams was "the only saint America has produced," and she has continued to be known as Saint Jane to millions around the world.

17–SCIENCE OF EFFICIENCY

FREDERICK WINSLOW TAYLOR'S
The Principles of Scientific Management

FREDERICK WINSLOW TAYLOR's approach to knowledge was strikingly similar to that of the seventeenth-century French philosopher René Descartes, who maintained that the unreliable, the vague, and the imaginary could be eliminated only by "methodical doubt," a systematic, all-encompassing skepticism. Taylor, too, held firmly to the belief that when starting an experiment in any field everything should be questioned—question the very foundations upon which the art rests, question the simplest, the most universally accepted facts; prove everything.

Taylor demonstrated conclusively that the scientific method could be applied to the practical problems of business and industry, to everyone's mutual benefit. The ideas of scientific management, such as time studies, were not new with Taylor, but his contributions to the field were highly original. In essence, he asserted, first, that every process of industry, however simple, could be subjected to scientific analysis to determine how it can be performed most efficiently, both from the point of view of maximum output and of minimum worker fatigue; and, second, that if industry were reorganized in harmony with the research findings, the workers and capitalists would profit through higher wages and increased dividends. It was Frederick Winslow Taylor who introduced the concept of scientific management to the world, thereby stirring up a ferment that has been a major force in shaping the twentieth century.

Taylor was a native of Pennsylvania, born in 1856, his father a Quaker and his mother from a family of New Bedford whalers. From early childhood he displayed inventive ability. At Exeter he was head of his class and captain of the baseball team, the first man to pitch overhand (because it was the most effective method); and later he designed a spoon-shaped racket with which he teamed with a friend to win the national doubles tennis championship in 1881.

At the age of eighteen, Taylor began an apprenticeship as a patternmaker and machinist in a small shop in Philadelphia. A few years afterward he went to work for the Midvale Steel Company, first as ordinary laborer and then, through successive promotions, as timekeeper, machinist, gang boss, foreman, assistant engineer, and chief engineer. Meanwhile, he earned a degree in mechanical engineering at Stevens Institute.

While still in his twenties, Taylor started to develop and prove the value of what he termed the task system, which others called the Taylor System, and which eventually became known as scientific management. As gang boss and foreman he began to ask himself such questions as "Which is the best way to do a particular job?" and "What is a reasonable day's work?" Taylor attempted to increase output by putting pressure on the men, and a power struggle erupted immediately between boss and workers. The boss won the battle, though not without leaving scars. Soon Taylor came to see that management lacked any scientific basis for pressurizing a worker for higher production without knowing what is a proper day's work. Experiments were begun to establish the facts, initially with the Midvale and later with the Bethlehem Steel Company. First there had to be discovered the best method of accomplishing the task at hand, followed by teaching workers the preferred method, the maintenance of suitable work conditions, setting of definite time standards, and finally paying the worker a premium in extra wages for doing the task according to specifications.

Taylor's objectives as he described them later in his best-known book, *The Principles of Scientific Management* (1911), were these:

First. The development of a science for each element of a man's work, thereby replacing the old rule-of-thumb methods.

Second. The selection of the best worker for each particular task and then training, teaching, and developing the workman; in place of the former practice of allowing the worker to select his own task and train himself as best he could.

Third. The development of a spirit of hearty cooperation between the management and the men in the carrying on of the activities in accordance with the principles of the developing science.

Fourth. The division of the work into almost equal shares between the management and the workers, each department taking over the work for which it is better fitted; instead of the former condition, in which almost all of the work and the greater part of the responsibility were thrown on the men.

Taylor realized that industrial management involved more than investigating methods of getting the work accomplished, but he insisted that one of management's first duties is "to develop a science for each element of a man's work," and a scientific approach should be used in solving every problem that arose.

An illustration of the Taylor method is an investigation for the Bethlehem Steel Works in 1898. One task that came to his attention was shoveling. From four hundred to six hundred men were employed in the yard, a majority of them engaged in shoveling iron ore or rice coal. Each man owned his own shovel, chosen because he liked its look or feel. Taylor found that shovelers were lifting four or five pounds when handling rice coal and up to forty pounds when moving ore. He immediately set out to determine what is an ideal shovel-load to move the most weight in a day, regardless of the material. Two good shovelers were set to work in different parts of the yard and two time-study men with stop-watches were assigned to study their work. At first, large shovels, holding thirty-eight pounds of ore, were used, and the number of shovelfuls and tonnage for the day counted. The next day a shorter shovel holding thirty-four pounds was used and the tonnage moved increased. The procedure was continued, from very heavy to very light loads, until it was found that the ideal—the level at which the worker moved a maximum amount of material—was twenty-two and a half pounds.

Thereafter, the company supplied the shovels, designed for the type of work to be done. The production of each man was measured or weighed at the end of the day and if he came up to the established standard, he was paid a

60 per cent bonus. If a man failed to earn the bonus, an instructor was sent out to show the worker how to do his job in the proper way and so earn the extra pay. After three and a half years, Taylor was doing the same amount of work in the yards with 140 men as was formerly done by four hundred to six hundred. After paying all added expenses, such as planning the work, measuring the workers' output, paying a bonus each day, and maintaining the toolroom, there remained a savings of $78,000 per year.

It has been suggested that even if Frederick Winslow Taylor had never lived, scientific management would have developed, sooner or later. Industry had grown by leaps and bounds during the nineteenth century, the number of wage earners had increased, invested capital was gaining, and manufacturing was expanding. The American phenomenon of mass production was well on its way. Prior to Taylor, during the first century of the Industrial Revolution, industrial methods had proceeded by trial and error. The sole guide was experience, rather than scientific study and experimentation. The wide attention received by Taylor's theories and their practical application in numerous plants undoubtedly hastened industry's adoption of the principles of scientific management. Great gains in productivity grew out of the techniques, not from increased pressure on the workers, but from elimination of the waste of workers' time and machine time, getting rid of lost motion, the co-ordination of materials, and generally sound planning.

One of Taylor's associates summed up the phase through which industry was then passing as follows: "We are passing from a stage in which there was a simple and unconscious following of tradition into a stage of self-consciousness in which we are moved to subject our habits and our motives to severe self-scrutiny. It is a very painful stage to have arrived at."

As a witness before a Special House Committee in 1912, Taylor was asked to define "scientific management," as conceived by him. His reply was stated first in negative terms:

Scientific management is not any efficiency device, not a device of any kind for securing efficiency; nor is it any bunch or group of efficiency devices. It is not a new system of figuring costs; it is not a new scheme of paying men; it is not a piecework system;

it is not a bonus system; it is not a premium system; it is no scheme for paying men; it is not holding a stop watch on a man and writing things down about him; it is not time study; it is not motion study nor an analysis of the movements of men; it is not the printing and ruling and unloading of a ton or two of blanks on a set of men and saying, "Here's your system; go use it." It is not divided foremanship or functional foremanship; it is not any of the devices which the average man calls to mind when scientific management is spoken of.

All of these ideas and devices were considered to be "useful adjuncts" to scientific management. The essence of scientific management in Taylor's mind, however, was a complete mental revolution on the part of both workers and management. It is in the interest of workers, management, and society in general, he held, to increase the production of needed commodities. The avoidance of waste of human and material resources, therefore, should be the goal of labor and management. The workman must keep in mind his duties toward his work, his fellowmen, and his employers; on management's side—the foreman, the superintendent, the owner of the business, the board of directors—there must be recognition of their duties toward their fellow workers in management, toward their workmen, and toward all of their daily problems. "Without this complete mental revolution on both sides," Taylor asserts categorically, "scientific management does not exist."

The primary objective of every manufacturing or business enterprise under the capitalist system, Taylor stresses, is to produce a profit, a "surplus." On the size of the surplus will depend the return for management and the level of wages for the workmen. The division of the surplus, as between profits and wages, is the chief source of dissension between employers and employees. Gradually the two sides come to look upon each other as antagonists—"pulling apart and matching the strength of the one against the strength of the other."

It is these attitudes which Taylor seeks to change through his "mental revolution." By substituting friendly co-operation and mutual helpfulness for antagonism and strife, the surplus may be vastly increased and become adequate to provide for the needs of both capital and labor.

A corollary principle, Taylor states, is that "both sides must recognize as essential the substitution of exact scientific investigation and knowledge for the old individual judgement or opinion, either of the workman or the boss, in all matters relating to the work done in the establishment. And this applies both as to the methods to be employed in doing the work and the time in which each job should be done."

These two principles, then, are regarded by Taylor as the absolutely essential elements of scientific management: the co-operation of management and labor to produce the largest possible surplus and the substitution of exact scientific knowledge for opinions or the old rule of thumb or individual knowledge.

The responsibilities of management are emphasized in no uncertain terms by Taylor. He notes that under the old "initiative and incentive" arrangement, the worker carried practically the entire responsibility for the details of his work and frequently for his implements as well. All that is changed under scientific management, which requires an equal division of responsibility between management and workmen. The planning done by the worker under the former system is done under the new system by the management, in accordance with the rules, laws, and formulas of scientific management. The work of every employee is fully planned out by the management at least one day in advance, and each man receives complete written instructions, describing in detail the task which he is to accomplish, as well as the means to be used in doing the work.

Summing up, in his *The Principles of Scientific Management*, Taylor points out that there is no single element but a combination of elements which constitute sound scientific management:

Science, not a rule of thumb.
Harmony, not discord.
Cooperation, not individualism.
Maximum output, in place of restricted output.
The development of each man to his greatest efficiency and prosperity.

The Principles of Scientific Management became the

bible of modern management and within a short time was translated into a dozen languages. Opposition from labor, however, developed almost immediately. Particular objections were raised to Taylor's incentive wage system, which penalized substandard performance, and to his emphasis on time and motion studies. Hostility to increased production was general. As Taylor stated in his testimony before a Special House Committee in 1912, "Each man in a particular working group feels that in his town or section or particular industry there is, in the coming year, only about so much work to be done. As far as he can see, if he were to double his output, and if the rest of the men were to double their output tomorrow or next week or next month or next year, he can see no other outcome except that one-half of the workmen engaged with him would be thrown out of work."

Taylor confessed to a certain amount of sympathy with this point of view, or at least understanding of it, though he insisted "that in no case has the permanent effect of increasing the output per individual in the trade been that of throwing men out of work, but the effect has always been to make work for more men."

Labor opposition resulted in part from misuse of the Taylor system. After standards had been established, factory managers would attempt to reduce labor costs by unscrupulous wage cuts, if they felt workmen were being paid too much. The result sometimes was harder work at no more take-home pay. Worker reaction, naturally, was violent. Thus, despite the many favorable installations started by Taylor, Congress was influenced in 1913 to pass legislation banning time-study work in government-operated plants. The provision, added as a rider to an appropriation bill, read as follows:

No part of the appropriation made in this Act shall be available for the salary or pay of any officer, manager, superintendent, foreman or other person having charge of the work of any employee of the United States Government while making or causing to be made with a stopwatch, or other time-measuring device, a time study of any job of any such employee between the starting and completion thereof, or of the movements of any such employee while engaged upon such work; nor shall any part of the appropriation made in this Act be available to pay any premiums or bonus or cash reward to any employee in addition to his regular wages, except as may be otherwise authorized in this Act.

As one commentator suggested, "Probably no scientist since the days of witchcraft has been so condemned by having his scientific methods legislated against by a great nation." Not until 1947 did the House of Representatives pass a bill which allowed the use of time study, and in 1949 the prohibition against the use of stopwatches was dropped from appropriation language.

Taylor, of course, defended the use of a stopwatch in determining how fast work ought to be done. Time, he said, remains one of the most important elements, and is a frequent matter of dispute between employer and employee. "The old way of guessing as to how fast a man ought to do a thing," he maintained, "is quite as unsatisfactory to the workmen as to those on the management's side."

Fundamental to the Taylor system was the standardization of both men and machines for maximum efficiency in production. On the machine side, the most advanced technology was required, developed in innumerable laboratory experiments, all directed toward speeding up and increasing the volume of output. The human side is far more complex. The workmen considered that time studies, for example, were an infringement on their right to decide for themselves how much work they could do in a given period. Taylor saw that special incentives had to be offered the workers, if their ill will, efforts at sabotage, and general opposition were to be overcome. Higher wages would be paid to the workmen who came up to performance standards and labor would share with management the responsibility for obtaining the largest output. "I think," said Taylor, "that the time will come when the trade-unionist will realize that the true and permanent road to prosperity lies in so educating themselves that they will be able and willing to do more work in return for larger pay, rather than to do less work for the same pay, or the same work for larger pay."

One of Taylor's warm admirers, Associate Supreme Court Justice Louis D. Brandeis, noted at the time of Taylor's death in 1915: "We who have had occasion to consider the hostility of labor leaders to the introduction of scientific management know that the hostility has in large measure been due to misunderstanding. Much of all the waste which Taylor undertook to eliminate has no direct relation to the specific functions for the working-man. It deals with waste in machinery, in supplies, in planning, in adjustment of production and distribution—matters in which changes cannot possibly affect the workman injuriously." Labor's attitude, Brandeis believed, could be changed by education and through securing the affirmative co-operation of the labor organizations.

Taylor was accused on various occasions of animosity toward labor unions—a charge which he vigorously denied. In his testimony before the Special House Committee, he declared himself in favor of unions, adding, "they have done a great amount of good in this country and in England; I am heartily in favor of those elements of trade unions which are good, and I am equally opposed to those elements of trade unions which are bad; and they have bad elements just as they have good." Taylor supported the unions in their demands for high wages and short hours, but took strong issue with them on their policy of deliberately restricting output.

It is of interest to compare Taylor's views on scientific management with those of his contemporary, Henry Ford. In the same year that Taylor's *Principles* appeared, Ford introduced the assembly line in the production of motor-cars. Ford's aim was to eliminate manpower as far as possible and to replace it by automatic or semiautomatic machines. While Taylor was trying to improve efficiency by reducing laziness and waste, Ford was working toward the same objective with machines. The two men shared a common economic philosophy, however, as is revealed by a statement in Ford's book *Moving Forward,* wherein his goals were defined: "To make an ever-increasing large quantity of goods of the best possible quality, to make them in the best and most economical fashion, and to force them on the market. To strive always for higher quality and lower prices as well as lower costs." Both Ford and Taylor believed that industrial progress could abolish poverty.

In his 1912 testimony before the congressional committee, Taylor summarized the accomplishments of scientific management up to that point. He reported that the system had been "introduced in a great number and variety of industries in this country"; the output of the individual workman had doubled, on the average; in most cases, savings had resulted in material reductions in selling costs;

wages had increased 30 to 100 per cent; and hours of work were being shortened. Further, despite the difficulties in changing from the old to the new type of management, there had not been a single strike among the men working under scientific management.

The development and promotion of the concept of scientific management was only one of Taylor's accomplishments. To him also goes the credit for inventing high-speed steel, a revolutionary process based on some forty-thousand experiments over a period of twenty-six years. In addition, he standardized tools and equipment, invented or improved steam hammers, experimented in growing synthetic golf greens, and devised methods for moving full-grown trees and plants without injury.

The profound impact of Frederick Winslow Taylor in influencing the history of industry, in America and abroad, is unquestioned. He was the first to bring the scientific spirit directly to bear upon the problems of managing men and materials. His most lasting achievement was the establishment of business research. In the complexities of modern life, Roger Burlingame pointed out in reviewing Taylor's career, "with its vast coordination of enterprises, its mathematics of cost accounting, its on-the-nose production, buying and selling, a business or industry without a planning department would be about as effective as a car without a steering wheel." Taylor visualized these future trends and laid the foundation for the new era.

A more severe critic, Gerhard Masur, sees Taylorism as "one more step toward the ever-growing rationalization of the world," both in democratic and socialistic societies. Taylor thought that maximum production demanded standardization of labor, which in turn meant mechanization followed by depersonalization. While recognizing the drawbacks, Taylor was convinced they would be compensated for by higher wages and long hours of leisure, and freedom from drudgery, want, and famine around the world. But Masur contends that "Taylor and his followers were prone to close their eyes to the dreary side of industrialization and technocracy ... in all too many instances men and women have been converted into the cogs and wheels of a machinery which they neither understand nor control." Masur argues, too, that the greater output in industrial goods has not been followed by a rise in cultural standards nor by more meaningful use of leisure.

"The concentration on material goods," he thinks, "has unleashed a greed for more material goods"—a thesis continued by John Kenneth Galbraith's *The Affluent Society*.

Taylor's reputation and prestige in his own time are attested to by the organization in 1914 of the Taylor Society, which subsequently united with the Society of Industrial Engineers to form the Society for Advancement of Management, with a current membership of sixteen thousand and 280 local chapters.

18–ECONOMIC DETERMINISM IN PHILADELPHIA

CHARLES A. BEARD'S
An Economic Interpretation of the Constitution of the United States

COMPARABLE TO Turner's essay on the frontier, in its impact on the writing and teaching of American history, is Charles A. Beard's *An Economic Interpretation of the Constitution of the United States,* first published in 1913. No American historian in the twentieth century has had a wider following than Beard, who has exerted a large influence on scholars, students, and the general public. A prolific writer, the total sales of Beard's books are estimated at fifteen million copies. Though only thirty-nine years of age, he had become an established historian by the time his *Economic Interpretation of the Constitution* appeared. The book fitted the mood of the Populist movement—Roosevelt's Progressive Party—muckraking era, and created an immediate sensation.

The heart of Beard's "economic interpretation" is that the Constitution as adopted by the delegates meeting in Independence Hall in Philadelphia in 1787 represented a triumph of personal property interests, i.e., moneylenders, capitalists, security holders, and manufacturers, over the interests of small farmers and debtors. As seen by Beard, the Constitution was backed by merchants, moneylenders, and public creditors who were "constantly urged to support the Constitution on the ground that their economic security depended upon the establishment of the new national government." The opposing group was the agrarian interests who favored paper money as an easy way to pay off their debts. Most active on behalf of the Constitution, according to Beard, were those who wanted the interest and principal paid on the public debt and those working for commercial regulations favorable to shipping, manufacturing, and western land speculation.

In his opening chapter, Beard deals with certain historical interpretations of American beginnings. Spokesman for the first was the nineteenth-century historian George Bancroft, who believed that the Founding Fathers had acted under divine guidance, that they had been directed by God first to stage a democratic revolution and then to write a democratic constitution.

A second school of historial interpretation Beard calls the Teutonic, "because it ascribes the wonderful achievements of the English-speaking peoples to the peculiar political genius of the Germanic race." The innate racial qualities of the Anglo-Saxon world, in short, account for such phenomena as the development of the American Government.

Still another approach is made by so-called objective or scientific writers who avoid theories, concentrate upon facts, and occupy themselves with producing critical editions of documents.

All three schools of thought are rejected in whole or part by Beard in favor of economic interpretations of history, growing out of social controversies. Beard had evidently been influenced by reading Edwin R. A. Seligman's *The Economic Interpretation of History*, a popular little book issued a decade earlier. Also helping to shape his views were John Marshall's biography of George Washington and James Madison's writings on constitutional questions as presented in the *Federalist Papers*.

Particularly relevant in Beard's view was the Tenth Number of the *Federalist Papers*, by Madison, "the father of the Constitution" and later President of the United States. Therein Madison states:

> The diversity in the faculties of men, from which the rights of property originate, is not less an insuperable obstacle to a uniformity of interests. The protection of these faculties is the first object of government. From the protection of different and unequal faculties of acquiring property, the possession of different degrees and kinds of property immediately results; and from the influence of these on the sentiments and views of the respective proprietors, ensues a division of society into different interests and parties. . . . The most common and durable source of factions has

been the various and unequal distribution of property. Those who hold and those who are without property have ever formed distinct interests in society. Those who are creditors, and those who are debtors, fall under a like discrimination. A landed interest, a manufacturing interest, a mercantile interest, a moneyed interest, with many lesser interests, grow up of necessity in civilized nations and divide them into different classes, actuated by different sentiments and views. The regulation of these various and interfering interests form the principal task of modern legislation, and involves the spirit of party and faction in the necessary and ordinary operations of government.

Lending further substance to Beard's thesis were comments by John Marshall, Chief Justice of the U. S. Supreme Court, in his *The Life of George Washington*, published about twenty years after ratification of the Constitution. Marshall believed that economic conflict led to adoption of the Constitution. Previous to the meeting of the Convention in Philadelphia, the conflict was raging on several fronts: (1) extreme dissatisfaction on the part of the mercantile interest with the progress of trade under the Articles of Confederation, and increasing sentiment for vesting in Congress the necessary powers over the commerce of the United States; (2) the loss of faith in the old government by the public creditors, that is, investors in government securities ("That the debt of the United States should have greatly depreciated will excite no surprise," wrote Marshall, "when it is recollected that the government of the Union possessed no funds, and without the assent of jealous and independent sovereigns could acquire none to pay the accruing interest"); (3) different views of the rights of property, causing two parties to form in every state, one believing that public and private obligations should be met through the sound administration of justice and levying of taxes, and the second urging relaxation of rules to ease the debtor's burdens and the suspension of taxes. So sharp was the difference of views on property rights, Marshall noted, the Constitution barely escaped defeat altogether.

To substantiate his hypothesis that economic factors were of primary importance in the making of the Constitution, Beard undertook a survey of economic interests in 1787. The forces to be analyzed were five in number: the geographic distribution of money on hand and loaned and the names of the holders; the geographic distribution and ownership of the public securities; the geographic distribution of small mortgaged farms and their connection with various schemes for depreciation of the currency and impairment of the obligation of contract; the owners and operators in western lands, since speculation in these lands was one of the leading activities of capitalists of the time; and the geographic distribution of manufacturing establishments and the names of owners and investors.

Also having a direct bearing on the conception and ratification of the Constitution was the position of the disfranchised. Four major groups in the population had no vote: the slaves, the indentured servants, men unable to meet the property tests imposed by state constitutions and laws, and women. Naturally, none of these groups was represented in the Convention which drafted the Constitution. Furthermore, some members of the Convention were resolved to deny the ballot to such persons. James Madison, for example, warned his colleagues against the industrial masses of coming generations, in these terms:

> Viewing the subject in its merits alone, the freeholders of the country would be the safest depositories of Republican liberty. In future times a great majority of the people will not only be without landed, but any sort of property. These will either combine under the influence of their common situation; in which case, the rights of property and the public liberty will not be secure in their hands, or, which is more probable, they will become the tools of opulence and ambition; in which case there will be equal danger on another side.

Defenders of democracy, however, were not wholly lacking in the Convention. James Wilson of Pennsylvania asserted, "The majority of people wherever found ought in all questions to govern the minority. . . . Furthermore, if numbers be not a proper rule, why is not some better rule pointed out? No one has yet ventured to attempt it."

Nevertheless, in the government of checks and balances adopted by the Constitutional Convention, carefully drawn rules restricted the powers of majorities: The House of Representatives alone was subject to direct election by the mass of the people; the Senate was elected by the legislatures of the states, membership in which was almost uniformly based on property qualifications; the President was chosen by electors selected by the legislatures of the states; and the judiciary was chosen by the President and the Senate. In addition, terms of office were staggered, to prevent a complete change of government at one time, and a system of judicial control, rated by Beard as "the most unique contribution to the science of government which has been made by American political genius," was provided.

The possessors of property in 1787 were classified by Beard into several distinct groups. The holders of real property included first the small farmers, generally antagonistic to the seaboard groups, frequently in debt for their land, dependent upon the towns for capital to develop their resources, and constituting in general a large debtor class. A second group was the landed proprietors, "the manorial lords of the Hudson valley region," a peculiar aristocracy dominant in New York politics, opposed to land taxation and strong for states' rights. Finally, there were the slaveholders of the South, also landed proprietors, who were inclined to favor the Constitution because, for the most part, it would strengthen their economic interest.

Personal property owners could be divided into four groups. Money holders were less powerful than they subsequently became, but they were not insignificant. Under the Articles of Confederation, they were handicapped by the lack of protection for manufacturers, the absence of security in investments in western lands, discrimination against American shipping by foreign countries, attempts to depreciate the currency and to delay the collection of debts, and the lack of uniformity and stability in the monetary systems of the individual states. For this class a strong national government was obviously desirable. Even more directly concerned in the establishment of a stable national government were the holders of public securities, state and continental, for the government was not paying the interest on its debt and the securities had depreciated to a fraction of their par value. The third important group of personal property owners were the manufacturing and shipping population. A large amount of capital had been invested in the several branches of industry, and innumerable manufacturing, shipping, trading, and commercial interests looked upon the adoption of the Constitution as a sure guarantee that they could obtain tariff protection against foreign competition. The fourth and last group was composed of investors in western lands, mainly through great land companies. These individuals, too, saw the benefits which might be expected from a new and stable government. Their attitude was reflected in a letter to Madison from Hugh Williamson, a member of the Convention from North Carolina: "For myself, I conceive that my opinions are not biased by private Interests, but having claims to a considerable Quantity of Land in the Western Country, I am fully persuaded that the Value of those Lands must be increased by an efficient federal Government."

Having demonstrated to his own satisfaction that four groups of property rights were adversely affected by the government, or lack of government, under the Articles of Confederation and that economic motives were behind the movement for a general reorganization of government, Beard went on to inquire whether members of the Convention which drafted the Constitution belonged to any or all of these groups:

In other words, did the men who formulated the fundamental law of the land possess the kinds of property which were immediately and directly increased in value or made more secure by the results of their labors at Philadelphia? Did they have money at interest? Did they own public securities? Did they hold western lands for appreciation? Were they interested in shipping and manufactures?

The purpose of the inquiry, Beard insisted, was not to show that the Constitution was made for the personal benefit of the members of the Convention. Nevertheless, after examining in detail the economic interests and experience of each delegate, he concludes that "not one member represented in his immediate personal economic interests the small farming or mechanic classes," while at least five sixths (including the Convention's leaders) "were immediately, directly and personally interested in the outcome of their labors at Philadelphia, and were to a greater or lesser extent economic beneficiaries from the adoption of the Constitution." A majority of the Convention delegates were lawyers by profession, and most of the members came from towns on or near the coast, that is, from the regions in which personal property interests were largely concentrated.

Member by member, insofar as surviving records were available, Beard reviewed the amount and geographical distribution of money and public securities held by the men who sat in the Constitutional Convention. He disclaimed any intention of writing a muckraking book, recalling the "names of hundreds of patriots who risked their money in original certificates or received certificates for services rendered." Beard's primary interest was to show that the Founding Fathers were fully aware of economic realities, and he admired them for it. "As a group of doctrinaires, like the Frankfort assembly of 1848, they would have failed miserably," he states, "but as practical men they were able to build the new government upon the only foundation which would be stable: fundamental economic interests."

Frequent reference is made by Beard to the *Federalist Papers* by Hamilton, Madison, and Jay, written to convince the voters that the Constitution should be ratified. Subtly in most instances, because they are appealing to the nation, but yet clearly they point out to large economic groups that safety and strength lie in the adoption of the new system.

As summed up by Beard, "These are the great powers conferred on the new government: taxation, war, commercial control, and disposition of western lands. Through them public creditors may be paid in full, domestic peace maintained, advantages obtained in dealing with foreign nations, manufactures protected, and the development of the territories go forward with full swing." The Constitution, concludes Beard, "was an economic document drawn with superb skill by men whose property interests were immediately at stake; and as such it appealed directly and unerringly to identical interests in the country at large."

On September 17, 1787, the Convention at Philadelphia completed its work and forwarded the new Constitution to Congress, which in turn voted to send the document to the state legislatures to be transmitted by them to conventions chosen by the voters of the several commonwealths. It has been estimated that, because of property disqualifications, ignorance, or indifference, the state ratifying conventions were chosen by a vote of not more than one sixth of the adult males. The voters, especially their leaders, were representative of the same economic groups as the members of the original Convention. Like the Philadelphia group, delegates to the state conventions were drawn predominantly from the personal property-public security holders, according to Beard's findings. They were fully aware of the economic value of the new Constitution to them, they were well informed and well organized, and mainly resided in the towns. Talent, wealth, and professional abilities were generally on the side of those who favored the Constitution. Opponents, on the other hand, representing the debtor class, were poor and uninfluential, and had serious practical difficulties in getting out the backwoods vote. "The wonder," comments Beard, "is that they came so near defeating the Constitution at the polls."

In his state-by-state analysis of the process of ratification Beard notes that the battle was hottest in those states where there was frank recognition of the fact that one class of property interests was in conflict with another. "Virulent abuse of debtors and paper money advocates is quite common." At the same time, "Merchants, money lenders, public creditors are constantly urged to support the Constitution on the ground that their economic security depends upon the establishment of the new national government." Holders of personal property were linked with the professional classes and controlled the press "not only through ownership, but also through advertising and other patronage."

Beard characterized his study as a "long and arid survey—partaking of the nature of catalogue." He did not regard his investigation as exhaustive or definitive; his desire was to encourage "a few of this generation of historical scholars . . . to turn away from barren political history" to something more fruitful.

On the basis of his findings, Beard draws a number of conclusions. First, the movement for the Constitution was originated and carried through principally by four groups whose interests had suffered under the Articles of Confederation: money, public securities, manufactures, and trade and shipping. Steps toward forming the Constitution were first taken by a group of men "immediately interested through their personal possessions in the outcome of their labors." No popular vote was taken on the proposition to call a Constitutional Convention. The mass of the population was not represented in framing the Constitution because it could not meet property qualifications for voting. The members of the Philadelphia Convention which drafted the Constitution were with few exceptions "immediately, directly, and personally interested in, and derived economic advantages from, the establishment of the new system." Examining the product of their labor, Beard states unequivocally that "the Constitution was essentially an economic document based upon the concept that the fundamental private rights of property are anterior to government and morally beyond the reach of popular majorities." The record reveals further that most members of the Convention recognized "the claim of property to a special and defensive position in the Constitution."

Additional conclusions at which Beard arrives are the following: (1) In the ratification of the Constitution, about three fourths of the adult males failed to vote because of their indifference or disfranchisement by property qualifications; (2) the Constitution was ratified by a vote of probably not more than one sixth of the adult males; (3) it is doubtful whether the voters in New York, Massachusetts, New Hampshire, Virginia, and South Carolina actually approved the ratification of the Constitution; (4) the leaders in the state ratifying conventions represented the same economic interests as the Philadelphia Convention members; (5) the proponents of the Constitution were chiefly personal property holders and the opponents were the small farming and debtor interests; (6) the Constitution was not created by "the whole people," but on the contrary "it was the work of a consolidated group whose interests knew no state boundaries and were truly national in their scope."

Attacks on the Beard thesis were not long in coming. The author himself later recalled the storm that he had stirred up:

> When my book appeared it was roundly condemned by conservative Republicans, including ex-President Taft, and praised, with about the same amount of discrimination, by Progressives and others on the left wing. Perhaps no other book on the Constitution has been more severely criticized, and so little read. Perhaps no other book on the subject has been used to justify opinions and projects so utterly beyond its necessary implications.

A self-formed committee of the New York Bar Association summoned Beard to appear before it and defend his book, "and when I declined," wrote Beard, "they treated my reply as a kind of contempt of court." Albert Bushnell Hart, elder statesman among historians, damned the work in an article entitled "Baseless Slanders on Great Men." *The Nation* published a scathing editorial, "Muckraking the Fathers." Nicholas Murray Butler of Columbia looked upon the book as something almost indecent.

The attacks on Beard and his *Economic Interpretation* have continued down through the years. An extreme right-winger, Harold Lord Varney, writing in *The American Mercury* in 1957, declares "The impact of this devastating book upon a whole generation of inquiring Americans was immense. Few books of our times have ever created in student minds such a stabbing skepticism concerning the basic postulates of American patriotism. After Beard got through with them, the American fathers who drafted the Constitution were cut down to the ignoble size of self-seekers and promoters of cynical special interests."

Scarcely less critical is the well-known American historian Henry Steele Commager, writing for *American Heritage* in 1958, who charges that Beard's emphasis on the economic motivation of the Founding Fathers "suggested that all earlier idealisms and patriotisms—even the idealisms and patriotisms of the framers" were "flawed by selfishness and hypocrisy." Commager concludes: "The idea that property considerations were paramount in the minds of those assembled in Philadelphia is misleading and unsound and is borne out by neither the evidence of the debates in the Convention nor by the Constitution itself." As Commager sees it, "The Constitution was not *essentially* an economic document. It was and is essentially a political document."

At least two full-fledged books have joined in the assault on Beard's controversial thesis: Robert E. Brown's *Charles Beard and the Constitution* (1956), and Forrest McDonald's *We the People; the Economic Origins of the Constitution* (1959).

Beard did not lack for defenders. Such eminent historians as William Dunning, William E. Dodd, Edward Channing, and Max Farrand and the brilliant journalist Walter Lippmann praised his book highly.

The problem remains: How valid is Beard's interpretation of the work of the Philadelphia Convention? In his Introduction to the 1935 edition of the book, Beard pointed out that he had used the title *an* economic interpretation, not *the* economic interpretation, and he had regarded other interpretations as possible. What he had sought to do was to bring out "those realistic features of economic conflict, stress, and strain" which other historians had ignored or omitted. Further, Beard asserts:

Whoever leaves economic pressures out of history or out of the discussion of public questions is in mortal peril of substituting mythology for reality and confusing issues instead of clarifying them. It was largely by recognizing the power of economic interests in the field of politics and making skillful use of them that the Fathers of the American Constitution placed themselves among the great practicing statesmen of all ages and gave instructions to succeeding generations in the art of government.

There is no concrete evidence that Beard had anything but admiration for the work done at Philadelphia. In later writings he describes the Fathers as "courageous," "brilliant," and "profound." His judgment of the Philadelphia Convention was that "never has there been a convention of men richer in political experience and in practical knowledge, or endowed with a profounder insight into the springs of human action and the intimate essence of government," and the Constitution endures as "a monument to their amazing wisdom." Though the framers of the Constitution had constructed a government with their own interests foremost in view, in Beard's view they had built the only kind of government which could be stable, that is, one based on a sound economic foundation.

Even one of Beard's severe critics Robert E. Brown, concedes that economic factors were important at Philadelphia: "Since most of the people were middle-class and had private property, practically everybody was interested in the protection of property." But there were motives other than economic, Brown insists, including disinterested patriotism, which the Fathers recognized as equally important. The point of view that the Philadelphia Convention was composed primarily of great patriots is strongly supported also by Henry Steele Commager, who concludes, "Not a government cunningly contrived to protect the interests of property, but one capable of extending to its citizens the blessings of liberty and happiness—was that not, after all, what the framers created?"

One of the principal foundations for Beard's thesis, that the members of the Convention had large investments in public securities, was invalidated by a leading constitutional authority, Edward S. Corwin. Beard's figures were based on 1791 records, four years after the Philadelphia Convention. Corwin showed, however, that only a few of the Convention members held public securities at the time of the Convention, and the largest holder, Elbridge Gerry, was "so little influenced by this consideration that he refused to sign the Constitution and opposed its adoption."

A wise judgment on the Beard book came from the eminent historian Arthur Schlesinger, Sr., about a decade after its appearance: "No discriminating reader need feel that such a presentation carries with it the imputation of ignoble or unworthy motives to the Fathers of the Constitution; rather it forms an illuminating commentary on the fact that intelligent self-interest, whether conscious or instinctive, is one of the motive forces of human progress."

Despite criticisms of its basic tenets, the importance and influence of Beard's *An Economic Interpretation of the Constitution of the United States* should not be underrated. As Malcolm Cowley commented, "It cut through the whole tissue of liberal idealism and rhetoric to the economic realities in American history." The book continues to generate lively reactions more than a half-century after its original publication. Its originality, insights, and cirtical spirit will continue to challenge the imagination of historians.

19–THE GREAT DEBUNKER

HENRY LOUIS MENCKEN'S *Prejudices*

SINCE THE END of World War I, a strong breeze of iconoclasm has blown through American literature. Biographers have stripped the national heroes of all legend and romantic glamor. Historians have been chiefly preoccupied with debunking America's past. No less irreverent in tearing down accepted dogma, destroying sacred cows, and wrecking popular images have been the novelists, poets, playwrights, and essayists.

Setting the tone for the new breed of social critics, and by far the most influential of the lot, from the mid-teens into the thirties, was H. L. Mencken, "The Sage of Baltimore." Among his prolific writings, the six volumes of *Prejudices* (1919-27) are representative of Mencken's extremely catholic interests and of subjects on which he held vehement views, pro and con. A satirist, humorist, devastating critic, and word juggler supreme, Mencken attracted readers by the thousands as he damned ignorance and dishonesty in American politics, hypocrisy in the church, sham in the educational system, puritanism in every form, provincialism, arty art, do-goodism among social reformers, racial discrimination, and superpatriotism, while defending with equal vigor the right of the individual to live his life without interference from bureaucrats, prohibitionists, censors, bluenoses, and their like. Through his editorship of *The American Mercury,* the series of *Prejudices,* and other writings, Mencken became a rallying point for the literature of protest in the United States; at one time he was described by the New York *Times* as "the most powerful private citizen" in the country. Mencken dedicated himself, in his own words, "to the

most noble and sublime task possible to mere human
beings: the overthrow of superstition and unreasoning
faith."

Did the times make the man or vice versa? is a per-
tinent question to ask of Mencken's career. Unquestionably the period in which he flourished was ripe for his
message. The nation after World War I was rich and
complacent; the *nouveaux riches* had pretensions toward
art, mainly as importers and collectors; literature had
become increasingly trite, unimaginative, and platitudi-
nous; and busybody reformers were prohibiting alcoholic
drinks, censoring books and moving pictures, and
preaching a jingoistic brand of Americanism. Mencken
concluded that "what ails the beautiful letters of the
Republic is what ails the general culture of the Republic—
the lack of a body of sophisticated and civilized public
opinion, independent of plutocratic control and superior to
the infantile philosophies of the mob—a body of opinion
showing the eager curiosity, the educated skepticism and
hospitality to ideas of a true aristocracy." Mencken set
himself the task of creating such a body of opinion, aided
by the poets Carl Sandburg, Vachel Lindsay, Wallace
Stevens, Ezra Pound, T. S. Eliot, and Robert Frost, and
the novelists Scott Fitzgerald, Ernest Hemingway, John
Dos Passos, Sinclair Lewis, Thomas Wolfe, and William
Faulkner.

Henry Louis Mencken, a native of Baltimore, born in
1880, was of German, Scotch, and English descent. At the
age of sixteen, he graduated from the Baltimore Polytech-
nic Institute, but his first love was journalism. At nineteen,
he was on the staff of the Baltimore *Morning Herald*,
began writing a weekly column the following year, and
within a short time was successively city editor and managing editor. After the *Herald* suspended publication in
1906, Mencken went over to the *Sun* papers of Baltimore
and remained there intermittently and in various capacities for the next thirty-five years. Meanwhile, he was per-
fecting his razor-sharp writing style and expanding his
ideas with studies on George Bernard Shaw, Friedrich
Nietzsche, and the American language, and serving, with
George Jean Nathan, as co-editor of the *Smart Set* magazine.

Mencken's weapons as he criticized and lampooned
contemporary American culture have been variously described as the blackjack, the ax, and the hammer. Among

his favorite targets were professors, academicians, Baptists, Methodists, Rotarians, Kiwanians, Elks, schoolteachers, Ph.D.'s, YMCA secretaries, philosophers, political leaders, radicals, clergymen, and the "booboisie" in general. His comments were invariably lively, witty, acidulous, prejudiced, full of exaggerations, and almost calculatedly unfair. His political views were conservative, if not downright reactionary. Characteristic is his definition of democracy:

Democracy is that system of government under which the people, having 35,717,342 native-born adult whites to choose from, including thousands who are handsome and many who are wise, pick out a Coolidge to be head of the State. It is as if a hungry man, set before a banquet prepared by master cooks and covering a table an acre in area, should turn his back upon the feast and stay his stomach by catching and eating flies.

Mencken was essentially a libertarian, a believer in complete liberty, adamantly opposed to overcentralized government and excessive bureaucracy because he was convinced that these represented the forces that were continually encroaching on the freedom of the individual. If anything was sacred to Mencken, it was liberty of thought, and he asserted his own right to this privilege by holding up to derision other people's prejudices, popular ideas, and sacred beliefs, by labeling political leaders as frauds, charlatans, and quacks, and by vigorously smiting any institution or movement of which he disapproved.

An admirer, James T. Farrell, in his *Reflections at Fifty* gives a cogent summary of Mencken's impact on his own era:

Mencken's attacks on Babbittry, on politicians like Coolidge and Harding, on business, on the cravenness of many newspapers, all contributed toward alerting a generation of writers, reporters, and college students who later went into public life. His contempt for quackery, his exposure of lies and evasions, his witty and pungent manner of taking all the stuffing out of stuffed shirts aided many of us in our youth. He helped us to grasp what was going on about us. He gave us a means for seeing through pretensions, pompositics, follies, deceits, and empty public shows. Like him, we were disillusioned by World War I. Like him, we found that the malignant parochialism of American life was frustrating many creative spirits. Like him, we saw that life could be more civilized than it was. And his good-natured assaults taught us how to laugh at all this. He strengthened our liberal attitude.

In the nineteen twenties, Mencken's writings became the bible of college and university students—in fact, of practically all readers under thirty. They responded with enthusiasm to his ridicule of jargon, pedantry, and obscurantism in education; to his belief that the scientist "who yields anything to theology, however slight, is yielding to ignorance and false pretenses"; to his contention that God had made a bungling job of the human body, forcing man "to lug around a frame packed with defects, from imperfectly centered eyes to weakly arched feet"; to his caustic comment that in a democracy "the man who is barely human is treated as if he were the peer of Aristotle"; to his claim that Christianity has more trouble with the sex question than does any other religion; and to similar Menckenisms. Yet, despite such essentially destructive slaughtering of sacred cows, a leading historian, Julian P. Boyd, holds that Mencken's "belaboring of theologians, politicians and pedagogues was in truth a defense of religion, democracy and learning."

As an attention-getting device, Mencken's manner of writing was a stroke of genius. "Menckenese" was imitated by many, but none ever used it with the facility and force of its inventor. His prose was unique, dynamic, packed with explosive and provocative phrases, high in shock content, often hilariously amusing. His essays were peppered with such terms as Uplifters, Yahoos, Wowsers, and Booboisie, as well as coney-catchers, bawds, and pimps; zanies and yokels; literary pallbearers; scoundrels, rascals, and poltroons; Christian Endeavor belt, foreign mission belt, and alfalfa colleges. Reminiscent of Rabelais is the way that Mencken revives archaic words, combining them with vernacular phrases and scholarly, scientific terminology to produce a scintillating effect overall, with never a dull moment for the reader.

The six series of *Prejudices*, issued from 1919 to 1927, were made up of essays on a variety of topics, book reviews, critiques on literature and music, and editorials, frequently reprinted from the *Smart Set* or *The American Mercury*. Often the pieces deal with personalities—H. G. Wells, Arnold Bennett, George Ade, George Jean Nathan, Jack London, Theodore Roosevelt, Joseph Hergesheimer, Ring Lardner, William Jennings Bryan, Beethoven; or social problems—war, censorship, birth control, prohibition; or literature and music; or political, religious, or educational matters—any subject, indeed, which provided Mencken with a likely target for his verbal pyrotechnics. Brickbats rather than words of praise predominate. The first volume of *Prejudices* was a collection of book reviews; beginning with the second, however, the series was broadened to pay Mencken's respects not only to the Humanists "and other such grave and glittering fish" but to the whole range of American culture, or at least those aspects which interested the author.

The full flavor of Mencken's prose style and iconoclastic ideas can only be obtained from direct quotation. Herewith, then, is a sampling:

Shakespeare—"The virtue of such great poets as Shakespeare does not lie in the content of their poetry, but in its music. The content of the Shakespearean plays, in fact, is often puerile, and sometimes quite incomprehensible. . . . One moans sourly over the spectacle of generations of pedants debating the question of Hamlet's mental processes; the fact is that Shakespeare gave him no more mental processes than a bishop has, but merely employed him as a convenient spout for some of the finest music ever got into words."

Martyrs—"To die for an idea: it is unquestionably noble. But how much nobler it would be if men died for ideas that were true. Searching history, I find no such case. All the great martyrs of the books died for sheer nonsense—often for trivial matters of doctrine and ceremonial, too absurd to be stated in plain terms."

American Aristocrat—"He must exhibit exactly the right social habits, appetites and prejudices, public and private. He must harbor exactly the right political enthusiasms and indignations. He must have a hearty taste for exactly the right sports. His attitude toward the fine arts must be properly tolerant and yet not a shade too eager. He must read and like exactly the right books, pamphlets and public journals. He must put up at the right hotels when he travels. His wife must patronize the right milliners. He himself must stick to the right haberdashery. He must live in the right neighborhood. . . . To hang back, to challenge and dispute, to preach reforms and revolutions. These are crimes against the brummagen Holy Ghost of the order."

Philosophy—"If you want to find out how a philosopher feels when he is engaged in the practice of his profession, go to the nearest zoo and watch a chimpanzee at the wearying and hopeless job of chasing fleas. Both suffer damnably and neither can win. . . . For the absolute, of course, is a mere banshee. No such thing exists. Philosophy in the narrow technical sense is largely moonshine and wind music."

Lincoln's Gettysburg Address—"It is eloquence brought to a pellucid and almost child-like perfection—the highest emotion reduced to one graceful and irresistible gesture. . . . But let us not forget that it is oratory, not logic; beauty, not sense. . . . The doctrine is simply this: that the Union soldiers who died at Gettysburg sacrificed their lives to the cause of self-determination—'that government of the people, by the people, for the people' should not perish from the earth. It is difficult to imagine anything more untrue. The Union soldiers in that battle actually fought against self-determination; it was the Confederates who fought for the right of their people to govern themselves."

Virginia—"Her education has sunk to the Baptist seminary level; not a single contribution to human knowledge has come out of her colleges in twenty-five years; she spends less than half upon her common schools, *per capita*, than any northern state spends. In brief, an intellectual Gobi or Lapland. Urbanity, *politesse*, chivalry? Go to! It was in Virginia that they invented the device of searching for contraband whiskey in women's underwear."

The lover—"The lover sees with an eye that is both opaque and out of focus. Thus he begins the familiar process of editing and improving his girl. . . . While the spell lasts his lady could shave her head or take to rubbing snuff, or scratch her leg at a communion service, or smear her hair with bear's grease, and yet not disgust him. Here the paralysis of the faculties is again chiefly physical—a matter of obscure secretions, of shifting pressure, of metabolism. Nature is at her tricks. The fever of love is upon its victim. His guard down, he is little more than a pathetic automaton."

Theodore Roosevelt—"A glorified longshoreman engaged eternally in cleaning out bar-rooms—and not too proud to gouge when the inspiration came to him, or to bite in the clinches, or to oppose the relatively fragile brass knuckles of the code with chair-legs, bung-starters, cuspidors, demi-johns, and ice-picks."

America—"The United States in my eye is incomparably the greatest show on earth. It is a show which avoids diligently all the kinds of clowning which tire me most quickly—for example, royal ceremonials, the tedious hocuspocus of *haut-politique,* the taking of politics seriously—and lays chief stress upon the kinds which delight me unceasingly—for example, the ribald combats of demagogues, the exquisitely ingenious operations of master rogues, the pursuit of witches and heretics, the desperate struggles of inferior men to claw their way into Heaven."

Rotary Clubs—"Rotary is as old as Christianity. The first Rotarian was the first man to call John the Baptist, Jack."

In his wide-sweeping onslaughts upon the status quo, upon genteel professors and clergymen, the provincial bourgeois and politicians, democracy and social reform, and favorite targets of a like sort, Mencken inevitably created enemies, who were as unsparing in their denunciations as Mencken himself had been. A compilation of such highly intemperate remarks was edited by Mencken and brought out in 1928 under the title *Menckeniana: A Schimpflexikon.* The content may be judged by the following representative selections: "I will content myself with the bald statement that he is a weasel"; "a pole-cat"; "Mencken's mental tastes remind me of the physical appetite of a sea-gull"; "a disappointed, dishonest, distruthful, disgraceful, degraded, degenerate evolute of a species fifty-seven varieties lower than a turkey buzzard"; "Mencken has dysentery of the mouth"; "Mencken is half-baked spiritually"; "his writing is the gibberish of an imbecile"; "why, I tell you folks, Mencken is just a dirty buzzard and the folks that follow him are no more than damn scoundrels"; "Mencken appeals to bootleggers, street walkers and the like"; "an 18-carat, 23-jewel, 33rd degree, bred in the bone and dyed in the wool moron."

More judicious, better-balanced valuations came from more literate critics. Edmund Wilson, writing in 1921, stated, "Mencken, in spite of all his protestations of realistic resignation, is actually a militant idealist. Most Americans—even of fine standards—have long ago resigned themselves to the cheapness and ugliness of America, but Mencken has never resigned himself. He has never ceased to regard his native country with wounded and outraged eyes. The shabby politics, the childish books, the factories turning out wooden nutmegs have never lost their power to offend him. At this late date, he is, I suppose, almost the only man in the country who still expects American novelists to be artists and politicians gentlemen." Walter Lippmann added: "Mr. Mencken is so effective . . . because his appeal is not from mind to mind but from viscera to viscera. If you analyze his arguments you destroy their effect . . . you have to judge him totally, roughly, approximately, without definition, as you would a barrage of artillery, for the general destruction rather than for the accuracy of the individual shots." A third commentator, Van Wyck Brooks, concluded that Mencken "was a social critic and a literary showman who had taken lessons from Macaulay, as well as from Nietzsche, Huneker and Bierce, and he fought with all his masculine force against the elements in American society that impeded the creative life and stifled its growth. A transatlantic Attila, with his own Teutonic fury, a coarse mind that had undertaken a literary spadesman's work, he accomplished a task that only a coarse mind could do."

Mencken's greatest impact on the literary scene of his time was as a book reviewer and commentator on authors —in essence creating literary trends and reputations. He championed Dreiser, Cabell, and Hergesheimer, contributed to Sinclair Lewis' early success by his enthusiasm for *Main Street* and *Babbitt*, and praised Sherwood Anderson and F. Scott Fitzgerald. His verdicts were by no means infallible, however, as, for example, in his rating of George Ade ahead of Ring Lardner as a humorist, and his characterization of Robert Frost as "a Whittier without the whiskers," while extolling such minor poets as John McClure and Lizette Woodworth Reese.

In Malcolm Cowley's view, "Mencken's most valuable contribution to American criticism was his fight to purge our literature of its puritanism and gentility. By jumping on the bodies of timid critics and timid novelists alike, by discrediting their flabby values and bloodless evasions, he more than any other man opened up pioneer spaces, and enabled us, at least technically, to come of age. Sex ceased to be a bugaboo, squalor a tabu, decorum a virtue, iconoclasm a subversion of ethics."

In long-range significance, present-day critics are agreed that Mencken's vitalizing effect on the American language, as writer and lexicographer, is pre-eminent. The first edition of his monumental study of *The American Language* appeared in 1919 and grew steadily in size. The fourth edition, 1936, filled 798 pages, and was followed by two sizable supplementary volumes, 1945-48. As Noah Webster had done a century earlier, Mencken argued that the American language was separate and different from the English and he assembled a wealth of material and information to support his case.

In a statement written by Mencken in 1931 he set forth a credo which he endeavored to follow in his writings and in his daily life: "I believe that it is better to tell the truth than to lie. I believe that it is better to be free than to be a slave, and I believe that it is better to know than to be ignorant." On another occasion he remarked, "As a critic, I regret nothing. I have made some mistakes, but on the whole I have been on the side of sound artists and against frauds." Mencken had an avid appetite for life, wishing, he said, that he might attain the "worldly wisdom of a police lieutenant, a bartender, a shyster lawyer, and a midwife."

Mencken has been compared, in each instance with considerable justification, with Juvenal, Dryden, Swift, Voltaire, Ambrose Bierce, and Philip Wylie. Most aptly, however, the current tendency is to liken him to Dr. Samuel Johnson, who played a similar role in eighteenth-century English literary circles. For Mencken, Edmund Wilson summed up the case with his comment, "it is astonishing that one independent critic, writing mainly in newspapers and magazines, should have fought so many successful fights and grown to be so powerful a figure," frequently in the face of powerful opposition.

When Mencken died in 1956, no one was better qualified to write his obituary than a longtime friend and associate on the Baltimore *Sun* staff, Gerald W. Johnson:

Something was subtracted from American freedom when Mencken died. He stood on his own feet, and however wrong-headed his philosophy it was not designed to appease, nor to curry favor with any man. Since the truly free spirit is rare, the loss of even one is serious; but in this case the loss is multiplied, for the man was not only free but gifted with a flaming literary style that made his freedom glaringly apparent. That style was imitated incessantly, but always lamentably, because its essence was a perception clear of conventional illusions lodged in a man whose independence was too complete for petty spite to be worth his while. So his most violent assaults on men—and some were violent beyond all precedent—were so void of furtive malice that his cuts were clean and healed rapidly. Many men whom he denounced held him in extraordinary personal esteem.

It was his good fortune to flourish in an era with great need of the service that he was supremely qualified to render, that of puncturing frauds. But he was also capable of stupendous labor of which *The American Language* is the monumental result, but which also transformed the American review. Physical collapse silenced him seven years ago, but he has not been forgotten for in his day he was unique and invaluable.

20–LEGAL MIND AT WORK

BENJAMIN N. CARDOZO'S
The Nature of the Judicial Process

BENJAMIN CARDOZO was rated by Roscoe Pound, an eminent legal scholar himself, as one of the ten greatest judges produced by the American bench. The names included in the illustrious line, beginning with John Marshall, shared certain common characteristics, according to Pound: "First of all, they were great lawyers, masters of their craft, masters of the authoritative materials in which judges in the English-speaking world are expected, as a duty of their office, to find the grounds of decision, and masters of the technique of applying those materials to the decision of cases."

Cardozo's American ancestry antedates by well over a century the beginnings of the nation. Forebears on his mother's side came from Portugal to America in 1654. His paternal ancestors left the Spanish peninsula during the expulsion of the Jews in the sixteenth century, migrating first to Holland and then to England. The founder of the American line came to the Colonies about 1752. For the next two centuries the family produced a succession of distinguished patriots and cultural leaders.

The first of the Cardozos to gain prominence—though not honor—in judicial circles was Benjamin's father, who cast an unfortunate blight on the family name. Judge Albert Cardozo was a member of the infamous Tweed Ring in New York, where his conduct finally led to charges of malfeasance and corruption being filed against him; in order to escape impeachment he resigned. It has been remarked that much of Benjamin Cardozo's life was devoted to the atonement of his father's sins.

As a child Benjamin was taught by a tutor, Horatio

Alger, who later became famous as the author of the most popular books for boys of the period, in all of which the hero triumphed over poverty and adversity by courage and hard work. Benjamin was a voracious reader of the Alger thrillers, and he credited his admittance to Columbia University at the early age of fifteen to the preparation for college received from Alger.

Cardozo's rise in the legal profession was rapid and brilliant. He served successively as a justice of the Supreme Court of New York, associate judge of the Court of Appeals, and finally as associate justice of the United States Supreme Court. Throughout his career his opinions, numbering some 470 in written form, are monuments of legal scholarship. Further, they are famous for literary style— in Santayana's words "clothed in a language that lends the message an intrinsic value, and makes it delightful to apprehend, apart from its importance in ultimate theory or practice."

Aside from the opinions, scattered through the *New York Reports* and *United States Reports* from 1914 to 1938, Cardozo's writings were not voluminous. Most widely known are four small books: *The Nature of the Judicial Process, The Growth of the Law, The Paradoxes of Legal Science,* and *Law and Literature.* It is generally agreed that the most original and significant of these works, the one exerting greatest influence on the legal profession and giving laymen the clearest insight into the workings of the law, is the first, *The Nature of the Judicial Process* (1921).

The extraordinary success of *The Nature of the Judicial Process* was due in part to the charm of the author's style, but more importantly to Cardozo's careful analysis of the factors, conscious and unconscious, which guide a judge in reaching his decisions. Previous to the appearance of this unique picture of the operations of the law, there was a widely prevailing belief that the legal process consisted primarily in drawing logical deductions from established precedents. Cardozo's interpretation showed that the matter was far more complex and by implication that the case method of teaching law has distinct limitations. As viewed by Cardozo, law is a living body of principles capable of growth and change.

"The work of deciding cases," states Cardozo, "goes on every day in hundreds of courts throughout the land. Any judge, one might suppose, would find it easy to describe the process which he had followed a thousand times and more. Nothing could be farther from the truth. Let some intelligent layman ask him to explain: he will not go very far before taking refuge in the excuse that the language of craftsmen is unintelligible to those untutored in the craft." Such an answer is unsatisfying to Cardozo and no doubt to the inquirer.

Consequently, the author indulges in introspection, asking himself such searching questions as: "What is it that I do when I decide a case? To what sources of information do I appeal for guidance? In what proportions do I permit them to contribute to the result? In what proportions ought they to contribute? If a precedent is applicable, when do I refuse to follow it. If no precedent is applicable, how do I reach the rule that will make a precedent for the future? If I am seeking logical consistency, the symmetry of the legal structure, how far shall I seek it? At what point shall the quest be halted by some discrepant custom, by some consideration of the social welfare, by my own or the common standards of justice and morals?" All these varying considerations, Cardozo points out, may and should influence the judge's decisions. By "introspective searchings of the spirit" he seeks to weigh the "strange compound," to discover the relative significance of the ingredients which enter into the judicial process. It may be doubted, suggests Cardozo, whether judges ought to be allowed to brew such a compound at all; nevertheless, he says, "I take judge-made law as one of the existing realities of life. . . . Not a judge on the bench but has had a hand in the making."

The first question for which Cardozo seeks an answer is "Where does the judge find the law which he embodies in his judgment?" The rule that fits the case may be found in the Constitution or a statute. Even so, there may be gaps to fill, doubts and ambiguities to be cleared, hardships and wrongs to be mitigated or avoided. Thus arises the need for judicial interpretation. More troublesome is "the land of mystery where constitution and statute are silent, and the judge must look to the common law for the rule that fits the case." In these instances, the first step is to compare the pending case with precedents, for "in a system so highly developed as our own, precedents have so covered the ground that they fix the point of departure from which the labor of the judge begins."

If the judge relies entirely upon the Constitution, statutes, and precedents, however, no system of living law could be evolved, and judges of high courts do not view their function so narrowly. "It is when the colors do not match, when the references in the index fail, when there is no decisive precedent, that the serious business of the judge begins. He must then fashion law for the litigants before him. In fashioning it for them, he will be fashioning it for others."

The assumption is erroneous, Cardozo emphasizes, that law is unchangeable and everlasting. Nothing is stable or absolute, even principles. Decade by decade and century by century, law is being modified, with the result that "hardly a rule of today but may be matched by its opposite of yesterday." Most of the changes have been wrought by judges. Still, the search must go on for "the essential and the permanent" in the field of justice.

Four primary approaches, as applied to the judicial process, are analyzed in detail by Cardozo: (1) the method of philosophy or the rule of analogy; (2) the method of evolution or historical development; (3) the method of tradition or the customs of the community; and (4) the method of sociology or of justice, morals, and social welfare.

The first principle is based on logic, analogy, or resemblance of relations, a method which is useful in eliminating favoritism and chance, enabling the judge to reach decisions with "serene and impartial uniformity." Logical development of the law, Cardozo asserts, requires consistency: "If a group of cases involve the same point, the parties expect the same decision. It would be a gross injustice to decide alternate cases on opposite principles. If a case was decided against me yesterday when I was a defendant, I shall look for the same judgment today if I am a plaintiff. To decide differently would raise a feeling of resentment and wrong in my breast; it would be an infringement, material and moral, of my rights." Therefore, adherence to precedent must be the rule rather than the exception in courts of law.

On occasion, logical principles may conflict. As an illustration, Cardozo cites the case of a legatee who had murdered his testator. One principle would recognize that an estate must be disposed of in conformity with a legal will. Another principle is that civil courts may not add to the pains and penalties of crime. But superseding these two concepts is another principle, "its roots deeply fastened in universal sentiments of justice, the principle that no man should profit from his own inequity or take advantage of his own wrong." The court so held in deciding the case, motivated by a "compelling sentiment of justice" more powerful than the preservation and enforcement of legal rights of ownership.

Cardozo proceeds next to an examination of the historical method, or the method of evolution, as applied to law. Occasionally this approach is in conflict with the philosophical method, though more often "the effect of history is to make the path of logic clear." The law of the future should not necessarily consist of an "uninspired repetition of the present and the past," Cardozo insists, but "history, in illuminating the past, illuminates the present, and in illuminating the present, illuminates the future." The most striking example is the law of real property, wherein Cardozo holds "there can be no progress without history." The law of contract is full of history, as are "the powers and functions of an executor, the distinctions between larceny and embezzlement, the rules of venue and the jurisdiction over foreign trespass."

A third force, after history and philosophy, having a bearing upon the establishment of judicial principles, Cardozo notes, is custom. Here he quotes Blackstone, who concluded that there are three kinds of common law: "(1) General customs, which are the universal rule of the whole Kingdom, and form the Common Law, in its stricter and more usual signification. (2) Particular customs, which for the most part affect only the inhabitants of particular districts. (3) Certain particular laws, which by custom are adopted and used by some particular courts of pretty general and extensive jurisdiction." Cardozo is inclined to play down the influence of custom in the development of law, though it may be an important factor in shaping legislation. "It is, however," he remarks, "not so much in the making of new rules as in the application of old ones that the creative energy of custom most often manifests itself today. General standards of right and duty are established." In this sense custom becomes identified with "customary morality, the prevaling standard of right conduct, the *mores* of the time. . . . Life casts the moulds of conduct, which will some day become fixed as law." Thus custom is gradually transformed by the people, or their representatives, into law.

From history, philosophy, and custom, Cardozo goes on to "the force which in our day and generation is becoming the greatest of them all," the power of social justice which finds its outlet and expression in the method of sociology. "Fundamentally," he insists, "the final cause of law is the welfare of society." Even though judges may not lightly set aside existing rules, they should not indulge in formalism for its own sake but rather interpret the rules as far as possible for the public good. "When the social needs demand one settlement rather than another," Cardozo declares, "there are times when we must bend symmetry, ignore history and sacrifice custom in the pursuit of other and larger ends." This statment is an accurate reflection of the attitude of the United States Supreme Court in recent years, which Cardozo helped to shape.

Judges have greater flexibility and freedom of choice in dealing with constitutions than with statutes, because "statutes are designed to meet the fugitive exigencies of the hour," while "a *constitution* states or ought to state not rules for the passing hour, but principles for an expanding future." Cardozo calls particular attention to the "great immunities" with which the Constitution surrounds the individual. How the immunities are to be defined frequently becomes a matter of judicial interpretation. Here, too, liberal views predominate among today's Supreme Court justices. As seen by Cardozo, it is the duty of the courts to examine statutes not in isolation or as abstract principles "but in the setting and the framework of present-day conditions, as revealed by the labors of economists and students of the social sciences in our own country and abroad."

The position of property under the law is clarified by Cardozo. He points out that "property, like liberty, though immune under the Constitution from destruction, is not immune from regulation essential for the common good. What that regulation shall be, every generation must work out for itself." Property has a social function to perform and legislation toward that end is an appropriate exercise of governmental power.

Altogether in the field of law, Cardozo observes, "the tendency today is in the direction of a growing liberalism. The new spirit has made its way gradually; and its progress, unnoticed step by step, is visible in retrospect as we look back upon the distance traversed. The old forms remain, but they are filled with a new content."

Summing up, Cardozo concludes:

My analysis of the judicial process comes then to this, and little more: logic, and history, and custom,

and utility, and the accepted standards of right conduct, are the forces which singly or in combination
shape the progress of the law. Which of these forces
shall dominate in any case, must depend largely upon
the comparative importance or value of the social
interests that will be thereby promoted or impaired.
One of the most fundamental social interests is that
law shall be uniform and impartial. There must be
nothing in its action that savors of prejudice or favor
or even arbitrary whim or fitfulness. Therefore in the
main there shall be adherence to precedent.

In a separate chapter, Cardozo deals with "the judge as
a legislator." Therein he finds that "in countless litigations,
the law is so clear that judges have no discretion." Their
right to legislate becomes evident when there are gaps in
the law, and rules and precedents must be established.
Certain general precepts, however, must be adhered to,
Cardozo observes:

The judge, even when he is free, is still not wholly
free. He is not a knight-errant, roaming at will in
pursuit of his own ideal of beauty or of goodness. He
is to draw his inspiration from consecrated principles.
He is not to yield to spasmodic sentiment, to vague
and unregulated benevolence. He is to exercise a
discretion informed by tradition, methodized by analogy, disciplined by system, and subordinated to "the
primordial necessity of order in the social life." Wide
enough in all conscience is the field of discretion that
remains.

The final chapter of *The Nature of the Judicial Process*
is devoted in part to a discussion of the place of precedent in our legal system. While noting valid objections
to a strict adherence to precedent, Cardozo still holds
that the rule should generally prevail, varying only in
exceptional cases. As a practical matter, he warns that
"the labor of judges would be increased almost to the
breaking point if every past decision could be reopened in
every case, and one could not lay one's own course of
bricks on the secure foundation of the courses laid by
others who had gone before him." Cardozo points out that
the rule of adherence to precedent is applied with less
rigidity in the United States than in England. Also, "the

United States Supreme Court and the highest courts of several states overrule their own prior decisions when manifestly erroneous," as was done in 1954, for example, when the Supreme Court ruled segregation in public schools unconstitutional, thereby reversing its own "separate but equal" dictum of 1896.

A majority of the cases which come before the courts can reasonably be decided only one way, in Cardozo's opinion. A small percentage, however, are less clear-cut, and "these are the cases where the creative element in the judicial process finds its opportunity and power ... where a decision one way or the other, will count for the future." It is in such instances that the judge assumes the role of a lawgiver. Looking back upon his own career, Cardozo recalls, "I was much troubled in spirit, in my first years upon the bench, to find how trackless was the ocean on which I had embarked. I sought for certainty. I was oppressed and disheartened when I found that the quest for it was futile. . . . I have become reconciled to the uncertainty, because I have grown to see it as inevitable."

Cardozo concedes that the power placed in the hands of judges is great and subject to possible abuse. He quotes Ehrlich to the effect that "there is no guaranty of justice except the personality of the judge." Below the more or less tangible factors which influence judgments are subconscious forces far more difficult to appraise. As expressed by Cardozo, "Deep below consciousness are other forces, the likes and the dislikes, the predilections and the prejudices, the complex of instincts and emotions and habits and convictions, which make the man, whether he be litigant or judge."

In conclusion, Cardozo cites with approval a statement by Theodore Roosevelt, "whose intuitions and perceptions were deep and brilliant," in the author's eyes: "The chief lawmakers in our country may be, and often are, the judges, because they are the final seat of authority. Every time they interpret contract, vested right, due process of law, liberty, they necessarily enact into law parts of a system of social philosophy; and as such interpretation is fundamental, they give direction to all law-making."

Benjamin Cardozo is most frequently bracketed with Oliver Wendell Holmes as the two pre-eminent American judges of the past fifty years. Cardozo's enduring reputation will doubtless be as an interpreter of the common law. In reviewing *Selected Writings of Benjamin Nathan*

Cardozo, published posthumously, Newman Levy concluded that "no judge in our history, with the possible exception of Holmes, offered such a rare combination of legal erudition, judicial poise, and broad, humanistic culture." These qualities are demonstrated on every page of *The Nature of the Judicial Process*.

21–VENTURE IN CONTEMPORARY ANTHROPOLOGY

ROBERT S. & HELEN MERRELL LYND'S
Middletown

TRADITIONALLY, anthropology has been concerned with the study of primitive peoples. The cultures of Samoans, Central Africans, Australian aborigines, Amerindians, and Patagonians have been explored in depth. Two social scientists, Robert and Helen Lynd, conceived the brilliant idea of applying the austere, objective principles of anthropological research to a moden community, scanning its mores, taboos, and living conditions as dispassionately as they would those of a savage tribe in the New Hebrides.

The Lynds began their sociological safari in January 1924. As amusingly described by an economist, C. E. Ayres:

> Having established their expedition headquarters in a centrally located native *kraal,* the field staff labored diligently throughout 1924 and well into 1925 studying the various types of natives, observing native customs and ceremonials, and tracing the complex pattern of interweaving motives and dominating sanctions by which the lives of all the members of the tribe are ruled. Thereafter they returned to civilization and spent three more years digesting their bulging portfolios of data and writing up the final report of the expedition.

For laboratory purposes, the Lynds needed a typical small American city, though they conceded that "a typical city, strictly speaking, does not exist, but the city studied was selected as having many features common to a wide group of communities." The city chosen was labeled

"Middletown" (later revealed to be Muncie, Indiana), selected because it was as close to the average as could be attained. Its population of thirty-eight thousand was 95 per cent native-born and less than 4 per cent Negro. A more typical city would probably have had a higher ratio of Negroes and foreigners. Middletown lies within fifty miles of Indianapolis, and more than a hundred miles from Cincinnati; it is a prairie town in the Corn Belt. There is no dominant industry in the area, but Middletown is an industrial center with eleven large and twenty-five small factories and assorted samples of modern high-speed machine production.

Other more or less typical features of "Magic Middletown," at the time of the Lynd study, were a Chamber of Commerce, the best basketball team in the state of Indiana, an Ad Club, a Kill Kare Club, a Sew We Do Club (membership limited to the elite ladies of the town), and 454 other active clubs. There were also forty-two churches, representing twenty-eight denominations, a flourishing Ku Klux Klan, sixty-three hundred automobiles, and nine motion picture palaces.

For convenience, the Lynds divided their investigation into six "main-trunk activities": getting a living, making a home, training the young, using leisure, engaging in religious practices, and engaging in community activities. It is assumed that everything people do in Middletown falls under one or another of these headings.

To obtain better perspective, the Lynds use two points of reference: Middletown as it was in 1890 and as it is in 1924–25. A few years earlier than the beginning period, in 1886, natural gas was struck in the area and the resulting boom transformed the placid county seat into a manufacturing city. From surviving documents, we discover how Middletown's six thousand people got their living in 1890; how financial wealth was less significant then and the machine was in its infancy; what patent medicines were being advertised and how the newspapers carried more fiery editorials; how houses and the lots they stood on were larger; we feel the excitement of elections; how trade unions were much stronger than thirty-five years later; how professional rather than business men were the community leaders; how clubs were fewer but livelier; and we see other striking contrasts between the two eras.

By 1924, a tremendous change, perhaps in part superficial, had occurred in the life of Middletown. The nature of the evolutionary process will be considered here under the Lynds' six divisions.

Without question, the business of getting a living dominates the lives, thoughts, and much of the behavior of the town's citizens. Somewhat arbitrarily, the Lynds divide Middletown into two classes—the business or professional class and the working class. No real upper class exists. The community is industrialized and its thirty-six factories form the backbone of the economic system. The craft workman has disappeared since 1890, replaced by a routinized, semiskilled machine tender doing the same operation over and over again, year after year, until he is tossed on the scrap heap at age forty-five. No matter how hard he works or how loyal he is to his employer, no member of the working class can ensure himself against the loss of his job. As periodic depressions come, the worker's job simply evaporates, and he must turn to the Social Service Bureau for charity. There is deep resentment against the continual process of speeding-up in the factories and among the workers generally a dull acceptance of being doomed to remain in the class of wage earners, perpetually in fear of the periodic layoff, to which the employers resort so mercilessly when slack times come.

The average worker in Middletown receives less than enough to meet the demands of a minimum standard of living. In 1924, it was estimated that a family of five required $1921 per year. But the shocking fact was that of one hundred typical workers, forty-two with families of five earned less than the minimum, and only ten with families of five earned over the minimum. Eighty-five per cent of Middletown's population did not file an income tax return, and of 2245 forms returned, 1036 were not taxable after deductions and exemptions for dependents were made. Even if allowances are made for those who evaded taxes, for small families, and for families with several wage earners, it appears that half of the community was living on less than the income officially declared necessary for health and decency. There were no old-age pensions, no unemployment insurance, and little free medical care.

Middletown's workers are employed in more than four hundred different occupations. Few of them can expect promotion or better wages and most of the work is unskilled. The introduction of machinery has multiplied the average worker's productivity twenty-fold, yet most of them still work over fifty-five hours per week.

Not only is the workman poorly paid, at the mercy of business cycles, and doing a dull, routine, mechanical job, but practically he cannot bargain collectively to improve his lot. In 1893, Middletown was described by a union leader as "next to Rochester, N.Y., the best organized town in the country." By 1924, unionism was practically dead. For years, the businessmen of Middletown had pointed with pride and joy to their labor market as untainted by unionism. The preponderantly native-born workers in the early days had been drawn from the cornfields, and were referred to by the manufacturers as "corn-feds." As industry expanded, mountain men from Kentucky and West Virginia, known as "green-peas," were brought in. Middletown presented an almost solid front against trade unionism and with extraordinary success. A typical attitude was reflected by the pastor of a working-class church who advised his parishioners to be very cautious about exposing their families to the probable consequences of union affliation, and the Lynds report that the Middletown pulpit in general was highly sensitive to the risk of moral degradation by listening to outside agitators.

Of one hundred working-class families in 1924, only eleven were contributing anything to the support of labor unions. As the unions declined, social activities disappeared. Formerly the unions had been centers for picnics, parties, benefits, and discussion groups, but those activities have virtually vanished and the unions can get out only a handful of members even for important meetings.

The failure of unionization in Middletown can be attributed to a variety of factors. The business class was solidly opposed, from the standpoint of ideology and self-interest; the police force stood ready to move against any invading union organizer; the newspapers editorialized and filled their news columns against the "'Red Menace." Also contributing were the apathy of the workers, labor racketeering, and incompetent labor leaders.

The Lynds' two major groups—the business class and the working class—are more sharply differentiated than one would expect in people with a supposed common heritage and common environment. As observed by the authors:

The mere fact of being born upon one or the other side of the watershed roughly formed by these two groups is the most significant single cultural factor tending to influence what one does all day long through one's life; whom one marries; when one gets up in the morning; whether one belongs to the Holy Rollers or Presbyterian Church; or drives a Ford or a Buick; whether or not one's daughter makes the desirable high-school Violet Club; or one's wife meets with the Sew We Do Club or with the Art Students' League; whether one belongs to the Odd Fellows or to the Masonic Shrine; whether one sits about evenings with one's necktie off; and so indefinitely throughout the daily comings and goings of a Middletown man, woman or child.

The bourgeois members of Middletown society labor less than the working-class members and are better paid, but they have their share of anxieties. They are even more dominated by the herd spirit than are members of the proletariat. They must play golf, vote the Republican ticket, and enthusiastically applaud the Bear Cat basketball team. They must also support the churches, though they are not required to attend them. They must be boosters of the Chamber of Commerce—Rotarian type, totally convinced that they live in the most progressive city in the finest country in the world.

A relatively new phenomenon in Middletown life is a credit economy. Mass production demands mass purchasing for its support. Hence the business regime exhorts the good citizen to "Buy! Buy! Buy-on-credit if necessary, but Buy." The rise and spread of installment buying, the dollar-down-and-so-much-per-week-or-month plan, affects nearly every family in the community. The Lynds view credit as a principal reason for social conformity—why everybody in Middletown is inclined to think alike and to act alike. Credit serves "as a repressive agent tending to standardize widening sectors of the habits of the business class—to vote the Republican ticket, to adopt golf as their recreation and to refrain from 'queer'—i.e., atypical behavior." Credit and snobbery appear to rule the lives of Middletown's business class. The working class are naturally not so much in the power of this elaborate system of credit, but they use it frequently enough to become involved in financial difficulties.

All the popular channels of communication in Middletown—large-scale advertising, magazines, movies, and radio—are directed toward making the citizens more aware of material things, to make them feel that semiluxuries are essential to living, and to be dissatisfied if they do not possess them. New tools and services commonly used in Middletown today were either unknown or little used in the nineties.

Middletown's thirty-eight thousand people live in 9200 homes, predominately one-family houses built of wood. Only 1 per cent of the inhabitants are apartment dwellers. Paradoxically, the smallest families live in the largest houses and there is unemployment in the building trade alongside a housing shortage. Housing lots are small, the standard frontage a mere forty feet; consequently, play room for children and for family leisure-time activities is lacking, and there is little family privacy. All new houses, except the very cheapest, have bathrooms and the improvement is being installed in many old houses. Electric lighting has become commonplace. A group of wealthy families live in large houses in the "East End," often heavy brick or stone affairs; others are building homes in the newer college district, low structures of brick or fieldstone or of white Dutch colonial type, with all modern conveniences.

A family has to sacrifice more than a full year's income to own a home or the income from one week of every four to rent a house. An important psychological factor is that sentiment in Middletown is deep-rooted in considering home ownership a mark of independence, of respectability, and of belonging.

The essential functions of the family, according to Middletown thinking, are childbearing and child-rearing. Childbearing is a moral obligation, though there are fewer children per family than in earlier generations. The voluntary limitation of parenthood is almost universally practiced among the business group, who have access to reasonably efficient contraceptive methods. Less than half the working class, however, use contraceptives, in large part because of ignorance, though somewhat deterred also by social and religious taboos. Strict rules frown on illicit and extramarital sexual relations, but the ban is widely disregarded clandestinely. Nearly 50 per cent of Middletown marriages end in divorce, the usual excuse being cruelty, though the actual reason is more likely to be financial woes. The incidence of divorce is highest among working wives, presumably less dependent economically on their husbands.

Child-rearing in Middletown presents problems unknown in a simpler age. The traditional method was to make children conform to the community's mores. Controls have been loosened by working mothers, by more time spent in schools and clubs, the limitations on play space at home, and for high school level children by athletics, dramatics, parties, dances, the movies, and auto riding. Use of the family automobile is a major source of disagreement between children and parents. Unchaperoned automobile parties may travel long distances and stay out as late as midnight. A judge of the juvenile court denounced the automobile as "a house of prostitution on wheels."

The automobile is also blamed by union officials for destroying the unions, condemned by the clergy for decreasing church attendance, and is responsible for "the not uncommon practice of mortgaging a home (to buy an automobile)." Nevertheless, the car is a status symbol to which all classes are loyal. The poorer people often buy a car to help their children's social position at school. Several working women state that in bad times they preferred to do with less food rather than give up their automobiles. A Ford is more valued than a bathroom. The fact that two out of three Middletown families own cars would seem to point toward a considerable degree of affluence in the community; in reality, many aged models rattling along the streets were long overdue at the junk yard. To the working man and his family, a car is the chief means of escaping, no matter how temporarily, the squalor of their home.

Other vehicles for escape are the telephone, the phonograph, the movie, and the radio. A total of 4348 Middletown homes have a telephone, leaving about five thousand without this facility. All the business-class families have telephones, but only 55 per cent of the working-class families.

Middletown is solicitous that all its young receive "an education," reflected in the fact that 45 per cent of money spent by the city is devoted to its schools. The school year has increased in length, children remain in school more years, and attendance in school and college is larger. The number of students graduating from high school has increased nineteenfold since 1890, while the city's population has increased only three and a half times. Furthermore, over a third of the high school graduates go on to college or normal school. Middletown believes in education, for education makes it possible for one's child to be assured of a place in the business or professional class and to escape working-class drudgery. "If education is sometimes taken for granted by the business class," the Lynds comment, "it is no exaggeration to say that it evokes the fervor of a religion, a means of salvation, among a large section of the working class." The fact that the high school has become the center of social life for Middletown's young also adds to its popularity.

Vocational work for boys in the high schools "is the darling of Middletown's eye," even though some teachers and parents feel that such courses lower academic standards. There is new emphasis on courses in history and civics, one of the main purposes of which is to inoculate students against subversive ideas. Traditional values and "right" attitudes are stressed throughout the curriculum. The conservatism of the students is reflected in their appraisal of the statement: "The theory of evolution offers a more accurate account of the origin and history of mankind than that offered by a literal interpretation of the Bible"; only 19 per cent marked the statement as true.

Four fifths of Middletown's teachers are women, a majority unmarried women under forty, with preference given to graduates of Middletown's own teachers' training college. Salaries for both men and women are too low to attract the ablest people. The citizens are inclined to disregard teachers and the content of books, while giving an exalted place to the schools' social and athletic activities.

The Lynds dwell at length on the use of leisure in Middletown, beginning with a discussion of the traditional ways of spending leisure. The great outdoors has little to offer, e.g., "A small river wanders through Middletown, and in 1890 when timber still stood on its banks, White River was a pleasant stream for picnics, fishing, and boating, but it has shrunk today to a creek discolored by industrial chemicals and malodorous with the city's sewage." A form of recreation still in vogue is talking—lectures, sermons, and gossip,—but speeches are shorter. Patterns of sociability are much influenced by the telephone, the phonograph, the radio, and the movie. Social life is more active than in 1890, but now takes different forms—the dance, the tea, the bridge party, and the country club luncheon. The old practice of dropping in on neighbors for a social visit has virtually disappeared, as have family reunions.

Middletown is "clubbed to death," beginning with the young people in school and continuing for the rest of their lives. Represented among 458 clubs are numerous women's organizations, church societies, the Rotary Club and its rivals, the Chamber of Commerce, the lodges of the secret orders bearing fantastic names, the YM and YWCA, the Ku Klux Klan. The club, in effect, has absorbed the functions of the church, and the church itself has become an aggregation of clubs.

It is rare in Middletown for a male to read a book. Culture, like embroidery, is a feminine activity. There are 40,000 books in the Middletown Public Library, but the library is starved for funds for new books. Eighty-three per cent of all books borrowed from the library are fiction, as are magazines subscribed to, for "Middletown appears to read magazines primarily for the vicarious living in fictional form they contain." The business class buys books in limited number, and the working class scarcely at all, except those relating to religion or for the children. Among 9200 homes in the city, 1840 subscribe to the *American Magazine;* 1530 to *The Saturday Evening Post;* between 900 and 1500 to the *Delineator, Ladies' Home Journal, McCall's; Physical Culture, True Story, Woman's Home Companion;* between 200 and 500 to *Collier's, College Humor, Cosmopolitan, Motion Picture Magazine, Dream World, National Geographic, Popular Science, True Romance;* 60 to *Vogue* and *Vanity Fair;* 35 to *The Atlantic Monthly,* 20 to *Harper's,* and 15 to *Century.*

The people of Middletown seem to have little interest in art. Music, like poetry and the other arts, is almost nonexistent among the men of the city. "It has ceased to be a matter of spontaneous active participation," as it was in the eighteen nineties, with its singing societies, "and has become largely a passive matter of listening to others." The Art Students' League has neither brushes nor easels, but listens to lectures on "The Character of the Early Christian, Byzantine, Romanesque, and Gothic Periods" and "Medieval Sculpture and Painting."

The most extended section of the Lynds' book deals with religion—dominant religious beliefs, where and how religious rites are carried on, leaders and participants in religious rites, and religious observances. Membership in one of the religious groups is generally taken for granted, particularly among the business class. The congregations of the forty-two churches in town range from two thousand down to twenty-four in number. The Protestants outnumber Catholics about fifteen to one. Skepticism is on the rise: "Questioning of the dominant Christian beliefs in public appears to have declined since the nineties, but one infers that doubts and uneasiness among individuals may be greater than a generation ago." Religious observances are a less spontaneous and pervasive part of the city's life than formerly, and there has been a decline in church attendance. The question of what religion means in the lives of the individuals concerned is treated at length by the Lynds on the basis of personal interviews, questionnaires, and direct observation.

Government and politics are viewed with apathy or distaste by most citizens of Middletown. Politics is equated with fraud, dishonesty, and corruption in the mind of the average Middletowner, and there is substantial evidence in the history of the city's municipal affairs to support his jaundiced views. Nevertheless, the community is deeply loyal to the Republican Party except at rare intervals. In the business of dispensing justice a rich man or a corporation stands a better chance in Middletown courts than a poor man, and "Save in the case of the judge of the superior court, neither juries nor judges have the confidence of the city." Meantime, the citizens delegate their interests in government to others and busy themselves with more pressing and immediate concerns.

Middletown's health is cared for by a group of more or less well-trained doctors operating individually and competitively. The papers are full of patent medicine advertisements, and believers in folk medicine and superstitious practices are numerous. Opposition to any form of socialized medicine is strong, though a high proportion of the population is unable to afford expert medical care.

The same philosophy of rugged individualism governs social welfare measures, for the community does not wish to encourage dependence. As stated by the Lynds, "Middletown's working philosophy in the matter tends to be: People in actual need must be helped, because you wouldn't let a *dog* starve, but we must not make it too easy for them, and by all means let's get the unpleasant business over with and out of sight as soon as possible!"

The Lynds attempt to draw few conclusions from their comprehensive study, preferring to let the facts speak for themselves. They try to bring out all significant aspects of Middletown's life, to reveal the complex interrelationships in this one reasonably typical American community, and to indicate some of the problems confronting government, industry, the medical and ministerial professions, education, and social science in general.

Ten years after their original investigation, the Lynds returned to Middletown. The result was a second book, *Middletown in Transition*, issued in 1937. The Great Depression had come and was near an end. In many ways the Middletown scene remained unchanged. There were now nearly 50,000 people. The leading industry, the manufacture of glass jars for household use for preserving food, had thrived during the depression years. A General Motors plant had opened to take advantage of Middletown's cheap labor.

But now it appears that a "Royal Family" had assumed a dominant position in Middletown social, business, and industrial life, the X (Ball) family, owners of the jar factory, whose fortunes had grown tremendously in the intervening years. The extent of the X family's control may be judged by a comment from one Middletown citizen:

> If I'm out of work, I go to the X plant; if I need money I go to the X bank, and if they don't like me I don't get it; my children go to the X college; when I get sick I go to the X hospital; I buy a building lot or house in an X subdivision; my wife goes down town to buy clothes at the X department store; if my dog stays away he is put in the X pound; I buy X milk; I drink X beer, vote for X political parties, and get help from X charities; my boy goes to their Y.M.C.A. and my girl to their Y.W.C.A.; I listen to the word of God in X-subsidized churches; if I'm a Mason I go to X Masonic Temple; I read the news from the X morning newspaper; and, if I am rich enough, I travel via the X airport.

Middletown has now become a college town. A state normal school, started in 1896, had survived numerous vicissitudes, and is operating as X State Teachers College, soon to emerge as X State University. The land on which the college stands was donated by the X family, probably to lend prestige to a new real estate subdivision.

The Lynds are convinced that "the business class in Middletown runs the city. The nucleus of business-class control is the X family." The dictatorship, however, is a benevolent one, for the X's are "alert, capable, democratic, Christian gentlemen, trained in the school of rugged individualism, patrons of art, education, religion and a long list of philanthropies; men who have never spared themselves in business or civic affairs; high exemplars of the successful, responsible manipulators of the American formulas of business enterprise ... conscientious and utterly unhypocritical in their combination of high profits, great philanthropy, and a low wage scale."

The power of the X family was demonstrated in its successful opposition to the entry of a Ford Plant into Middletown. Rather than exposing the city's present industries to the disturbing influence of the Ford wage scale, this important addition to the community's industrial expansion was deliberately sacrificed. No wonder some citizens felt that they would be better off with less philanthropy and fatter wage envelopes.

Still, the X family and its business associates are not omnipotent. Some years earlier, Middletown had built sewers through the streets, and naturally arranged to have them empty into the river. Now the sewage-loaded river flows past the beautiful new homes of Middletown's royalty, and the owners feel strongly that something should be done. They want a modern sewage disposal plant for the city. But the working class, living on the South Side, comprising 65 per cent of the population and outvoting the North Side, refuses to pay higher taxes for the improvement. Thus, Middletown continues to stink.

"The line between working class and business class, though vague and blurred still," report the Lynds, "is more apparent than it was ten years before." There are signs of a growing class consciousness, especially among women and children. The two principal classes are also being subdivided. The working class now consists of three distinct layers: foremen and skilled mechanics, semiskilled factory workers, and untrained laborers, without regular jobs. In a culture which emphasizes getting ahead in the world, few of the working class are likely to rise as high as even a foremanship. The business class has split into two main divisions: a less privileged group, composed of clerical workers, salespeople, and small retailers, a new middle class; and, at the top, a "business control group," headed by the X family, who have emerged as a local aristocracy.

Middletown itself has become more attractive since the twenties. Government relief money has financed many public improvements. Flower growing as a hobby is more common, encouraged by the leisure time forced on people by the depression years.

Politically, too, Middletown is changing. In 1932, the county in which Middletown is located was the only one in Indiana to go for Hoover against Roosevelt, but in 1936 Roosevelt received 59 per cent of the city's votes, even though "the weight of frightened hope with which the city's leading businessmen backed Landon to defeat Roosevelt was almost literally beyond exaggeration." One of the humorous stories going around town on election day was about a man down at the X plant who broke his leg falling over the pile of Landon buttons discarded by the men outside the plant door.

Some critics have suggested that the Lynds overestimated the power of Middletown's business elite and underrated the politicians. They offer such evidence as the election of a mayor who fought the business interests, the defeat of the city manager form of government through the concerted effort of the political machine, the rejection of the sewage disposal plant because the politicians representing the South Side could see no advantage to them and to their constituents, and government approval of projects which had popular but not business support.

The Lynds see under-the-surface conflicts in Middletown as "not so much new as more insistent, more difficult to avoid, harder to smooth over." The differences, aggravated by the Depression, include conflicts among economic and political, economic and educational and religious, economic and familial institutions, and conflicts among groups in the community. "Compromise and expediency rule Middletown's course. At point after point—in its handling of relief, in city government, in its dealings with dissent—it deals with present situations simply as it must, using the old words." In final analysis, Middletown is viewed as a "sober, hopeful, well-meaning city, caught in its institutional conflicts, caught between past and future and not knowing which way to move."

Middletown and *Middletown in Transition* have been widely and deservedly acclaimed as classics in their field, pioneer additions to the literature of social anthropology, the most exhaustive and systematic study of American folkways yet produced. Their influence on social scientists continues to be pervasive.

22-NATION WITHIN A NATION

W. J. CASH'S *The Mind of the South*

Is THE SOUTH fundamentally different from other regions of the United States—in effect a nation within a nation? W. J. Cash returned a positive answer to the question in his *The Mind of the South*, a work widely recognized by students of regional analysis as a classic. Cash's essential thesis is that, despite enormous physical and social differences, there can be traced throughout the former Confederate States "a fairly definite mental pattern, associated with a fairly definite social pattern." Common to an overwhelming majority of Southern white people, the author maintains, is "a complex of established relationships and habits of thought, sentiments, prejudices, standards and values, and association of ideas."

Carl Carmer, a Southerner by adoption, once made the remark that "the Congo is not more different from Massachusetts or Kansas or California than Alabama." Carmer could as logically have pointed out the divergencies between Mississippi and North Carolina. "Nevertheless," asserts Cash, "if it can be said that there are many Souths, the fact remains that there is also only one South," shaped by the peculiar history of the region. To illuminate and to validate his theory, Cash presents a fascinating ideological and social history of the South from colonial times until the beginning of World War II. The emphasis, notwithstanding the book's title, is sociological, rather than psychological or intellectual.

At the outset Cash explodes two legends, one of the Old and the other of the New South. The first is a throwback to the eighteenth century, when there flourished a culture of elegant gentlemen and lovely ladies, a ruling class of cavaliers, aristocrats dwelling in stately mansions, possessing vast estates and innumerable slaves, immersed in brilliant social activities. Beneath the elite class, the myth goes, were the poor whites, physically inferior and descended from lower classes.

The legend of the Old South is dismissed by Cash in large part as moonshine. The colonial gentry were a much more homespun lot than one would gather from a visit to the Williamsburg Restoration or from talking to members of the Colonial Dames. The frontier tradition remained strong and there was no great gap between the common whites and the owners of large plantations. In fact, the two were frequently blood relations. By accident, fate, and the process of natural selection, the common whites were "the less industrious and thrifty, the less ambitious and pushing, the less cunning and lucky." Cash does not, however, reject the romantic concept of Southern aristocracy as unadulterated bunk. There were enough genuine gentlemen to provide a basis for the legend. The number was relatively small. William E. Dodd, U.S. historian, states that in 1860 there were no more than four or five thousand of the greater planters. Cash guesses that "the total number of families in Virginia, South Carolina, Louisiana—in all the regions of the little aristocracies— who were rationally to be reckoned as proper aristocrats came to less than five hundred—and maybe not more than half that number."

Both the aristocrats and the poor whites had one common tenet, the "vastly ego-warming and ego-expanding distinction between the white man and the black." No matter what his station in life, the white man would always be a member of the dominant race. "And before that vast and capacious distinction," comments Cash, "all others were foreshortened, dwarfed, and all but obliterated." Thus was democracy preserved, insofar as the white man was concerned.

As for the New South, Cash maintains that a legend has arisen based on the erroneous view that the Civil War simply obliterated the civilization of the antebellum period and established a new order dominated by industrialism. In Cash's eyes, the distinction between the Old and the New South is largely imaginary. The South is substantially what it always was, if allowance is made for the effect of new factors in its environment. The mind of the South survived virtually unchanged into recent times in its attitude toward race and politics, its intolerance of "wrong thinking," its religious conservatism. In Southern economy, as seen by Cash, the cotton mill village was organized in much the same fashion as the plantation and the owners' modes of thought toward their workers closely paralleled those of the great plantation proprietors. Thus it is argued that industrialism did not lead to a revolution in the South's ingrained ideology, but placed more power in the hands of "the hard, pushing, horse-trading type of man" and confirmed the exaggerated individualism of the Old South.

Intense individualism as a factor in the development of the Southern mind is constantly stressed by Cash. The impact of the frontier may be clearly discerned here, a rough-and-ready setting in which every man was forced to stand on his own feet in order to survive. Independence and self-sufficiency worked against the development of law and order. As Cash notes, the Southerner has "an intense distrust of, and, indeed, downright aversion to, any actual exercise of authority beyond the barest minimum essential to the existence of the social organism." As a natural corollary, the Southerner is quick to resent any encroachment on his freedom and to boast "that he would knock hell out of whoever dared to cross him." Hence, we see "the perpetuation and acceleration of the tendency to violence which had grown up in the Southern backwoods as it naturally grows up on all frontiers." Also traceable to the frontier mentality is the tradition of vigilante action, represented in the South by lynchings.

A second Southern characteristic, dealt with at length by Cash, is the strong tendency toward romanticism and hedonism, i.e., the belief that pleasure is the chief good in life. The Southerner spurns realism, lives much in a self-created world of imagination and fantasy, and "he likes naively to play, to expand his ego, his senses, his emotions . . . he will accept what pleases him and reject what does not . . . and in general he will prefer the extravagant, the flashing, and the brightly colored." Aspects of this attitude are contempt for certain types of hard labor, referred to as "nigger work"; devotion to horse racing, listening to brass bands, making love, dancing, and extravagant play; a fondness for rhetoric, especially the high-flown oratory of demagogic politicians.

Romanticism and escapism also account for the South's

religious pattern, as seen by Cash. The Southerner's "chief blood-strain was likely to be the Celtic—of all Western strains the most susceptible to suggestions of the supernatural." Consequently, "what our Southerner required was a faith as simple and emotional as himself. A faith to draw men together in hordes, to terrify them with Apocalyptic rhetoric, to cast them into the pit, rescue them, and at last bring them shouting into the fold of Grace." For these reasons, the appeal of the revivalistic sects—the Methodists, the Baptists, and the Presbyterians—to the Southern mind is obvious.

Toward the institution of slavery, the churches displayed a curious ambivalence. The evangelical religious sects had all begun by denouncing it. Before 1830, a majority of the abolition societies were in the South. But placed on the defense by bitter attacks from the North, viewpoints started to change and justifications for slavery, characteristically romantic in nature, began to emerge. To palliate what Cash calls "that eternal uneasiness of the South's conscience over slavery," churchmen began referring to it as a "providential trust" and "God's plan for instructing the black man in the Gospel and securing him entry into eternal bliss."

From colonial days forward, miscegenation was a striking feature of the slave system, beginning with the Portuguese, Spanish, and Yankee slave traders and continuing with the Southern planters. Melville Herskovits, American anthropologist, states that only 20 per cent of American Negroes are unmixed, while almost 80 per cent show mixture with whites or American Indians. The Southerner's reaction in antebellum days, writes Cash, was typically romantic, first by inventing the fiction that miscegenation did not exist, and second to place the white woman on a pedestal to compensate her for so cruelly wounding the sentiments she held most sacred.

Having viewed the region's characteristics, Cash turns to a critical examination of the South's claim to a superior culture. By and large, the claim is disallowed. Prior to the Civil War's outbreak, the South's colleges "were no more than academies"; illiteracy was far above the American average; the only novelist of distinction, William Gilmore Simms, was snubbed; the only able painter, Washington Allston, achieved his first recognition abroad; the only poet deserving the name, Edgar Allan Poe, was left to starve; and any books except the Bible were rare, even in the homes of wealthy planters.

And so Cash arrives at a harsh judgment: "In general, the intellectual and aesthetic culture of the Old South was a superficial and jejune thing, borrowed from without and worn as a political armor and a badge of rank; and hence ... not a true culture at all." Cash considers the situation the more amazing because the South "had enjoyed riches, rank, and a leisure perhaps unmatched elsewhere in the world, for more than a hundred years at least," and ought to have progressed to a complex and important intellectual culture. In seeking an explanation, Cash believes that conflict with the Yankee was a primary factor. The defense of slavery led to a taboo on criticism, a ban on all analysis and inquiry, and an opposition to new ideas and every innovation. Given his environment, the Southerner "developed no need or desire for intellectual culture in its own right—none, at least, powerful enough to drive him past his taboos to its actual achievement."

The Civil War and Reconstruction are seen by Cash as an attempt by the Yankee to achieve by force what he had failed to accomplish by political means, namely to give the "tariff gang" a free hand and to force the South into the prevailing American mold. At Appomattox the Southern world seemed to have been destroyed, but the victory was an illusion. The war "left the essential Southern mind and will ... entirely unshaken." Reconstruction made the region more self-conscious, more united than ever, filled with fear, rage, indignation, and resentment, and patriotic passion, determined to reassert white superiority and to resume mastery of the Negro.

Out of Reconstruction and the decade or so of Negro-carpetbagger dominance developed two complexes in the Southern mind. The first was the fear of Negro rape of white women, the other control of government in the South by the Yankee operating through the Negro. Only resort to naked force, the white Southerners felt, could again make them the ruling class. Hence the coming of the Ku Klux Klan and the rise of a tradition of violence which has marked Southern culture for more than a century. The Negro, caught in the middle, became the scapegoat. No matter how damnable the means, they were justified and even glorified if the end to be attained was good.

In later decades the traumatic effects of the Civil War

and Reconstruction and their aftermath were felt through a repression of liberal ideas and speech, most specifically through a repudiation of Yankee thought and indeed the thought of the outside world. "Darwin, Huxley, Ben Butler, Sherman, Satan," notes Cash, "came to figure in Southern feeling as very nearly a single person." Further, "even first-rate minds were so tightly bound in the ruling pattern that the hospitality to novel notions normal to such minds was almost fully paralyzed."

Paradoxically, however, the South at last began to develop a literature, as an increasing number of authors devoted themselves to the writing and publishing of novels, stories, essays, and poetry, beginning with Sidney Lanier, Joel Chandler Harris, George W. Cable, Thomas Nelson Page, and Ellen Glasgow.

Then came Progress. To meet the Yankee on his own ground, and perhaps even excel him, the Southern leaders decided late in the nineteenth century that the region must industrialize. With the factory—chiefly the cotton mill—rose the myth that the South had "suffered a change of heart," had acquired "a completely new viewpoint," and henceforth would be just like Yankeedom. In fact, Cash maintains, with much supporting evidence, "there was no revolution in basic ideology and no intention of relinquishing the central Southern positions and surrendering bodily to Yankee civilization." By the beginning of the new century, for example, the South had effectively nullified the Fourteenth Amendment and formally disfranchised the Negro.

As they viewed their own actions, the cotton mill owners and founders, mainly the old "Confederate captains," built the factories for humanitarian reasons, to salvage the sinking tenant farmer from economic ruin. In practical operation, Cash iterates again and again, "the economic benefit of the new industrialism were far from distributing themselves equitably down the social scale. Whatever the intent of the original founders of Progress, the plain truth is that everything here rested finally upon one fact alone: cheap labor."

The Mind of the South shows an obsession with cotton. Cash was born and spent his boyhood in a South Carolina cotton mill town, where his father operated a company store. The cotton mill whistles calling the "lintheads" to the spindles were Cash's association with cotton—not wide fields covered with white blossoms. When he thought of cotton, Cash visualized company houses, clouds of lint, and lung diseases, and a general physical deterioration of the workers.

By the 1920s King Cotton was ill, both in the factory and on the farm, a result of European and Japanese competition, over-production, economic depression, loss of foreign markets, poor management, and related factors. For these conditions, the worker paid the main part of the price.

Nevertheless, Southern industry continued to expand. New England mills were enticed southward by the promise of cheap, contented labor, free factory buildings and sites, and the waiving of taxes. The consequence, Cash was convinced, was that "Dixie was now being worse exploited than ever the tariff gang had dreamed of." There was increased employment, but it was "a boon purchased at the appalling price of virtually giving away the inherent resources of the section, physical and human."

Meantime, the small farmers, the tenants, and the sharecroppers—the dwellers on the land who outnumbered the industrial workers by more than two to one in 1930—were having their share of trouble. The depredations of the boll weevil, starting in the early twenties, price slumps, increasing foreign competition for the cotton market of the world, and expanding production of the staple in India, China, South America, and the Soviet Union were crowding the Southern farmer to the wall. Thousands of landowners in the deep South were reduced to bankruptcy by the boll weevil and many more thousands of tenants and sharecroppers were driven to emigrate.

The rise and fall of labor unions in the South is traced in graphic detail by Cash. Unionism from the beginning was equated with Communism by the Southern industrialists, and even among the working men themselves there was long a curious, widespread, and active antagonism to unionization, explained in part by their old intense individualism. Faced with exploitation by Yankee manufacturers, wage cuts, and work speedups in the late twenties and thirties, however, the workers reacted with strikes and attempts to form unions. The movement had too many forces arrayed against it to hope for success, including economic depression, a surplus of labor willing to serve as strikebreakers, the whole business community, the evangelical clergy, the police and other government agencies, the press with few exceptions, and the farmers. And so the strikes failed and the unions promptly collapsed.

In another area of "The Sahara of the Bozart" (H. L. Mencken's epithet for the South), an oasis had come into being. A powerful new school of writers was making itself heard at home and abroad, notably James Branch Cabell, Elizabeth Madox Roberts, Julia Peterkin, DuBose Heyward, Conrad Aiken, Roark Bradford, Thomas Wolfe, Erskine Caldwell, and William Faulkner. In the twenties the Southern agrarians appeared, led by John Crowe Ransom, Allen Tate, and Donald Davidson, moving, as Cash notes, "toward a more clear-eyed view of the Southern world."

Political leadership, on the other hand, showed little or no improvement. Demagogues of the Right and Left proliferated—Cotton Ed Smith of South Carolina, whipping up hatred of the Negro and preaching states' rights; Huey Long of Louisiana, declaiming "Every Man a King"; Bilbo of Mississippi, promoting a movement to deport all Negroes to Africa; Robert Rice Reynolds of North Carolina, leading a crusade of hatred against aliens, of which his state had the smallest proportion in the nation; "Red Gallus" Gene Talmadge, rabble-rousing hero of the Georgia crackers. More decent individuals, such as Carter Glass and Harry Byrd of Virginia, and Josiah William Bailey of North Carolina, were ultraconservatives, but a few social-minded individuals were beginning to emerge, notably the Bankheads and Lister Hill of Alabama.

Cash's concluding "basic picture of the South" has been often quoted:

> Proud, brave, honorable by its lights, courteous, personally generous, loyal, swift to act, often too swift, but signally effective, sometimes terrible, in its action —such was the South at its best. And such at its best it remains today, despite the great falling away in some of its virtues. Violence, intolerance, aversion and suspicion toward new ideas, an incapacity for analysis, an inclination to act from feeling rather than from thought, an exaggerated individualism and a too narrow concept of social responsibility, attachment to fictitious and false values, above all too great attachment to racial values and a tendency to justify cruelty and injustice in the name of those values, sentimentality and a lack of realism—these have been its

characteristic vices in the past. And, despite changes for the better, they remain its characteristic vices today.

In a chapter of Morris' *The South Today: 100 Years After Appomattox* (1965), Edwin M. Yoder, Jr., re-examines "W. J. Cash After a Quarter Century." Yoder notes that after twenty-five years, historians differ with Cash on several points. Some argue that there was more to the Reconstruction period than Yankee piracy and brutal economic imperialism, and others hold that Cash's bitter treatment of Southern religion is superficial and biased. Nonetheless, Yoder believes that the essential character of the South has not changed radically in the quarter century since Cash described it, despite economic and social modifications, the spread of television, and jet air travel. Race is as much or more a Southern preoccupation as it was before World War II, and fundamental changes in racial attitudes and practices are exceedingly slow in coming, regardless of federal legislation.

No less snail-paced from the standpoint of any basic alteration is what Cash called "the savage ideal," defined as "that ideal whereunder dissent and variety are completely suppressed and men become, for all their attitudes, professions, and actions, virtual replicas of one another." Motivations, however, continue to be of the highest, for as Yoder notes, "when repression-minded Southern legislators curtail freedoms of speech, organization, teaching, or movement, it is usually, so they say, in all good faith, for the sake of a higher good."

Cash believed that unionization of cotton mill workers would herald a new day for the South, a belief that Yoder considers naïve, given the fierce individualism and aversion to regimentation characteristic of the Southern cracker. In any event, the wholesale unionization predicted by Cash never came, beaten back by right-to-work laws, a mass of cheap labor out of the hills, and high-priced lawyers hired by the corporations.

A novel explanation of the Southern mind, differing somewhat from Cash's analysis, is offered by C. Vann Woodward in his *The Burden of Southern History*. Unlike the rest of the nation, which has been historically conditioned to victory, plenty, and optimism about the possibility of solving human problems, Woodward holds, the South has experienced defeat, poverty, and tragedy on a large scale. An atmosphere of abiding tragedy permeates Southern fiction, with a background always of inability to resolve the great social dilemma of race relations.

In a recent biography, *W. J. Cash: Southern Prophet* (1967), Joseph L. Morrison concludes, "During this second half of the twentieth century, it has been accepted by virtually everyone that studies of the South—and, by extension, of the Negro revolution—must begin where Cash left off." By writing his book, Cash contributed in no small degree to regional self-consciousness. The pattern he designed has since influenced a multitude of investigators of regional problems, in the South and elsewhere.

23–DEED VERSUS CREED

GUNNAR MYRDAL'S *An American Dilemma*

IN SUPPORT of the psychological and sociological bases for its celebrated decision banning racial segregation in public schools, the United States Supreme Court cited various authorities, concluding with "And see generally Myrdal, *An American Dilemma* (1944)."

The significance of Gunnar Myrdal's *An American Dilemma* was perceived by a reviewer in the *Political Science Quarterly* when the book first appeared: "It is predictable," wrote Frank Tannenbaum, "that in the future it will be classed with Tocqueville's *American Democracy* and Bryce's *American Commonwealth*. This is high praise, but the achievement is so clear and so broadly based that it has wider scope than the problem it is devoted to—the Negro. It is, in fact, a critical evaluation of American civilization."

When, in 1937, the Carnegie Corporation of New York decided to sponsor "a comprehensive study of the Negro in the United States, to be undertaken in a wholly objective and dispassionate way as a social phenomenon," the key problem was to find a competent director. There was no lack of able American scholars who were deeply interested in the field and who had devoted years of their time to it, but as Frederick P. Keppel, President of the Corporation, commented, "the whole question had been for nearly a hundred years so charged with emotion that it appeared wise to seek as the responsible head of the undertaking someone who could approach his task with a fresh mind, uninfluenced by traditional attitudes or by earlier conclusions." Such objectivity was possible only for a man from Mars; as the nearest practical alternative, a distinguished Swedish scholar was chosen. Gunnar Myrdal had already achieved an international reputation as a social economist, a university professor, economic adviser to the Swedish Government, and a member of the Swedish Senate.

The "dilemma" analyzed and described by Myrdal is the failure of the American credo as it applies to the Negro. The prevailing theme of the book is the contrast between the fundamental American faith in freedom, equality, justice, opportunity, and the right of every man to strive for the good things of life and our sense of inner defeat and frustration that comes from the failure to practice our high ideals. This is the American dilemma. On the one hand, as a people we are under the influence of high national and Christian precepts, but these are counteracted by personal and local interests; economic, social, and sexual jealousies; matters of community prestige and conformity; group prejudices against races of people; and other desires, impulses, and habits.

Myrdal's concern for the white man as well as for the Negro stands out. Studies of the Negro problem have concentrated traditionally on industrial, educational, economic, and biological aspects, disregarding the effects on the white American living in a democratic society. "What do the millions of white people in the South and in the North actually think when, year after year, on the national holidays dedicated to the service of democratic ideals, they read, recite and listen to the Declaration of Independence and the Constitution? Do they, or do they not, include Negroes among all men?" In actuality, Myrdal credits Americans with an uncommon sensitivity to their creed, which causes them acute embarrassment when they are caught violating it. A skeptic viewing the mass of evidence presented by Myrdal may, on the contrary, be left with lingering doubts whether the American people are indeed influenced by profound moral convictions in the field of race relations.

In trying to defend their behavior to themselves and to others, Myrdal believes that "people will twist and mutilate their beliefs" of social reality. Thus, he found numerous solidly entrenched popular beliefs about the Negro which are demonstrably false, but which are loaded with emotions and understandable as devices used to excuse the white man's mistreatment of the Negro.

Myrdal was convinced that American culture had to be

studied in its entirety in order to determine the place of
the Negro, for "the Negro problem is an integral part of,
or a special phase of, the whole complex of problems in
the larger American civilization. It cannot be treated in
isolation." Seen in the context of the American society at
large, the problem of the Negro can be viewed in broader
perspective. Just as the conditions and forces at work in
the larger American society react on the Negro, so the
presence of millions of colored citizens constantly affects
the American way of life. Nevertheless, the author warns
that despite the fact that he has been forced "to dig in
dark corners and to wash dirty linen in public" in the
course of his investigation, no one should "regard our
analysis as a complete evaluation of America." By concentrating on problem groups and areas, "a delusion is easily
created that the situation in America is worse than it
actually is."

For background purposes, Myrdal devotes his opening
chapter to his basic thesis, "American Ideals and the
American Conscience." He finds, perhaps not surprisingly,
"that America, compared to every other country in
Western civilization, large or small, has the *most explicitly
expressed* system of general ideals in reference to human
interrelations." The creed developed out of the Era of
Enlightenment and the American Revolution and from
Christianity, especially Protestant sects split off from the
Anglican Church, and it has strong roots in English law.
Because these inspiring principles are a common heritage,
Myrdal notes that there is "a strong unity in this nation
and a basic homogeneity and stability in its valuations." In
brief, "the American Creed is the cement in the structure
of this great and disparate nation."

But from the point of view of the American creed, the
status of the Negro in America leaves much to be desired;
in fact, Myrdal holds, it "represents nothing more and
nothing less than a century-long lag of public morals." The
Negro problem was solved long ago in principle; the
practice is vastly different, for "the Negro in America has
not yet been given the elemental civil and political rights
of formal democracy, including a fair opportunity to earn
his living."

What is described as the "American Creed," Myrdal is
careful to explain, is not an American monopoly; it is the
common democratic creed as it has developed over a
period of centuries in Western Civilization.

America has had, and continues to have, other minority groups and minority problems. Within one or two generations, however, the "melting pot" absorbs the newcomers into the dominant majority. The general pattern of assimilating minorities into a homogeneous nation breaks down, states Myrdal, in the case of Negroes, who are commonly assumed to be unassimilable, because of color prejudices, opposition to mixed marriages, and concern for "race purity." The extensive miscegenation which has proceeded from the earliest slave days to the present has been principally extralegal in character. The assumption that Negroes cannot be merged into the total population led to their segregation. As summarized by Myrdal, the caste system is rationalized and defended by the white man on these grounds: The Negro people belongs to a separate race of mankind; the Negro race has an entirely different ancestry; the Negro race is inferior in all important respects; biologically, the Negro race belongs somewhere between the white man and the anthropoids; all white people in America can be considered a homogeneous race while the Negro race is different both in ancestry and characteristics. These popular beliefs bear directly upon interracial relations.

That there are differences between the races is conceded by Myrdal, but he is strongly inclined, after citing numerous authoritative studies, to account for them by environmental conditions: "When we approach those problems on the hypothesis that differences in behavior are to be explained largely in terms of social and cultural factors, we are on scientifically safe ground. If we should, however, approach them on the hypothesis that they are to be explained primarily in terms of heredity, we do not have any scientific basis for our assumption."

Questions relating to Negro population and migration are discussed by Myrdal in minute detail. At the time of his study, the 1940 census had reported Negroes were 9.8 per cent of the American population, contrasted to 19.3 per cent in 1790. The proportion had steadily declined over those 150 years. For social reasons, the author strongly advocates voluntary birth control by Negroes, in order to relieve the poverty of the Negro masses, to protect the health of working mothers, to reduce the high disease rate, especially from venereal cases, and to decrease the extremely high illegitimacy rate among Negroes. Stated broadly, "the reasons for birth control among

Negroes is due only to the fact that, as a group, they are more touched by poverty, disease, and family disorganization than is common among the whites in America."

Since first brought to this country as slaves, the Negro population has been heavily concentrated in the South. It is a curious phenomenon that each of the major wars in which the United States has engaged since the Revolution has resulted in large Negro migrations. The movement did not reach flood tide, however, until World War I. "The Great Migration," as Myrdal calls it, starting in 1915 and continuing in waves since then, has brought about dramatic changes in the distribution of Negroes in the United States. World War II, which was in progress when Myrdal was writing, vastly accelerated the steady drift toward the North and West. The Negro problem was no longer wholly Southern but quickly became national in scope. Furthermore, the removal from a rural to an urban environment added to Negro unrest. In any case, Myrdal believes that "migration to the North and West is a tremendous force in the general amelioration of the Negro's position." At the same time, he stresses that a "solution" of the Negro problem "is much too complicated to be solved by migration."

Myrdal dwells at length on the Negro's economic plight—Negro poverty; economic exploitation; the Southern plantation economy in relation to the Negro farmer, especially sharecroppers; jobs for Negroes outside agriculture; the Negro in business, the professions, public service, and other white-collar occupations; and family income, food consumption, and housing conditions. In a chapter on "The Negro in the Public Economy" consideration is given to such vital matters as discrimination in public service, education, public health, recreational facilities, public housing policies, social security, and social welfare programs.

From the preceding analyses, Myrdal concludes that the picture for the Negro people is dark from an economic standpoint. They are kept out of certain industries, North and South; in industries where they are employed, they are often segregated; and in practically all industries where they are accepted, they are confined to unskilled occupations and to such semiskilled and skilled occupations as are unattractive to white people.

Even in the early forties, when Myrdal was writing, the outlook for the Negro in Southern agriculture was bleak, because of overpopulation, soil erosion, the boll weevil's depredations, lack of land ownership, white exploitation of tenants, increasing mechanization, and the movement of cotton cultivation westward. In 1968, the President's National Advisory Commission on Rural Poverty found that the situation had deteriorated further. Negro farmers in the deep South, for example, were being pushed off the land at an increasing rate, their work being taken over by chemical weed killers and tractor-drawn cotton-picking machines.

Acute observers of the American scene are convinced that the Negro's best opportunity for improving his lot is through political action. His right to vote in the North, states Myrdal, is unquestioned, though obstacles in the Southern states are numerous. "Negroes can feel sure that, unless this country undergoes a veritable revolution, their right to vote will remain unquestioned in the North, independent of any increase due to continued migration from the South." Myrdal believes that "without any doubt, this is one of the strategic protections of the Negro people in American society." In the South, however, the matter of suffrage was found to be quite different for the would-be Negro voter. Largely for historical reasons dating back to slavery, Civil War, and Reconstruction, the Negro was effectually disfranchised in many areas; liberal voices were weak; and the region was mainly ruled by its conservatives.

Myrdal asserts that "there is not going to be a Negro party in American politics," and the Negro vote will continue to be divided between the Democratic and Republican Parties. In the competition for the vote, "the question arises whether, in this haggling and bargaining, the Negroes will be able to extract the maximum advantage by acting as a political unit, nationally and locally." The legal foundations for Negro disfranchisement were found to be gradually withering away—a trend which has since removed all legal bases, though not the tactics of intimidation, subterfuge, or violence.

Closely related to political factors is the inequality of justice for the Negro, principally in the South, a subject to which Myrdal devotes four hard-hitting chapters. Again, the breakdowns and failures in legal machinery have their roots in the past—the relation between master and slave; the systematic exclusion of Negroes from the judiciary, juries, and law-enforcement agencies; and restrictions on political participation. The weakest link in the legal system is seen by Myrdal to be the typical Southern policeman—low-paid, with little general education, no special police schooling, low in social prestige, and violently prejudiced against the Negro. Conditions in Southern prisons are also roundly condemned. There are few kind words, too, for the Southern judiciary, which in general is inclined to be far harsher on Negroes than on whites accused of crime. In fact, concludes Myrdal, "this whole judicial system of courts, sentences and prisons in the South is overripe for fundamental reform. It represents a tremendous cultural lag in progressive twentieth century America." The author is encouraged to find that "in principle, the average white Southerner is no longer prepared to defend racial inequality of justice."

Brief attention is paid by Myrdal to race riots, a phenomenon terrifyingly common in recent years. Here Myrdal failed in his role of prophet, for to him the future looked peaceful in the North while there were many signs of growing racial tension in the South. He was perceptive, however, in recognizing that if riots occur, "they will be due to continuing discrimination from the whites and to growing realization by Negroes that peaceful requests for their rights are not getting them anywhere." The effects of riots on amicable race relations are extremely serious, notes Myrdal, and the memory of them, among both whites and Negroes, is long-lasting.

Hardly less irksome and aggravating to the Negro than economic, political, and legal inequalities are social inequalities in the American culture. The historical antecedents in the pre-Civil War slave system again are clearly evident. Social segregation and discrimination are regarded by Myrdal as a challenge to the American creed. To salve their consciences, the whites devised the "separate, but equal" doctrine, now invalidated by the highest court in the field of education and in various other applications. Certain popular beliefs supporting social inequality are cited by Myrdal: Many Negroes are poor, uneducated, and deficient in health, morals, and manners; Negroes prefer their own company, separate from other people; and Negroes are basically inferior. This credo serves to explain "Jim Crow" laws, legal bans on intermarriage, and residential segregation.

Since Myrdal was writing, court decisions have banned the elaborate structure of state laws and municipal regulations which he described, designed to prohibit Negroes from using the same schools, libraries, parks, playgrounds, railroad cars, railroad stations, sections of streetcars and buses, hotels, restaurants, and other facilities as do the whites. Even in the early nineteen forties, it was observed that the system was "gradually losing its legal sanctions and increasingly depending upon extra-legal or illegal sanctions." From the viewpoint of the Negro, social discrimination is a powerful force in keeping him down in all other respects—not merely the social.

A consequence of the social, judicial, political, and economic inequalities and disabilities under which the Negro labors, Myrdal observed, is increasing isolation: "Voluntary withdrawal is now becoming a habit in all social classes of Negroes." Intimate and personal, friendly relations with white persons or families, prevalent in earlier times, are now rare. As Negroes absorb modern American culture, they are driven "to self-segregation to preserve self-respect." It is impossible "to educate the American Negroes and at the same time to keep them satisfied with their lower caste position."

A distinction is made by Myrdal between caste and class, as found in the United States. A man born a Negro or a white always retains that status, but he can pass from one class to another. Thus, the caste system of America is closed and rigid, while the class system is, in a measure, always open and mobile. Each caste has its own class system. A white person who breaks caste solidarity is damned with the epithet "nigger lover," and is liable to social and economic ostracism. Caste pressure, on the other side, produces Negro solidarity for individual and group protection. The Negro's only opportunity to break through the caste wall is limited to light-skinned individuals who may be able to cross the color line and "pass" as whites.

Since the end of the Civil War, Negroes have been fighting the caste system and Myrdal devotes several chapters to the Negro protest and its leaders, beginning with such great compromisers as Booker T. Washington and going on to the more radical spokesmen of recent years. Myrdal underlines the statement, "Generally speaking, every agency working for assimilation of the Negro people in the broader American civilization, which is democratic in its fundamental values, is bound to strengthen the Negro protest against caste." The two world wars fed the protest movement, gave the Negroes new confidence in themselves, and brought them to a realization of their own power. The sense of racial solidarity was also strengthened.

The caste system, in Myrdal's view, is essentially vicious and has an extremely deleterious effect on American civilization. "The tragedy of caste," he asserts, "is that it does not spare the integrity of the soul either of the Negro or of the white man." But any basic reforms must depend upon white co-operation, contrary to the rejection by Negro radical leaders of any white participation in the protest movement. "The Negroes' status in America is so precarious," Myrdal believes, "that they simply have to get the support of all possible allies in the white camp."

The activities of Negro improvement and protest organizations are reviewed critically by Myrdal, with particular attention to nationalist movements (such as the back-to-Africa plans), business and professional organizations, the National Negro Congress, the National Association for the Advancement of Colored People, the Urban League, and the Commission on Interracial Cooperation (an interracial group). Reverting to his earlier theme, Myrdal concludes that "only when Negroes have collaborated with whites have organizations been built up which have any strength and which have been able to do something practical." The effectiveness of the organizations has also been closely related to the integrity of their leaders: "To the Negro people dishonest leadership is a most important cause of weakness in concerted action."

Agencies of a non-political character, in their various capacities, also represent and speak for the Negro. Of particular significance are the Negro church, school, and press, all of which receive Myrdal's attention. The church has remained a largely segregated institution and the author found "astonishingly little interracial cooperation between the white and Negro churches of the same denomination." In total membership the churches are the largest of Negro organizations, but Myrdal points out that they suffer from numerous weaknesses: frequent schisms, poverty, the steady decline of the ministers' prestige and leadership, ideological backwardness, and the ministers' lack of education. Nevertheless, "it must never be forgotten that the Negro church fundamentally is an expression of the Negro community itself." The church is what it is because the Negroes wanted it that way—at least until recently.

Education as a factor in improving the Negro's status is stressed by Myrdal, for "the long-range effect of the rising level of education in the Negro people goes in the direction of nourishing and strengthening the Negro protest." And despite Southern suspicion of the effect of education on the Negro, "the Negroes' statutory right to public education remained unassailable." The emphasis, however, has been on "classical" education, and Myrdal regards it as an unfortunate fact that no effective industrial training was ever given the Negroes in the Southern public schools, except training for cooking and menial service. "What is needed is an education which makes the Negro child adaptable to and movable in the American culture at large." Myrdal also advocates a system of adult education for Negro immigrants who move from the South to the North, "to teach the migrating Negro masses the elements of American culture and also, perhaps, elements of vocational skills." Such a program, he suggests, may relieve the heavy burden on the social and economic order in the North.

The Negro press was found by Myrdal, not surprisingly, to be primarily controlled by the active members of the upper and middle classes of the Negro community, and a great part of the subscribers came from the same classes. "The importance of the Negro press for the formation of Negro opinion, for the functioning of all other Negro institutions, for Negro leadership and concerted action generally," states Myrdal, "is enormous."

In his concluding chapter, "America Again at the Crossroads," Myrdal summarizes his findings and draws certain conclusions concerning the future. The most striking social trend, he notes, is changes in white attitudes, North and South, and the decay of the caste theory: "The gradual destruction of the popular theory behind race prejudice is the most important of all social trends in the field of interracial relations," and further, "America can never more regard its Negroes as a patient, submissive minority."

The main trend in American history, in Myrdal's view, is the steady movement toward realization of the American creed. "In this sense the Negro problem is not only America's greatest failure but also America's incomparably great opportunity for the future." Myrdal closes with an inspiring declaration of faith:

Studying human beings and their behavior is not discouraging. When the author recalls the long gallery of persons whom, in the course of this inquiry, he has come to know with the impetuous but temporary intimacy of the stranger—sharecroppers and plantation owners, workers and employers, merchants and bankers, intellectuals, preachers, organization leaders, political bosses, gangsters, black and white, men and women, young and old, Southerners and Northerners—the general observation retained is the following: Behind all outward dissimilarities, behind their contradictory valuations, rationalizations, vested interests, group allegiances and animosities, behind fears and defense constructions, behind the role they play in life and the mask they wear, people are all much alike on a fundamental level. And they are all good people. They want to be rational and just. They all plead to their conscience that they meant well even when things went wrong.

In a "Postscript" to the twentieth-anniversary edition of *An American Dilemma*, published in 1962, Arnold Rose, who assisted Myrdal in the original investigation, reviews changes which had occurred during the twenty-year period. The rate of change was considerably more rapid than had been anticipated. Especially notable were the effects of industrialization and technological progress; "heightened group identification," represented by the Congress on Racial Equality (CORE), the Southern Christian Leadership Conference (SCLC), under Martin Luther King, Jr.'s leadership, and the Student Nonviolent Coordinating Committee (SNCC); and the impact of federal legislation, court decisions, and administrative actions on civil rights. Opposition continued, however, both in the South (mainly through the White Citizens' Councils) and in the North (principally from homeowners and labor unions). Nevertheless, there were improvements in employment opportunities for Negroes, Southern Negroes were being given the right to vote, law enforcement was improving, and such facilities as schools, playgrounds, restaurants, hotels, and other public and commercial establishments were being desegregated. Less progress had been made in housing, which remained largely segregated throughout the nation. In Rose's opinion, caste and racism in the country had become so "debilitated" that "I venture to predict the end of all formal segregation and discrimination within a decade, and the decline of informal segregation and discrimination so that it would be a mere shadow in two decades." Perhaps an overly optimistic prediction in the light of recent events.

Robert Lynd, author of *Middletown*, acclaimed *An American Dilemma* as "the most penetrating and important book on our contemporary American civilization that has been written. . . . No one at all concerned with American democracy can afford to miss reading and pondering this book." Myrdal sums up the nation's choice when he states, "America is free to choose whether the Negro shall remain her liability or become her opportunity." If the American creed prevails, world faith in democracy will be strengthened; its rejection would be a damaging blow to democratic principles everywhere.

24—PRIVATE OPULENCE AND PUBLIC POVERTY

JOHN KENNETH GALBRAITH'S
The Affluent Society

SINCE THE acid pen of Thomas Carlyle characterized it as "the dismal science," the study of economics has been trying to live down a reputation for dullness. Its most convincing exhibits to prove the contrary are the writings of Adam Smith, Thorstein Veblen, and John Kenneth Galbraith.

In terms of impact, the enormous, worldwide prestige of Smith's *The Wealth of Nations* did not come for some years after its publication, when Britain had become industrially revolutionized in the nineteenth century and, by following Smith's precepts, became for a time the world's richest nation. Veblen, an iconoclastic, original thinker, was widely read by scholars, writers, and teachers, but his influence is debatable. The third of the trio, J. K. Galbraith, has poured out a stream of economic treatises for more than two decades. One, *The Affluent Society* (1958), has already established itself as a classic. John Strachey predicted that "twenty years after its publication, *The Affluent Society* will be exercising an influence comparable, though of a very different kind, to that exercised by John Maynard Keynes' *The General Theory of Employment, Interest and Money*." As a high-level administrator in the Office of Price Administration, adviser to President Kennedy, Ambassador to India, Professor of Economics in Harvard University, and consultant on economic affairs to the governments of numerous underdeveloped nations, Galbraith has been in a position to help shape events directly, as well as through his writings.

The central theme of *The Affluent Society* can be briefly summed up: As long as there has been a science of economics, its practitioners have been almost wholly occupied with problems of scarcity and poverty, and, as corollaries, with how to increase production of needed goods, decrease inequality of income, and ensure personal security. The emphases were logical as long as a majority of the population needed food, shelter, and clothing. Thus we find the leading eighteenth- and nineteenth-century economists—Adam Smith, Ricardo, Malthus, and John Stuart Mill—concerned with the most urgent problems of their time: the high price of bread, the depreciation of English money, the grim poverty of the new industrial towns, and the appalling tendency of the poor to multiply.

Toward the end of the nineteenth century and through the early decades of the twentieth, the doctrines of the Social Darwinists were dominant in America. Their teachings, in essence, are that a constant struggle goes on in the economic arena. The winners survive and become wealthy; the weak are eliminated. Thus it was, as Galbraith notes, "In the half century following the Civil War in the United States, men accumulated fortunes of incredible size."

Throughout history, Galbraith points out, nearly all nations have been very poor. The exceptions, quite recent in date, are in western Europe and, especially, the United States. Economic thought has marked time, however, while events marched on, e.g., we continue to think and act as though we were living in a poverty-stricken culture. Following the precepts of what Galbraith ironically terms "conventional wisdom," economists urge maximum production to support full employment and economic security, despite the fact that already more than enough is being produced to supply reasonable needs.

Even after a majority of families have had satisfied their desires for television sets, automobiles, refrigerators, and other "consumer durables," they must be convinced that they should continue buying—another television set, another car, and another refrigerator. Otherwise, a recession sets in, profits fall off, and the number of unemployed rises. "Buy now" campaigns are announced to fight the slump.

Galbraith seeks to demonstrate that this type of economic thinking is outmoded in an affluent society such as ours. The important private needs are already satisfied and production has outstripped demand. A logical sequence is that high production and full employment can be maintained only if people are persuaded to buy articles for which they have no real need—what Galbraith describes as the "Dependence Effect." The demand for non-essentials is created almost entirely by the institution of advertising, as practiced in the United States. Advertising as a major social force, following the Galbraith thesis, cannot exist except in a society so affluent that the desire for goods must be artificially created. "There were few people at the beginning of the nineteenth century," writes Galbraith, "who needed an advertising man to tell them what they wanted." He adds, "A man who is hungry need never be told of his need for food." Those who are far removed from physical want are open to advertising's persuasion. The cost of stimulating the consumer is enormous. In 1956, when Galbraith was writing, total advertising expenditures in the United States amounted to about $10,000,000,000 annually and were growing at the rate of a billion dollars per year.

The popular belief that maximum production of private goods and services is *ipso facto* highly desirable leads to serious dangers, Galbraith holds. In time, the economy becomes overbalanced with a superfluity of private goods while public goods and services are being starved. Specifically, the people are giving first priority to such trivial rewards as fancy cigarette lighters, expensive perfumes, chrome on automobiles, excessive use of tobacco and alcohol, and breakfast foods shot out of guns, while neglecting to provide decent schools and housing, adequate public transporation, parks, efficient police protection, and even research and development programs for national security. The resulting contrast is scathingly described by Galbraith:

> The family which takes its mauve and cerise, air-conditioned power-steered, and power-braked automobile out for a tour passes through cities that are badly paved, made hideous by litter, blighted buildings, billboards, and posts for wires that should long since have been put underground. They pass on into a countryside that has been rendered largely invisible by commercial art. . . . They picnic on exquisitely packaged food from a portable icebox by a polluted stream and go on to spend the night at a park which is a menace to public health and morals. Just before dozing off on an air mattress, beneath a nylon tent,

amid the stench of decaying refuse, they may reflect vaguely on the curious unevenness of their blessings. Is this, indeed, the American dream?

The public attitude on these matters presents a curious contradiction, as seen by Galbraith. Thus, the nation may be saturated with homes, cars, and factories, but conservative forces will vigorously oppose changing the emphasis to the production of social goods, such as urban redevelopment, schools, and low-income housing. Projects of the latter nature are viewed as attacks on the free enterprise system, undermining American self-reliance, and frequently are damned as rankly socialistic. Anyway, it is asserted that the citizen knows better how to spend his money than does the government.

From a rational point of view it would not seem difficult to differentiate between what is frivolous and extravagant and what is basic and essential. The enlightened citizen would doubtless place oversized cars, rapid changes in fashions, and built-in obsolescence in the first group and water purification, housing, medical care, and education in the fundamental category. The choice, however, is not always so clear-cut and simple. For that reason Galbraith offers a detailed analysis of his "Theory of Social Balance," trying to strike a proper ratio between private and public needs. The city of Los Angeles, he concludes, "is a near-classic study of the problem of social balance. Magnificently efficient factories and oil refineries, a lavish supply of automobiles, a vast consumption of handsomely packaged products, coupled with the absence of a municipal trash collection service which forced the use of home incinerators, made the air nearly unbreathable for an appreciable part of each year. . . . The agony of a city without usable air was the result." Well-developed public services, such as more research, better policing, and a municipal trash collection system, could have controlled air pollution.

The overstress on production and private consumption produces a chain of evils, in Galbraith's view. First, the production system has not only to be run at full speed at all times but to undergo continuous expansion. Otherwise, wage earners join the ranks of the unemployed. On the other hand, a high rate of production, maintained without a break, leads inevitably to chronic inflation, as wages and prices chase each other in an upward spiral. Thus, a capitalistic society witnesses violent economic oscillations, from boom to bust. The profit motive which dominates the thinking of an affluent people has strongly negative implications—little or nothing should be produced which does not yield a profit, an explanation of the popular antagonism to expenditures for public services.

A related problem arises from a key method used to finance a high proportion of consumer purchasing: installment buying, discussed by Galbraith in a chapter entitled "The Bill Collector Cometh." "Consumer demand," he remarks, "comes to depend more and more on the ability and willingness of consumers to incur debt." As consumption increases, consumer debt rises. As Galbraith sees it, therefore, "Our march to higher living standards will be paced, as a matter of necessity, by an ever deeper plunge into debt." The dimensions of consumer credit outstanding may be judged from the figure of $92,519,000,000 reported by the *Federal Reserve Bulletin* in 1967. "The legacy of wants, which are themselves inspired," Galbraith writes, "are the bills which descend like the winter snow on those who are buying on the installment plan. By millions of hearths throughout the land it is known that when these harbingers arrive the repossession man cannot be far behind. Can the bill collector be the central figure in the good society?" The massive debt, a high proportion for non-essentials, hanging over the American people adds substantially to national tensions. It is a major factor, too, in causing economic instability.

Galbraith recognizes the necessity for providing full employment, or at least a regular income for workers and their families. Countering his proposal to eliminate superfluous production, the question naturally arises: How can employment be maintained without maximum production, both of necessities and luxuries? Galbraith's answer is to divorce production from security of employment. Let there be more unemployment from time to time, he says. This will have the incidental benefit of curbing inflation. To make the plan palatable to the unemployed, however, unemployment compensation should be raised to a large percentage of normal income, such benefits to increase as total unemployment rises, on the assumption that the worse the recession the harder it is to find a job and the most necessary is government aid. In periods of high employment, unemployment compensation should be reduced to circumvent malingering workers.

The Galbraith plan is similar in certain features to recent proposals by labor unions for a guaranteed annual wage and by federal officials for an income tax in reverse. A prime purpose in all is to eliminate the hazard of depression unemployment for the worker and to ensure a reasonable living standard.

Galbraith believes that labor has been overstressed at the expense of leisure in American society. A combination of such factors as the Puritan condemnation of idleness, the urge to produce, and a desire to accumulate wealth led to the undervaluation of the importance and rewards of leisure. It is Galbraith's contention that the American standard of life is far more significant than the American standard of living. "Why," he asks, "should men struggle to maximize income when the price is many dull and dark hours of labor?" The goal instead ought to be to find interesting and rewarding occupations while learning to enjoy leisure.

The proponents of "conventional wisdom" in economics insist that top production is essential to national security and defense, a concept which Galbraith dismisses as a delusion. He is highly skeptical of the frequently iterated proposition that a direct correlation exists between national power and economic output, and defense capability and external security increase in direct ratio with increases in the gross national product. In an extraordinary chapter, "The Illusion of National Security," Galbraith argues that America has fought her "last gross national product war," and that the old idea that the essential strength of the free world is American productive power has become a myth. "It is not gross output but usable military output which counts." An example is the Soviet Union, whose GNP is far below that of the United States, but which was able by concentrating scientific personnel and productive capacity to send its first Sputniks into space several months ahead of the American Explorer satellites. Actually, a nation's military might and potentials may be seriously weakened, Galbraith believes, by heavy stress on consumer production, especially of luxury goods.

As a method for financing much-needed public services, in order to achieve the kind of social balance that he advocates, Galbraith proposes a national sales tax. Though liberals usually attack sales taxes as regressive, education and other social services are of greatest benefit to the lowest income group. If the notion can be discarded that private output is sacred and public production somewhat disgraceful, wasted resources can more easily be diverted to the public area. "The relation of the sales tax to the problem of social balance," notes Galbraith, "is admirably direct. The community is affluent in privately produced goods. It is poor in public services. The obvious solution is to tax the former to provide the latter—by making private goods more expensive, public goods are made more abundant."

Critics of Galbraith take issue with his basic premise—that we are an affluent society. Millions of American families, they say, exist on submarginal incomes and are ground down by poverty. An American family with an income of $3000 a year or less is by no means affluent. If our society is truly affluent, why the federal government's obsession with a variety of poverty programs? Galbraith sees no incompatibility between these facts and his thesis. He concedes the existence of pockets of poverty in the southern Appalachians and other specific areas, mainly rural. "The modern locus of poverty," he finds, "is even more the rural than the urban slum." Present-day poverty falls into two categories: *case* poverty, afflicting particular individuals or families, and *insular* poverty, a kind of island of poverty in an otherwise prosperous region. The lot of these people is not improved by increased national production. In Galbraith's opinion, "The first and strategic step in an attack on poverty is to see that it is no longer self-perpetuating." The efficient elimination of poverty requires a disproportionate investment in the children of poor communities, through providing them with high-quality schools, strong health services, special programs of nutrition and health, and opportunities for advanced education for qualified students. The effect of the "investment in individuals is to enable them either to contend more effectively with their environment, or to escape it and take up life elsewhere on more or less equal terms with others."

In a 1964 interview, Galbraith suggested that today's concern over poverty can be traced to his book. "Up until then," he commented, "everyone wrote on the assumption that poverty was the general rule, that what this country needed was more for everybody. But *The Affluent Society* established affluence as the general case and allowed poverty to be seen as exceptional."

The Affluent Society is rich in quotable quotes, for

Galbraith is a gifted phrasemaker. Following, more or less at random, is a sampling of his witticisms and epigrams:

Wealth is not without its advantages and the case to the contrary, although it has often been made, has never proved widely persuasive.

It is a far, far better thing to have a firm anchor in nonsense than to put out on the troubled seas of thought.

The notion of a vested interest has an engaging flexibility in our social usage. In ordinary intercourse it is an improper advantage enjoyed by a political minority to which the speaker does not himself belong. When the speaker himself enjoys it, it ceases to be a vested interest and becomes a hard-won reward. When a vested interest is enjoyed not by a minority but by a majority, it is a human right.

A cat chasing its own tail may, by an extraordinary act of feline dexterity, on occasion succeed in catching it. To overcome inflation by increasing production, while superficially similar, will not so often be successful.

The gods are appeased by stern denunciations [in Congress] of public profligacy and inspired promises of vast economies. The ceremony is solemnly described to the people by press and radio. Thereafter the seemingly indispensable outlays are voted, and the result is more often to increase the budget than to reduce it.

Men of high position are allowed, by a special act of grace, to accommodate their reasoning to the answer they need. Logic is only required in those of lesser rank.

The shortcomings of economics are not original error but uncorrected obsolescence.

The business executive listening to a luncheon address on the virtues of free enterprise and the evils of Washington is already persuaded, and so are his fellow listeners, and all are secure in their convictions. ... Scholars gather in scholarly assemblages to hear in elegant statement what all have heard before. Yet it is not a negligible rite, for its purpose is not to convey knowledge but to beatify learning and the learned.

Galbraith sums up the main purpose of *The Affluent Society* in these words: "Its concern has been with the thralldom of a myth—the myth that production, by its overpowering importance and its ineluctable difficulty, is the central problem of our lives. We have now seen the sources of this myth. And we have seen some of the consequences—the tenuous and maybe dangerous process of consumer demand creation, recurrent inflation, social imbalance—to which the myth commits us."

The wide influence of *The Affluent Society* may be judged by the fact that the title of the book itself has become incorporated into popular speech as descriptive of advanced Western societies. One reviewer, Robert Lekachman, stated his conviction that "Galbraith has done an enormous service to the cause of intelligent economic and social debate. In the end, he may have done as substantial a service to the prestige of economics itself."

25-UPSETTING THE BALANCE OF NATURE

RACHEL CARSON'S *Silent Spring*

COMPARABLE in its impact on public consciousness, and demand for instant action, to Tom Paine's *Common Sense,* Harriet Beecher Stowe's *Uncle Tom's Cabin,* and Upton Sinclair's *The Jungle* was Rachel Carson's *Silent Spring* (1962), describing the disastrous effects on the balance of nature caused by the irresponsible use of insecticides and other pest controls.

Actually, the dark picture painted by Miss Carson, an eminent marine biologist, was part of a larger canvas—the overwhelming problem of pollution of the air, water, and land which was increasingly disturbing the conscience of the American people. Public-spirited citizens everywhere were realizing with alarm that man was ruining his environment by fouling the air he breathes, the water he drinks, the soil that produces his food, and the food itself. Automobiles were filling the cities with lethal fumes; smog was settling down in choking volume on virtually all large urban centers; human and industrial wastes were being dumped into lakes, rivers, and streams, killing fish and steadily reducing potable water resources; oil wastes dumped in the sea were killing millions of seabirds and ruining beaches, and further pollution of the ocean was resulting from the dumping of industrial atomic wastes. Beginning with World War II, the dangerous fallout from nuclear bomb explosions had posed an even more serious dilemma for the world at large.

This was the background against which Rachel Carson wrote. She begins her shocking story with a fable, in which she tells of a small American town, set in the heart of prosperous farmland, with its wild flowers, numerous songbirds, and well-stocked trout streams. "Then a strange blight crept over the area and everything began to change. Some evil spell had settled on the community: mysterious maladies swept the flocks of chickens; the cattle and sheep sickened and died. Everywhere was a shadow of death." Doctors discovered new kinds of sickness appearing among their patients. "There was a strange stillness. The birds, for example—where had they gone? . . . On the mornings that had once throbbed with the dawn chorus of robins, catbirds, doves, jays, wrens, and scores of other bird voices there was now no sound; only silence lay over the fields and woods and marsh."

The town described does not actually exist. "I know of no community that has experienced all the misfortunes," writes Miss Carson, "yet every one of these disasters has actually happened somewhere, and many real communities have already suffered a substantial number of them."

What has silenced the voice of spring in countless places, Miss Carson contends, is indiscriminate blanket spraying of vast areas from airplanes with potent chemicals, and similar misuses of insecticides and herbicides.

The beginnings of the devastation so graphically condemned by Miss Carson were a by-product of World War II. In experiments with agents intended for chemical warfare, it was found that some of the compounds were deadly to insects. After the war, chemical manufacturers, drug companies, agricultural schools, and government agencies started actively to develop and to promote the use of killers designed to exterminate various types of insects and undesirable plant growths. Handed these new weapons, the forester sprayed to protect his trees, the cranberry picker to protect his bogs, the cotton planter to save his cotton from the boll weevil, and so on down a long procession of farmers and gardeners—with little or no understanding of or concern for the consequences.

For thousands of years, man had fought to control pests—insects, rodents, weeds, bacteria, and other forms. Until World War II, the chief pesticides were arsenic, nicotine, and vegetable derivatives lethal to cold-blooded animals. The organic chemicals added to the plant growers' arsenal in the postwar period included the chlorinated hydrocarbons, such as DDT, and the organo-phosphorus substances, of which parathion is a common example. As a direct result, states Miss Carson:

For the first time in the history of the world, every human being is now subjected to contact with dangerous chemicals, from the moment of conception until death. In the less than two decades of their use, the synthetic pesticides have been so thoroughly distributed throughout the animate and inanimate world that they occur virtually everywhere. They have been recovered from most of the major river systems and even from streams of groundwater flowing unseen through the earth. Residues of these chemicals linger in soil to which they may have been applied a dozen years before. They have entered and lodged in the bodies of fish, birds, reptiles, and domestic and wild animals so universally that scientists carrying on animal experiments find it almost impossible to locate subjects free from such contamination. They have been found in fish in remote mountain lakes, in earthworms burrowing in soil, in the eggs of birds—and in man himself. For these chemicals are now stored in the bodies of the vast majority of human beings, regardless of age. They occur in the mother's milk, and probably in the tissues of the unborn child.

The sprays, dusts, and aerosols have the power to kill all insects, good and bad, Miss Carson points out, as well as the birds and the fish, and to poison the soil, perhaps permanently—all to get rid of a few weeds and insects. The poisons are insoluble in water and therefore pollute the surfaces of fruits, vegetables, grasses, and grains. Aiming at a troublesome beetle, the chemists have wiped out the bird life of whole regions; aiming at a weevil, they have exterminated the race of bald eagles; aiming to save man from malaria, they have put several known cancer-causing agents into permanent circulation; aiming at an insect which was destroying commercial spruce plantations, the Canadians killed off all the salmon of three generations in four large rivers.

Miss Carson builds a damning and persuasive case with innumerable other specific instances of the destruction being wrought by pesticides. In the mid-nineteen fififtes, the city of East Lansing, Michigan, began a massive spraying of the Michigan State University campus to kill beetles which carry Dutch elm disease. The sprayed leaves fell to the ground in the autumn, and were eaten by worms. In the spring, robins ate the worms and within a week nearly all the robins were dead. In eastern Canada, where budworms were gradually killing off the balsams, there was extensive spraying of the forests. "Soon after the spraying had ended," reports Miss Carson, "there were unmistakable signs that all was not well. Within two days dead and dying fish, including many young salmon, were found along the banks of the stream. Brook trout also appeared among the dead fish, and along the roads and in the woods birds were dying. All the life of the stream was stilled."

As a result of the spraying of Clear Lake, California, with DDT, to rid it of gnats for the comfort of fishermen, the swanlike western grebes began dying, until they had dwindled from one thousand to thirty pairs. In the National Wildlife Refuges at Tule Lake and the Lower Namath, also in California, herons, pelicans, grebes, and gulls died in great numbers—the victims of insecticide residue which had been building up to lethal strength in the water flowing from heavily sprayed agricultural lands. In the Midwest, indiscriminate spraying for the Japanese beetle virtually annihilated robins, meadowlarks, brown thrashers, and pheasants in Blue Island and Sheldon, Illinois.

In "A Postscript to Rachel Carson," Clark C. Van Fleet, California sportsman, author, and conservationist, commented on the increasing use of sodium fluoroacetate, known as 1080. "Used in conjunction with grain as a rodent bait," he observed, "a single kernel will immediately kill a mouse, a rat, or squirrel or a rabbit. . . . Over a hundred deer carcasses were found within a small compass where state agents had carelessly scattered poison grain. . . . Some three thousand ducks and geese in Siskiyou County, California, died as the result of improper spread of grain containing 1080 as a poison for ground squirrels. Hawks and eagles were also found dead."

Two years after the publication of *Silent Spring* the U.S. Public Health Service had positive proof that the pesticide endrin was responsible for the deaths of 10,000,000 fish in the lower Mississippi River and the Gulf of Mexico; the poison had reached the river through runoff from farms.

In July 1968, *Newsweek* reported, "In Borneo, health officials recently launched a campaign to rid rural villages of flies. DDT did the job quickly, but the cure turned out to be worse than the disease. Lizards who ate the flies accumulated the poison in their bodies. Cats ate the lizards and died. Soon the rat population started to proliferate, and plague threatened the entire region."

Miss Carson continually stresses the perils to man himself from the widespread use or misuse of pesticides. If the chemicals are deadly to animal and plant life, can man with impunity eat contaminated meats and vegetables? A few human victims had already died in convulsions from exposure to certain highly concentrated pesticides, the author points out, and she fears that many others will eventually die of cancer, leukemia, hepatitis, or other dread diseases possibly caused by pesticides. Lethal poisons spread across the land, are blown into farm homes, settle on food, and pollute tanks and ponds. Emphysema, a serious lung disorder, unheard of until recent years, is becoming common in country areas, and respiratory illnesses are increasing by leaps and bounds in orchard and berry country. Because of birth-to-death exposure to dangerous chemicals, there is a progressive buildup of poison in our bodies, and the cumulative effect may well be disastrous. Many common insecticides for household use are highly toxic.

An exclamation point was added to Miss Carson's warnings when, two years after the appearance of *Silent Spring*, she herself died of cancer.

The basic fallacy overlooked by those who make extensive use of pesticides, Rachel Carson holds, is that they are upsetting the balance of nature. A vital fact which they ignore is that all life is one life, that the countless species of animals and plants and the soil, water, and air they live on are all intimately interconnected and interdependent. The ancient network of living things, in which each animal and plant depended upon every other one, has been upset by man, who is continually engaged in molding the environment to his own advantage. He must be supreme in nature, the human egotist believes, and the changes he makes are often sudden and profound—and frequently irreversible. Too often, man has looked upon himself as opposed to nature, not as a part of her, and in his efforts to subdue, he has ravished and destroyed.

One of the frightening ways in which nature fights back is to produce new and more dangerous pests. Chemicals have quickly killed off the weak and feeble among the creatures attacked, but permanent control over the survivors is not gained. A thorough spraying may kill 90 per cent of a particular species. The hardier members, however, are resistant to the spray and survive; when they reproduce, most of their offspring inherit the immunity. Furthermore, the survivors often reproduce in fantastic numbers. To combat the new superpests, the chemists develop ever more poisonous sprays, thereby increasing the danger to all living things, including man. Thus, Miss Carson concludes, in upsetting the balance of nature, we are fighting a losing battle: "As crude a weapon as the cave man's club, the chemical barrage has been hurled against the fabric of life—a fabric on one hand delicate and destructible, on the other miraculously tough and resilient, and capable of striking back in unexpected ways."

As the author of two best sellers, *The Sea Around Us* and *The Edge of the Sea*, Miss Carson was already famous before *Silent Spring* was published. Readers had a foretaste of her newest book through partial serialization in *The New Yorker*. When *Silent Spring* came off the press, therefore, it was an instant best seller; it remained on the New York *Times* list for thirty-one weeks and sold 500,000 copies in hard cover before being brought out in paperback. The book had an immediate and profound effect on American opinion. The potential dangers of pesticides became known to all, and popular pressure speeded up industry and government research.

After *Silent Spring* was published, the federal government began an investigation of its pesticide control programs to find an answer to how to use chemical pesticides more safely. A world conference, called the United Nations Food and Agriculture Organization, met in Rome to study how pesticides can be used effectively without harming people. The British Ministry of Agriculture, Fisheries, and Food placed severe restrictions on the use of three widely used insecticides related to DDT—aldrin, dieldrin, and heptachlor. The U. S. Congress closed a loophole in the machinery for control by ending the "protest registration" system under which a manufacturer whose product was disapproved by the Department of Agriculture could continue to make and sell it. Legislatures in a number of states also tightened controls.

As could have been anticipated, the multi-million-dollar chemical industry, so vigorously attacked by Miss Carson, reacted violently. She had claimed that the industry's introduction of more and more chemicals was often based on profit rather than need. The Carson campaign was characterized by one commentator as "the most massive indictment of an entire industrial complex since the days of Ida Tarbell." The great corporations involved—mainly the major oil companies and their affiliates, the petrochemical companies—the economic entomologists, officials of the U.S. Department of Agriculture, and agricultural research workers generaly quite predictably did not submit tamely to the scathing criticisms aimed at them.

A spokesman for the chemical industry, Dr. Robert White-Stevens of the American Cyanamid Company, issued a blast stating that "the book's major claims . . . are gross distortions of the actual facts, completely unsupported by scientific, experimental evidence, and general practical experience in the field." Miss Carson was accused of unfairness, prejudice, and hysteria, and the image of a crackpot was built up by her enemies, who chose to ignore her long career as a professional biologist, her sixteen years' experience with the Fish and Wildlife Service, and other accomplishments.

Departing from personalities, the critics asserted that chemical herbicides and insecticides have become necessary to man's survival. Without them, in a short time there would be no more marketable fruit or vegetable crops. If chemical pesticides were discontinued, they added, the agricultural areas of the world would soon be ravaged by hordes of grasshoppers, weevils, and other insect invaders. Chemical sprays make possible the huge food crops that farmers can now grow. Lacking them, surplus food would vanish, whole populations would starve, rivers and fields would be choked with weeds, and certain diseases would get out of control. Thus, the commercial interests and their spokesmen among the scientists presented a picture as one-sided and scary as anything in *Silent Spring*.

A telling argument used by pesticide supporters is that such chemicals have virtually eradicated many diseases. Mosquitoes, lice, ticks, fleas, and other insects are carriers of malaria, yellow fever, sleeping sickness, typhus, and other scourges. Malaria, which was formerly widely prevalent, has been practically stamped out in the United States and a number of other countries through the use of insecticides.

In short, maintain the proponents of pesticides, man has no choice except to upset the balance of nature. Otherwise, the insects will eventually inherit the earth.

Propaganda is not expected to give both sides of an

argument, and *Silent Spring* is a fiercely passionate tract—emotional, dramatic, sensational in many respects. Nevertheless, Miss Carson concedes that farm chemicals have a place. "It is not my contention," she writes, "that chemical insecticides must never be used. I do contend that we have put poisonous and biologically potent chemicals indiscriminately into the hands of persons largely or wholly ignorant of their potentials for harm."

Miss Carson offers various constructive alternatives to the use of chemical pesticides. She feels that in many cases biological controls would be safer than chemical controls. The use of such natural controls has been limited; only about one hundred insect predators have been successfully introduced into the United States. Other alternates to insecticides are parasites, resistant crop varieties, sterilization of male insects by radiation, chemical sterilants, sex lures and physical attractants, such as light, to draw insects into traps. The potentialities of these approaches were shown by an English science writer, Edward Hyams, in an article for *The New Statesman:*

> Where biologists, and not commercially-interested chemists, have been in charge, methods used to control troublesome insects, and even weeds, have been ecologically sound: there have been some astonishing successes, for example, in inoculating communities of troublesome creatures with the parasites natural to them, often brought from overseas, and in establishing these parasites permanently so that the control is stable and continuous. It is also and invariably enormously cheaper than the chemical methods. Very little work has been done in this field; but there is no doubt at all that if it can be done by biologists and naturalists who understand the whole picture—and not, like the entomologists, only one small piece of it—biological control of most and perhaps all 'pests' can be achieved.

This is Miss Carson's vital solution: that insects, pests, and undesirable growths may be controlled by encouraging their enemies—a proposal offered at the beginning of the nineteenth century by Charles Darwin's grandfather, Erasmus. Ragweed causing hay fever can be fought, writes Miss Carson, by maintaining the dense shrubs and ferns that help to crowd it out; fight crabgrass by providing better soil for high-quality lawn grass; "fight insects by seeking to turn the strength of the species against itself," instead of by the careless, unrestrained use of chemicals. "As matters stand now," asserts Miss Carson, "we are in little better position than the guests of the Borgias."

The chief problem in applying biological controls appears to be a lack of research. According to a recent report only about one hundred biologists are actively engaged in such research, a majority of them in California. The reason is financial: The universities depend upon industry for research grants and the chemical industry provides 98 per cent of the funds for pest control research. Moreover, the lucrative positions are in chemical research, while biologists must be satisfied with lower-paid jobs as teachers, government workers, or with growers' associations.

Objective appraisals of the situation by scientists with no particular axes to grind have concluded that there is a middle ground where chemistry, biology, wildlife, and mankind can coexist. The complex problems, they say, must be attacked by ecologists and biologists, qualified to assess all factors in the environment; specialists in the medical profession must evaluate and control dangers to public health; and more federal and state funds must be provided for basic research.

In a front-page obituary, the New York *Times* called Rachel Carson "one of the most influential women of her time." Senator Abraham Ribicoff, former U. S. Secretary of Health, Education, and Welfare, summed up her career by stating: "This gentle lady, more than any other person of her time, aroused people everywhere to be concerned with one of the most significant problems of mid-20th century life—man's contamination of his environment." Stewart L. Udall, Secretary of the Interior, one of Miss Carson's warmest admirers and supporters, added: "In the success of *Silent Spring* was the hope that those who truly care about the land have a fighting chance to 'inherit' the earth. That the pen of one so unassuming should have such an impact on national events was remarkable, and a heartening sign to conservationists everywhere."

Bibliographical Notes

ADDAMS, JANE (1860-1935)
Twenty Years at Hull-House. New York: Macmillan, 1910.
462 pp. Continued by: *The Second Twenty Years at Hull-House, September 1909 to September 1929.* New York: Macmillan, 1930. 413 pp.

BEARD, CHARLES AUSTIN (1874-1948)
An Economic Interpretation of the Constitution of the United States. New York: Macmillan, 1913. 330 pp.

BEAUMONT, WILLIAM (1785-1853)
Experiments and Observations on the Gastric Juice and the Physiology of Digestion. Plattsburgh, New York: Printed by F. P. Allen, 1833. 280 pp.

BELLAMY, EDWARD (1850-98)
Looking Backward, 2000-1887. Boston: Tichnor, 1888. 470 pp.

CARDOZO, BENJAMIN (1870-1938)
The Nature of the Judicial Process. New Haven: Yale University Press, 1921. 181 pp.

CARSON, RACHEL (1907-64)
Silent Spring. Boston: Houghton Mifflin, 1962. 368 pp.

CASH, WILBUR JOSEPH (1901-41)
The Mind of the South. New York: Knopf, 1941. 429 pp.

FLEXNER, ABRAHAM (1866-1959)
Medical Education in the United States and Canada; a Report to the Carnegie Foundation for the Advancement of Teaching. New York, 1910. 346 pp. (Carnegie Foundation for the Advancement of Teaching, *Bulletin,* No. 4.)

GALBRAITH, JOHN KENNETH (1908-   )
The Affluent Society. Boston: Houghton Mifflin, 1958, 358 pp.

HOLMES, OLIVER WENDELL (1809-94)
The Contagiousness of Puerperal Fever. Boston, 1843. 28 pp.

(Reprinted from *The New England Quarterly Journal of Medicine and Surgery*, April 1843.)

LEWIS, MERIWETHER (1774-1809) and CLARK, WILLIAM (1770-1838)
History of the Expedition Under the Command of Captains Lewis and Clark. Philadelphia: Bradford and Inskeep, 1814. 2 vols.

LYND, ROBERT STAUGHTON (1892-   ) and LYND, HELEN (1896-   )
Middletown: a Study in Contemporary American Culture. New York: Harcourt, 1929. 550 pp.
Continued by *Middletown in Transition: a Study in Cultural Conflicts*. New York: Harcourt, 1937. 604 pp.

MAHAN, ALFRED THAYER (1840-1914)
The Influence of Sea Power upon History, 1660-1783. Boston: Little, Brown, 1890. 557 pp.

MANN, HORACE (1796-1859)
Report. In: Massachusetts Board of Education, *Report . . . Together with Report of the Secretary of the Board*, 1st-12th, 1837-48. Boston: 1838-49. 12 vols.

MENCKEN, HENRY LOUIS (1880-1956)
Prejudices, Series 1-6. New York: Knopf, 1919-27. 6 vols.

MYRDAL, GUNNAR (1898-   )
An American Dilemma; the Negro Problem and Modern Democracy. New York: Harper, 1944. 2 vols.

PAINE, THOMAS (1737-1809)
Common Sense, Addressed to the Inhabitants of America. Philadelphia: Robert Bell, 1776. 79 pp.

SINCLAIR, UPTON (1878-1968)
The Jungle. New York: Doubleday and Page, 1906. 413 pp.

SMITH, JOSEPH (1805-44)
The Book of Mormon: an Account Written by the Hand of Mormon, upon Plates Taken from the Plates of Nephi. Palmyra, New York, 1830. 588 pp.

STEFFENS, LINCOLN (1866-1936)
The Shame of the Cities. New York: McClure, Phillips, 1904. 306 pp. Reprinted from *McClure's Magazine*, 1903.

STOWE, HARRIET BEECHER (1811-96)
Uncle Tom's Cabin; or Life Among the Lowly. Boston: J. P. Jewett, 1852. 2 vols. First published serially in the *National Era*, June 5, 1851-April 1, 1852.

TAYLOR, FREDERICK WINSLOW (1856-1915)
The Principles of Scientific Management. New York: Harper, 1911. 77 pp.

THOREAU, HENRY DAVID (1817-62)
"Resistance to Civil Government." In: *Aesthetic Papers*, edited by Elizabeth P. Peabody. Boston, 1849, pp. 189-211.

Tocqueville, Alexis Charles Henri Maurice Clérel de
    (1805-59)
    De la Démocratie en Amérique. Paris: C. Gosselin, 1835-40.
    4 vols.
Turner, Frederick Jackson (1861-1932)
    "The Significance of the Frontier in American History."
    American Historical Association *Annual Report*, 1893, pp.
    197-227. Definitive edition: *The Frontier in American History*, New York: Holt, 1920. 375 pp.

INDEX

Aaron, Daniel, 127
Abbott, Grace and Edith, 194
Adams, John, 19
Adams, John Quincy, 85
Adams, Samuel, 19, 20
Adams, Samuel Hopkins, 166
Addams, Jane, *Twenty Years at Hull-House*, 185–195; *Second Twenty Years at Hull-House*, 192
Affluent Society, J. K. Galbraith, 274–282
Aiken, Conrad, 259
Aitken, Robert, 18
Alcott, Bronson, 98
Aldridge, Alfred Owen, 28
Alger, Horatio, xiii, 229–230
Allen, Paul, 41
Allston, Washington, 255
Altgeld, John Peter, 189–190
American Crisis, Thomas Paine, 27–28
American Dilemma, Gunnar Myrdal, 262–273
American Language, H. L. Mencken, 227
American Mercury, 216, 223
American Revolution, 17, 19–20
American Women's Peace Party, 192
Ames, Albert Alonzo, 155–156
Antioch College, 85
Appeal to Reason, 166
Arikara Indians, 35–36
Armour, J. Ogden, 168
Ashbridge, Samuel H., 160
Ayres, C. E., 238

Bache, Richard, 18
Bailey, Gamaliel, 109–110
Bailey, Josiah William, 259
Baker, Ray Stannard, 152

Bancroft, George, 208
Beard, Charles A., ix, 19, 149, *Economic Interpretation of the Constitution of the United States*, 207–218
Beaumont, Gustave de, 63
Beaumont, William, *Experiments and Observations*, 52–62, 94
Bellamy, Edward, *Looking Backward*, 119–129
Bethlehem Steel Company, 197
Biddle, Nicholas, 41
Billington, Ray Allen, 145, 146, 150
Billroth, Theodor, 173
Blackstone, William, 102, 106, 233
Book of Mormon, 42–51
Bowman, Sylvia E., 128
Boyd, Julian P., 222
Bradford, Roark, 259
Bradford, William, 142
Brandeis, Louis D., 203–204
Brooks, Van Wyck, 226
Brown, Robert E., 216, 217
Bryce, James, xiii
Burke, Edmund, 28
Burlingame, Roger, 205
Burns, John, 195
Butler, Edward R., 155
Butler, Nicholas Murray, 216
Byrd, Harry, 259
Byrd, William, 142

Cabell, James Branch, 259
Cable, George W., 257
Caldwell, Erskine, 117, 259
Calverton, V. F., 45
Cantwell, Robert, 164–165
Cardozo, Albert, 229

Cardozo, Benjamin N., *Nature of the Judicial Process*, 229–237

Carlyle, Thomas, 274

Carmer, Carl, 252

Carnegie Corporation of New York, 262

Carnegie Foundation for the Advancement of Teaching, 172

Carson, Rachel, *Silent Spring*, xii, 283–291

Cash, W. J., *Mind of the South*, 252–261

Church of Jesus Christ of Latterday Saints, 42–51

Civil disobedience, 96–107

Clark, William, 30–41

Clarke, Hovey C., 156

Clendening, Logan, 87

Commager, Henry Steele, 216, 217

Common School Journal, 78

Common Sense, Thomas Paine, 17–29

Congress on Racial Equality, 272

Constitution, U. S., 207–218

Contagiousness of Puerperal Fever, O. W. Holmes, 86–95

Continental Congress, First, 19; Second, 27

Conway, Jill, 194

Corwin, Edward S., 218

Coues, Elliott, 41

Cowdery, Oliver, 45

Cowley, Malcolm, ix–x, 218, 226

Craven, Avery, 144

Crèvecoeur, Michel Guillaume Jean de, 142

Dana, Richard Henry, Jr., xiii

Darrow, Clarence, 190

Darwin, Erasmus, 290

Davidson, Donald, 259

Declaration of Independence, 17, 27, 102

Democracy in America, Alexis de Tocqueville, 63–73

Descartes, René, 196

Dewey, John, ix

Digestion, physiology, 52–62

Dodd, William E., 253

Drayton, William Henry, 27

Dunglison, Robley, 57

Dunne, Finley Peter, 152–153, 167

Dwight, Edmund, 79

Eastman, George, 184

Eastman, Mary H., 114

Economic Interpretation of the Constitution of the United States, Charles A. Beard, 207–218

Education, public, 74–85

Eliot, Charles, 176

Emerson, Ralph Waldo, 96, 98

Evans, John Henry, 45

Experiments and Observations, William Beaumont, 52–62

Farrell, James T., 221–222

Faulkner, William, 117, 259

Federalist Papers, 208–209, 213

Flexner, Abraham, *Medical Education in the United States and Canada*, 172–184

Flexner, Simon, 172, 174

Flinn, William, 157

Floyd, Charles, 35

Folk, Joseph Wingate, 153–155

Ford, Henry, 204

Franklin, Benjamin, xiii, 18, 27, 29, 61, 146

French Revolution, 28

Fugitive Slave Law, 108

Fulton, John F., 61

Galbraith, John Kenneth, *Affluent Society*, 206, 274–282

Gandhi, Mahatma, 103–104

Garrison, William Lloyd, 114

George III, 19, 21–22

George, Henry, xiii

Gerry, Elbridge, 218

Gilbertson, Catherine, 116

Girson, Rochelle, x

Glasgow, Ellen, 257

Glass, Carter, 259

Goldman, Emma, 105

Gordon, Alexander, 87, 89

Grandin, Egbert B., 46

Grayson, William J., 113–114

Grizzly bears, 37–38

Grolier Club, x

Hale, Sarah Josepha, 114
Hamilton, Alice, 191, 194
Harding, Walter, 104
Harris, Joel Chandler, 113, 257
Harris, Martin, 45, 46
Hart, Albert Bushnell, 216
Herskovits, Melville, 255
Heyward, DuBose, 259
Hodge, Hugh Lenox, 92
Holmes, Oliver Wendell, *Contagiousness of Puerperal Fever*, 86–95
Holmes, Oliver Wendell, Jr., 236–237
Hoover, Herbert, 193
Hull House, 185–195
Hunter, William, 52
Hyams, Edward, 290

Influence of Sea Power upon History, Alfred T. Mahan, 130–141
Insecticides and herbicides, 283–291

Jackson, Andrew, 29, 143
Jackson, Donald, 41
Jaques, W. K. 166–167
Jefferson, Thomas, 19, 27, 30–33, 40–41, 98, 142–143, 146
Jewett, John P., 110
Johns Hopkins University Medical Department, 173
Johnson, Gerald W., 227–228
Johnson, Lyndon B., 171
Judicial process, 229–237
Jungle, Upton Sinclair, 164–171

Kelley, Florence, 194
Kennedy, John F., 150
Keppel, Frederick P., 262
Keynes, John Maynard, 274
King, Martin Luther, Jr., 105–106, 272
Kinsey, Alfred C., xiii–xiv
Koch, Robert, 86

Lanier, Sidney, 257
Larrabee, Eric, x
Lathrop, Julia, 194
Lawton, Thomas W., 166
Lee, Richard Henry, 26–27
Legal philosophy, 229–237
Lekachman, Robert, 282

Lerner, Max, 163
Levy, Newman, 237
Lewis, Meriwether, and Clark, William, *History of the Expedition*, 30–41
Lincoln, Abraham, 116, 143, 224
Lippmann, Walter, 226
Lister, Joseph, 86
Lodge, Henry Cabot, 139
London, Jack, 170
Long, Huey, 259
Longfellow, Henry W., 114–115
Looking Backward, Edward Bellamy, 119–129
Louisiana Territory, 30–31
Low, Seth, 161–162
Lynd, Robert S. and Helen M., *Middletown*, 238–251; *Middletown in Transition*, 248–251

McCarthy, Joseph, 105
McClure, S. S., 153
McDonald, Forrest, 216
MacLeish, Archibald, 190
McLuhan, Marshall, xi
McManes, James, 159
Madison, James, 208–209, 210
Magee, Christopher L., 157–158
Mahan, Alfred T., *Influence of Sea Power upon History*, 130–141
Malthus, Thomas, 275
Mann, Horace, *Annual Reports*, 74–85
Marcosson, Isaac F., 166–167
Marshall, John, 208, 209, 229
Martin, David, 159–160
Masur, Gerhard, 205–206
Meat packing industry, 165–171
Medical Education in the United States and Canada, Abraham Flexner, 172–184
Meigs, Charles D., 92, 93
Melville, Herman, xiv
Mencken, Henry Louis, 259; *Prejudices*, 219–228
Middletown, Robert S. and Helen M. Lynd, 238–251
Mill, John Stuart, 275
Mind of the South, W. J. Cash, 252–261
Mirsky, Jeannette, 34–35

Mitchell, Weir, 61
Mitford, Jessica, *American Way of Death*, xii
Mommsen, Theodor, 130
Monroe, James, 28
Mormons, 42–51
Morrison, Joseph L., 261
Morton, Marcus, 82
Mott, Frank Luther, 117
Municipal government, 152–163
Munson, Gorham, 116
Myrdal, Gunnar, xiv, *American Dilemma*, 262–273

Nader, Ralph, *Unsafe at Any Speed*, xii
Napoleon Bonaparte, 30
Nathan, George Jean, 220
Nation, 216
National Association for the Advancement of Colored People, 270
National Era, 110
National Negro Congress, 270
National Women's Trade Union League, 188
Nationalist, 127
Nature of the Judicial Process, Benjamin N. Cardozo, 229–237
Nauvoo, Illinois, 50
Negroes, American, 105–106, 262–273
Neill, Charles P., 169
New England Quarterly Journal of Medicine and Surgery, 88, 93
New Statesman, 290
New York Times, 219, 288, 291
New Yorker, The, 288
Newsweek, 286–287
Norris, Frank, 153

O'Dea, Thomas F., 49
Osler, William, 62

Page, Thomas Nelson, 116, 257
Paine, Thomas, 164, *Common Sense*, 17–29, 283; *Age of Reason*, 28–29; *Rights of Man*, 28
Parkman, Francis, 150
Parrington, Vernon L., 107
Pasteur, Louis, 86

Pavlov, Ivan Petrovich, 61
Peabody, Elizabeth, 97
Pennsylvania Magazine, 18
Penrose, Boies, 160
Pesticides, 283–291
Peterkin, Julia, 259
Philbrick, John D., 78
Phillips, David Graham, 153
Pierson, George Wilson, 65–66
Poe, Edgar Allan, 255–256
Polk, James K., 96
Poole, Ernest, 153
Pound, Roscoe, 229
Prejudices, H. L. Mencken, 219–228
Principles of Scientific Management, F. W. Taylor, 196–206
Pritchett, Henry, 172
Prout, William, 52–53
Puerperal fever, 86–95
Puleston, W. D., 137

Quay, Matthew S., 158

Ransom, John Crowe, 259
Réaumur, René, 52
Reed, Joseph, 26
Resistance to Civil Government, H. D. Thoreau, 96–107
Reynolds, James B., 169
Reynolds, Robert Rice, 259
Ribicoff, Abraham, 291
Ricardo, David, 275
Richmond, Mary, 194
Roberts, Elizabeth Madox, 259
Robinson, James, 105
Rockefeller Foundation, 183
Rocky Mountains, 38
Roosevelt, Franklin D., 149–150, 250
Roosevelt, Theodore, 17, 139, 143, 149, 152, 153, 165, 167, 190–191, 224–225, 236
Roper, Elmo, xii
Rose, Arnold, 272–273
Rosen, George, 61
Rush, Benjamin, 20, 32, 36
Russell, Charles Edward, 166
Russia, 71–72

Sabin, Florence, 194
Sacajawea, 36–37, 38, 39
St. Martin, Alexis, 53–62
Sandburg, Carl, 160

Santayana, George, 230
Saturday Review, x
Schlesinger, Arthur, Sr., 218
Schwann, Theodor, 57
Scientific management, 196–206
Sea power, 130–141
Seligman, Edwin R. A., 208
Semmelweis, Ignaz Philipp, 94–95
Shame of the Cities, Lincoln Steffens, 152–163
Shoshone Indians, 36, 38–39
Significance of the Frontier in American History, F. J. Turner, 142–151
Silent Spring, Rachel Carson, 283–291
Silliman, Benjamin, 57
Simms, William Gilmore, 255
Sinclair, Upton, 105, *The Jungle*, 164–171, 283
Slavery, U. S., 18, 71, 97, 108–118
Smith, Adam, 274, 275
Smith, Bernard, ix–x
Smith, Joseph, *Book of Mormon*, 42–51
Smith, Lillian, 117
Smith, Matthew Hale, 82
Snow, C. P., xi
Society for Advancement of Management, 206
Southern Christian Leadership Conference, 272
Southern states, 252–261
Spallanzani, Lazzaro, 52
Spock, Benjamin, xiv
Stalin, Joseph, xi
Staples, Samuel, 97
Starr, Ellen Gates, 186, 188
Steffens, Lincoln, *Shame of the Cities*, 152–163
Steinbeck, John, xiv
Stowe, Charles Edward, 109, 115
Stowe, Harriet Beecher, *Uncle Tom's Cabin*, 108–118; *Dred*, 117
Strachey, John, 274
Student Nonviolent Coordinating Committee, 272
Sullivan, Mark, 152

Talmadge, Eugene, 259

Tammany Hall, 161–162
Tannenbaum, Frank, 262
Tarbell, Ida, 152, 289
Tate, Allen, 259
Taylor, Frederick Winslow, *Principles of Scientific Management*, 196–206
Taylor, Walter Fuller, 128
Thomas, Norman, 105
Thoreau, Henry David, *Resistance to Civil Government*, 96–107
Thwaites, Reuben G., 41
Tocqueville, Alexis de, xiv, *Democracy in America*, 63–73
Tolstoy, Leo, 103
Toynbee Hall, 186–187
Trevelyan, George, 27
Turner, Frederick Jackson, *Significance of the Frontier in American History*, 142–151
Twain, Mark, xiv
Twenty Years at Hull-House, Jane Addams, 185–195

Udall, Stewart L., 291
Uncle Tom's Cabin, Harriet Beecher Stowe, 108–118
U. S. Supreme Court, 67, 106, 234, 236, 262
Urban League, 270
USA in Books, U. S. Information Agency, x
Utopias, 119–129

Van Fleet, Clark C., 286
Varney, Harold Lord, 216
Veblen, Thorstein, 274
Viets, Henry R., 94

Wald, Lillian, 194
Washington, Booker T., 269
Washington, George, 19, 23, 26
Webb, Walter Prescott, 150–151
Webster, Noah, 227
Weed, Thurlow, 46
Weeks, Edward, ix
Weld, Theodore, 110
Wetmore, Claude H., 154
White, Charles, 87
White Citizens' Councils, 272
White-Stevens, Robert, 289
Whitman, Walt, 103

Whitmer, David, 45
Wiley, Harvey W., 165
Wilhelm II, 138, 139
Williamson, Hugh, 212
Wilson, Edmund, 225–226, 227
Wilson, James, 210
Wilson, Woodrow, 149
Winthrop, John, 142
Wolfe, Thomas, 259

Women's International League
    for Peace and Freedom, 192–
    193
Woodward, C. Vann, 260–261

Yoder, Edwin M., Jr., 260
Young, Brigham, 49, 50

Ziegenhein, Henry, 154

PLUME BOOKS are part of New American Library's high quality paperback publishing program. The list includes important new books and carefully selected reprints ranging from art and the humanities to science. The high level of scholarship and writing that characterize Signet Classic and Mentor books will be continued and expanded in these large format editions.

___Z5001 MAKERS OF ENGLAND, Arthur Bryant. . .$3.50

___Z5002 AGE OF CHIVALRY, Arthur Bryant. $3.95

___Z5003 WILL TO MEANING, Viktor Frankl. $1.95

___Z5004 GREAT DIALOGUES OF PLATO,
            W. H. D. Rouse. . . . .[•]•]•. . . .$2.95

___Z5005 SCIENCE & CIVILIZATION IN ISLAM,
            Seyyed Hassein Nasr. $3.50

___Z5006 ORIGINS OF SCIENTIFIC THOUGHT,
            Giorgio de Santillana. $2.95

___Z5007 INFINITE VARIETY OF MUSIC,
            Leonard Bernstein . . . .[•]•]• . .$2.95

___Z5008 COLLECTED STORIES OF KATHERINE
            ANNE PORTER $2.95

___Z5009 DE-ROMANIZATION OF THE CATHOLIC
            CHURCH, Edward Wakin &
            Father Joseph F. Scheuer. $3.50

___Z5010 BREAKTHROUGHS IN MATHEMATICS,
            Peter Wolff $2.75

___Z5011 HISTORY OF POSTWAR RUSSIA,
            R. W. Pethybridge. $2.45

___Z5012 THE LIVING CITY, Frank Lloyd Wright. .$2.95

___Z5013 NATURAL HOUSE, Frank Lloyd Wright. .$2.95

___Z5014 FUTURE OF ARCHITECTURE,
               Frank Lloyd Wright. $2.95

___Z5019 THE SCOTCH, John Kenneth Galbraith. .$2.95

___Z5020 EPIGRAMS OF MARTIAL, Palmer Bovie. .$3.95

___Z5021 MARTHA QUEST, Doris Lessing. . . .•ːɵːɵ•. .$2.95

___Z5022 PRICKSONGS & DESCANTS,
               Robert Coover . . . .·:•·. $2.45

___Z5023 RIPPLE FROM THE STORM,
               Doris Lessing $3.50

___Z5024 ROOTS OF APPEASEMENT,
               Martin Gilbert . . . .·-•. $3.50

___Z5025 HERO ON A DONKEY, Miodrag Bulatovic $2.75

___Z5026 LANDLOCKED, Doris Lessing. $2.95

___Z5027 EUROPEAN POWERS 1900-1945,
               Martin Gilbert . . . .·ːɵ•.ɵːɵ•. .$3.50

___Z5028 A PROPER MARRIAGE, Doris Lessing. . .$3.50

___Z5029 CLIMAX OF ROME, Michael Grant. $3.95

___Z5030 HARD TRAVELLIN', Kenneth Allsop. .•ɵː•. .$3.75

___Z5031 GARIBALDI & HIS ENEMIES,
               Christopher Hilbert $3.95
